H EUR

Saving the Forsaken

PEARL M. OLINER

With statistical analysis by
JEANNE WIELGUS *and*
MARY B. GRUBER

Saving the Forsaken

RELIGIOUS CULTURE AND THE
RESCUE OF JEWS IN
NAZI EUROPE

Yale University Press
New Haven &
London

Set in Sabon type by Keystone Typesetting, Inc.
Printed in the United States of America.

Library of Congress Cataloging-in-Publication Data
Oliner, Pearl M.
Saving the forsaken : religious culture and the rescue of Jews in Nazi Europe /
Pearl M. Oliner.
        p.   cm.
Includes bibliographical references (p.   ) and index.
ISBN 0-300-10063-9 (cloth : alk. paper)
1. Righteous Gentiles in the Holocaust — Attitudes. 2. Righteous Gentiles in
the Holocaust — Psychology. 3. World War, 1939–1945 — Jews — Rescue.
4. Altruism. 5. Motivation (Psychology). 6. Religion and culture. 7. Personality
and culture. I. Title.
D804.65.O45 2004
940.53′1835′0922 — dc22
2004059403

A catalogue record for this book is available from the British Library.

The paper in this book meets the guidelines for permanence and durability of the
Committee on Production Guidelines for Book Longevity of the Council on
Library Resources.

10 9 8 7 6 5 4 3 2 1

Contents

Preface

I began writing this book some fifteen years ago. Sam Oliner, my husband, and I had just put the final touches on a book we wrote titled *The Altruistic Personality: Rescuers of Jews in Nazi Europe.* It had been a daunting project, one that took more than ten years to complete, and I was feeling somewhat drained.

As the subtitle suggests, the book was a study of non-Jewish rescuers of Jews during the Holocaust. It was an academically focused book, but one with strong emotional associations. Sam is a Jewish survivor of that period, the only survivor of his family. I, a first-generation American, daughter of Polish Jewish immigrants, had a vastly different life in Brooklyn, New York. Privileged as I was, I nonetheless share with many a powerful consciousness of that horrific time. As compared with those who write about the horrors of that period, a far more anguishing yet absolutely essential task, it was an easier emotional undertaking. The former have to deal with people and conditions that must be understood but can lead to despair. Those who study rescuers encounter that small minority of people who managed to be heroically human and give us all reason to be hopeful about the human experiment generally.

Yet even as we were completing the project, I knew it was not finished — or more accurately, that I had not finished with it. During the next few years I busied myself with other related projects but knew that I would take it up again. The Altruistic Personality and Prosocial Behavior Institute, of which Sam is executive director and I research director, had collected hundreds of interviews of rescuers, nonrescuers, and survivors of that period. Having pored over most of them, I felt I had gotten to know some interviewees intimately even though I had met only a few. I was appalled by nonrescuers who expressed bigotry and hate — and suspected some of having been perpetrators — but found myself empathizing with those nonrescuers who in many cases appeared to be very much like me. I was *awed* by rescuers. Would I have been one of them, I wondered? Although many people have contributed to an understanding of those times and people and continue to do so, I believe we need to know a great deal more if we hope to promote goodness.

One issue that frequently arises whenever we talk about rescuers is religion — "Who did more — religious or irreligious people?" is a common question, but concerns are not confined to this one. We had touched on religious issues only briefly in *The Altruistic Personality,* reporting no significant difference in religiosity between rescuers and nonrescuers — that finding is confirmed again here. If religiosity does not help explain the respective decisions, does that mean that religiosity did not count at all? Some rescuers had, in fact, given clearly religious reasons for rescue. Conversely, some rescuers, the majority of whom were irreligious, had given reasons for their activities having nothing to do with religion. How did their values compare with those of religious rescuers, and how did they differ from their nonrescuer counterparts? Questions such as these prompted this work. *The Altruistic Personality* focused on individuals; the focus here is on groups. And rather than asking who did more, the questions here center on the altruistic dispositions that characterized Christian rescuers and nonrescuers reflecting different levels of religiosity, as well as Protestant and Roman Catholic denominations, and how such group dispositions might help explain why participants in that group acted as they did.

While the data are derived from people who lived during a particular historical period and in particular geographical areas, I hope that the findings may be useful in furthering the understanding of predispositions in other cultures as they relate to outgroup altruism generally.

Religion and Culture

When we moved to Leidsche Dam, the Jews were not bothered yet. But within a year we received a letter from my brother-in-law that the Jews in Rijssen were having trouble: a doctor and a teacher had been arrested, and others too. We thought immediately of the Levin family. A few days later at the dinner table, we were reading as our daily Bible reading the passage in Isaiah 58 that talks about fasting, sharing your bread with the hungry, bringing the poor and persecuted to your house, clothing the naked and so on. The children were at the table, but my wife and I looked at each other and we knew what we had to do: this was our way.

— Alexander

I was in the military between 1939 to 1940. Then I was a student at engineering school at the Ponts et Chaussées from 1940 to 1942. Then I became an engineer, working at public highways and bridges, building roads at Nevers. I was also involved in building the channel there. Afterwards, I worked in the Department of the Seine, in the division of motor fuel and public transportation. My wife was home, busy raising the children.

— Jacques

I saw what was happening and talked with friends, fellow students and others. By chance, a farmer's son once said to me: "If expenses were paid, some farm workers would be willing to hide a child." I thought to myself what a great idea. So I went to talk to some of the farm workers and some of my friends agreed to supply the money. From then on I traveled around looking for places and distributing coupons. I was mostly involved with Jewish children, and some adults. I provided them with coupons, clothes, etc. Most important of course, was finding a hiding address of course, but school was also important. When I didn't have an address, I'd shove it on to a colleague or the colleague to me.

— Maartje

We left our flat in Warsaw and went to our summer place — we rented rooms there. And I helped the local people a lot. My first contact with the partisans was in our summer place. I also worked at a first-aid station in 1944 where different people came: Poles and Russians. My whole training amounted to a three-month first-aid course. I always took my baby along. I thought it better to die together than to leave her an orphan. I did it to help Poland — that was the most important thing, to help Poland.

— Gosha

These vignettes give a sense of the wartime activities of four people, all of whom lived in occupied Europe during World War II. In each of the countries they represent, Jewish inhabitants became victims of that horrendous event known as the *Shoah,* more commonly the Holocaust. Alexander, a very religious Christian, became a rescuer of Jews during the Holocaust, but Jacques, an equally religious Christian, did not. Irreligious Maartje became a rescuer, but equally irreligious Gosha did not. What led very religious Alexander and irreligious Maartje to become rescuers? Did they share similar values, and if so, how representative were they of their respective religious and irreligious groups? And what values influenced their counterparts — very religious Jacques and irreligious Gosha — to make different decisions?

Proposed answers to just such questions have often focused on values and attitudes commonly associated with altruism: values having to do with care and empathy, for example. Not uncommonly, too, values and attitudes have focused on personality, that is, attributes and experiences associated with individuals. This book also focuses on values and attitudes commonly associated with altruism, but rather than concentrating on individuals, its dominant concern is the religious cultural contexts from which individuals emerged.

The groups studied here reflect different levels of religiosity—the very religious, the moderately religious, and the irreligious—as well as two denominations—Protestants and Roman Catholics. What I will explore is how altruistically associated predispositions of these groups compared, concentrating particularly on their differences, and if differences among them reflected some discernible patterns that might help explain cultural influences on individual responses. While my specific focus here is on Christian culture and rescue of Jews during the Holocaust, my aspiration is to suggest some relationships between cultural values generally and altruism, and most particularly between cultural values and altruism toward outsiders (a phenomenon we call "outgroup altruism"). In that context, we will meet Alexander, Maartje, Jacques and Gosha again in the following chapters. It is my hope that by considering them in much greater detail, we will gain a better understanding of their responses in terms of the cultures from which they emerged.

"Christian" here includes Protestants and Roman Catholics of varying levels of religiosity—very religious, moderately religious, and irreligious—living in selected countries of Western, Central, and Eastern Europe during World War II. "Culture" refers to the more or less shared beliefs, attitudes, norms, and values of the various groups: the very religious, the moderately religious, and the irreligious, as well as Protestants and Catholics generally. Jews are the "outgroup": marginalized under the best of circumstances, they were increasingly persecuted and hunted as the Nazi terror spread.

Rescuers helped in diverse ways, among them escorting Jews to safety across borders, acting as couriers on their behalf, seeking hiding places, and providing shelter within their own homes, sometimes for several years. Undertaken without expectations of external rewards, and under threat of death in most cases, not only for rescuers but often for their families as well, rescue was an altruistic act of the highest level.[1] It was also a very rare act; even by the most generous standards, less than one-half of one percent of the population under Nazi occupation participated in it.

Historians and theologians—Jews and non-Jews—have given considerable attention to Christian behavior during the Holocaust, and their work has been invaluable for all scholars interested in this subject. Their primary concentration, however, has been on religious institutions and their leaders, as well as the theological underpinnings which may have underlain their respective behaviors. With mounting conviction, scholars generally point to an overall institutional failure. With a few notable local exceptions, religious institutions, Catholic and Protestant, failed to respond adequately to the unfolding Jewish genocide.[2] Religious institutions are an essential part of culture and play a critical role in influencing the decisions of their adherents. Institutional

leaders and their policies tell us a great deal about religious officials and religious elites, but they do not necessarily reflect the thinking of ordinary participants in that culture. They serve a peripheral role here, providing some
background material as may be necessary. My primary focus is on ordinary
Christians and how their values and attitudes may have affected their decision
to rescue or not to rescue.

As already noted, values and attitudes included in this study concentrate on
those orientations often associated with prosocial and altruistic behaviors.
Explicit theological beliefs are excluded, although they are assumed to have
influenced such cultural orientations and to have been influenced by them.
Psychologists and social psychologists largely pioneered the scientific study of
altruism and continue to make major contributions toward understanding it.
This work depends heavily on their efforts, but it differs in emphasis.

The primary unit of analysis among psychologists and social psychologists
tends to be individuals: their personality characteristics and, to a lesser degree,
the situational variables that influence them. Personality focuses on internal
characteristics of individuals, and those associated with altruism include
among others empathy, sense of personal responsibility, mood, and personal
norms. Personality variables associated with rescue have included similar attributes, with particular emphasis on attitudes toward Jews and other outsiders. Situational variables refer to external matters, among which relevant
skills (for example, knowing how to rescue a drowning person), the presence
of others (for example, when others are present, responsibility is often dif-
fused), the expressed emotions of victims (for example, victims who scream
are more likely to be helped than those who don't), and social norms (when
unwritten or written standards say helping is the right thing to do, people are
more likely to help) have been identified as encouraging altruistic responses.
External variables associated with rescue have included opportunity, avail-
ability of resources, networks, and normative considerations among others.
Several studies of rescuers have found evidence to support the importance of
the above-mentioned personality and external characteristics, including one
by my husband, Samuel P. Oliner, and myself.[3]

Yet despite the major contributions made by these investigators in helping
us understand attributes associated with altruism, psychological and social
psychological studies have some limitations. One of them is the often implicit
assumption that relevant personal attributes are similar across groups: that is,
qualities influencing men to behave altruistically would have the same effect
on women; the old and young would respond in like fashion given similar
attributes; and, in the context of this book, qualities influencing the very and
moderately religious would induce similar responses among the irreligious, as

well as among Catholics and Protestants. But is that indeed the case, or did these groups in fact approach their decisions differently? Phrased differently, did religious cultural context make a difference?

As defined here, culture means the more or less shared beliefs, attitudes, norms, and values found in a group of people who may or may not have contact with one another, but who nonetheless share a sense of common identity that makes them distinct from others. Culture is part of the external world from which people learn to interpret events and evaluate circumstances.

How is culture different from personality? Psychologists agree that at bottom all humankind shares a universal nature; a genetic inheritance that includes basic physical properties — sensory capacities, bodily systems — and basic psychological properties — the capacity to communicate, create and play, and feel emotions such as anger and love. The sense that individuals make of their physical properties, and how they communicate or feel about things, are functions of their culture and personality. Culture is learned and is not inherited genetically. While each culture is unique in the sense that no culture is exactly the same as any other culture, individuals in the same culture tend to share many of its major beliefs and values. Personality is also unique, but unlike culture, which marks a group of people as distinct from others, personality characterizes one person as distinct from all others. Personality results from learning and inheritance, and no single individual has exactly the same personality as any other individual. Personal and cultural experiences contribute to the development of personality, but so do genetic factors. Culture and personality have a reciprocal relationship; each is influenced by and influences the other, but personality is the particular constellation of psychological characteristics that mark one person as singular.

In keeping with the cultural focus of this exploration, the groups discussed here are people who lived in Europe during World War II, but who differed in terms of their degree of Christian religiosity and Christian denominational affiliation. The purpose of this book is to suggest how the cultural contexts of each religious group may have influenced the decision to rescue or not to rescue. I focus on answers to two broad questions: First, how did levels of religiosity — very religious, moderately religious, and irreligious — influence rescue? More specifically, what values and attitudes distinguished religious rescuers from less religious rescuers, and how did very religious, moderately religious and irreligious rescuers differ from one another and from their nonrescuer counterparts? Second, how did Catholics and Protestants approach rescue? More specifically, what values and attitudes distinguished Catholic rescuers from Protestant rescuers, and how did Catholic and Protestant rescuers differ from their similarly affiliated nonrescuer counterparts?

To answer these questions I relied on the database collected by the Altruistic Personality and Prosocial Behavior Institute. It includes interviews conducted in the late seventies and eighties with 510 persons living in several countries in Nazi-occupied Europe — 346 rescuers and 164 nonrescuers — as well as 150 survivors. Most of the respondents are from Poland, Germany, France, and Holland, but also included are representatives from Italy, Denmark, Belgium, and Norway. Most still lived in their native countries at the time the institute's associates interviewed them; some had emigrated to Canada and the United States.[4]

Approximately 95 percent of rescuers were authenticated as such by Yad Vashem; the remaining 5 percent are individuals the institute identified based on interviews with rescued survivors, using criteria similar to those established by Yad Vashem. Yad Vashem is Israel's memorial to the victims of the Holocaust. Part of its charge is to honor those who risked their lives to rescue Jews. To qualify as an honoree, the rescued survivor (or friends or relatives) needs to submit evidence of the deed to a Yad Vashem–appointed commission of eighteen members. In addition to examining submitted documents, the commission conducts interviews. Three overriding criteria determine selection: the rescuer had to be motivated by humanitarian considerations only, risked his or her own life, and received no remuneration of any kind for his or her act. Selections are made very carefully and take considerable time; in 1988, Yad Vashem had identified approximately 6,000 rescuers; as of the year 2002, that number had increased to more than 19,000.[5]

Nonrescuers include people not identified as rescuers by Yad Vashem and who lived in the same countries during the same period as rescuers. During the course of the interviews, an important difference emerged among respondents in this group in reaction to the question of whether they had done anything out of the ordinary during the war to help others or to resist the Nazis. Sixty-seven responded in the affirmative, several claiming they had helped Jews and/or participated in resistance activities. To distinguish between this group and those who claimed to have done nothing, the former were called "actives" and the latter "bystanders." Sample numbers include 67 in the active group and 97 in the bystander group. Statistical comparisons sometimes include rescuers and all nonrescuers (that is, actives and bystanders), as well as rescuers and bystanders only.

The interview schedule consisted of approximately 450 items, 75 percent of which were forced choices, the remainder open-ended. In addition, each respondent was asked to describe his or her wartime activities in detail. The questionnaire administered to nonrescuers was much the same as that given to rescuers, except that instead of being asked to describe their rescue activity and its setting, the nonrescuers were asked to describe their particular activities and lives during the war. Taped interviews, commmonly lasting several hours, were conducted in the native tongue of the respondents. They were subsequently transcribed and translated into English, coded, and analyzed. Analyses were both qualitative and quantitative in character. (For more on the questionnaire, see Oliner and Oliner, 1988.)[6]

The first book-length publication resulting from this effort occurred in 1988. Focusing on a comparison of personality characteristics between rescuers and nonrescuers, Sam Oliner and I concluded that rescuers as compared with nonrescuers had more "extensive" personalities, a concept we developed to mean stronger attachments to people in their immediate environments and in more powerful feelings of responsibility to those outside their immediate or familial circles. Their paths toward rescue varied; no one personality characteristic appeared to be critical, and no single constellation of personality characteristics, motivations, or situational contexts appeared entirely sufficient to explain it.

As we wrote in *The Altruistic Personality,* a major purpose of that work was to help identify altruistic personality attributes for the purpose of encouraging their development. In a similar vein and despite the focus of the present book on particular religious groups in a particular historical period, I hope this volume will suggest some broad relationships regarding culture generally and outgroup altruism specifically. Rescue is an example of heroic outgroup altruism, and if we can better understand the cultural contexts that contributed to it, we might be able to use such knowledge in cultivating and mobilizing similar predispositions within the particularities of different cultural contexts.

The concepts critical to this exploration, briefly defined above, are far more complex than indicated and often tend to be accompanied by controversy and unresolved issues. I raise them here so as to provide additional clarification regarding my perspective, and to indicate how I addressed them.

One unresolved issue relates to the concept of altruism itself. Is a "pure heart" required to fit the idea of altruism or is the deed sufficient? Some people propose that motivation is key, insisting that to qualify as altruistic the actor must have no interest other than the welfare of the receiver.[7] Others suggest that even if a pure heart does in fact exist, it would be difficult to locate scientifically. Many researchers accept a moderate position, asserting that an act that satisfies both the self and others can nonetheless be considered altruistic. Sam Oliner and I summarized these varied approaches as follows more than ten years ago, and little has changed since:

At one extreme are those who insist that the altruistic actor must have no concern for self and derive no benefit from the act; at the other are those who say that the act that satisfies both the self and the other can nonetheless be considered altruistic. In between are those who maintain that it is sufficient that costs outweigh gratification. Proposals regarding the types of motivations necessary range from mere intention to help, to helping for any reasons other than external rewards, to insistence on specific internal states (such as empathy, or lack of concern with restitution), specific values (such as love or compassion), personal norms, or principles of justice.[8]

Our definition, the one also accepted here, belongs to the moderate motivational standard. Altruism, we said, is a behavior "directed towards helping another, involves a high risk or sacrifice to the actor, is accompanied by no external reward and is voluntary."[9] With respect to motivation, the standard is minimalist, insisting only that the act be "directed towards helping another" and "accompanied by no external reward," thus implying that internal rewards are acceptable. With respect to cost, our definition approaches a maximalist position, insisting that the act involve "a high risk or sacrifice." Since it does not rule out exclusively self-centered reasons such as wanting to "look good" rather than "be good," or conforming to others' expectations rather than internalized principles, some people might prefer to call this "consequential altruism"; that is, an altruistic result but not necessarily based on an altruistic motivation. Since motivation at best can only be inferred rather than seen, even when the respondent reports her or his motivation, the focus on behavior continues to seem reasonable. These criteria are consistent with those of Yad Vashem, and on that basis all those identified as rescuers in this book behaved altruistically.

Rescuers behaved altruistically, but did they behave morally? A voluntary behavior directed toward helping another might appear self-evidently moral, but not everyone agrees on this point. Elliott Sober and David Wilson, for example, reject the idea that altruism requires all abdication of self-interest, but conclude that an altruistic act may *not* be moral. If helping someone means hurting another in equally needy circumstances, they say, then it not only does not qualify as a moral act but is in fact an immoral one. Morality, they argue, requires a moral principle, and "like all principles 'properly so called,' *are general*; they identify general criteria for decisions and cover all objects that have a certain property."[10] Morality, in other words, requires abstract principles as motivators that apply universally to all individuals in similar circumstances without regard for personal favorites. When parents help their own children more than other equally needy children, it can qualify as an altruistic act but not a moral one. Similarly, a rescuer who chose to help a

Jewish friend while ignoring a Jewish stranger, might be considered to have behaved altruistically but not morally.

Not so, argues philosopher Leonard Blum; such help lacks moral merit only if it denies the interests of others outside the relationship.[11] Yet the moral merit of singling out individuals or groups for special kindness while failing to bestow equal service to equally needy others remains problematic. It raises a related question: Is helping an "ingroup" member moral? Ingroups are people who perceive themselves as having a common fate, similar attributes, and a shared sense of identity from which they exclude others: they are the "us" as opposed to the "them." "Outgroups" are groups who are perceived as neither belonging to nor sharing a common fate with the ingroup, and thus excluded from a common identity; they are the "them" as opposed to the "us." Some groups are marginal, neither quite "in" nor "out," but those who are more "out" may be seen as sources of conflicts, often perceived as competitors and dangerous, and sometimes identified simply as enemies.[12] Not surprisingly, ingroup altruism is far more common than outgroup altruism, and marginal groups may be helped in some circumstances but not in others. If morality requires principles to be applied universally, then helping an ingroup is not moral if it does not confer similar help to outsiders.

Sociologist Geert Hofstede goes further, implying that helping members of an ingroup is neither moral nor altruistic. Ingroup helping, he says, is a form of "group worship" or "in-group egoism"; only outgroup helping merits the label "altruism."[13] While Hofstede's perspective remains a minority point of view, he does highlight a distinction that needs to be explored further. Helping an outsider is frequently far riskier than helping an insider: it often invites in-group disapproval and sometimes even ostracism; on rare occasions, such as the instances discussed in this book, it can mean death. Although helping is frequently discussed as a unitary phenomenon, it might be useful to distinguish between lower and higher levels of altruism. Rescue belongs to the higher level in terms of potential cost, and when bestowed on an outsider group, it meets Hofstede's criterion as an altruistic act.

Like altruism, ingroups, and outgroups, "culture" also is a complex concept, requiring some elaboration.

Anthropologists were the first to develop the idea of "culture"; it became a core concept in their early work and remains so today. One of the founders of anthropology, Edward B. Tylor, defined "culture" as "the knowledge, beliefs, art, morals, law, custom, and any other capabilities and habits acquired by a member of a society."[14] As Tylor suggests, culture is a comprehensive idea, including the totality of a group's material (e.g., physical objects such as tools, art, shelters) and nonmaterial (e.g., religious beliefs, moral values) world.

Although this definition remains largely intact today, with anthropologists continuing to study both material and nonmaterial culture, many today prefer to focus on material culture. Other kinds of social scientists concentrate more on nonmaterial culture.

In their early days, anthropologists were very interested in describing the relationship between personality and culture, and they had considerable success in persuasively demonstrating linkages between them. Margaret Mead and Ruth Benedict are among the most widely known writers in this tradition, but other intellectual pioneers among them include Franz Boas, Edward Sapir, and Clyde Kluckhohn.[15] The societies anthropologists studied in the twenties, thirties, and forties were relatively small, homogeneous, and remote from western experiences. When subsequent researchers attempted to apply similar principles to the study of contemporary cultures, particularly minority and nonwestern cultures, they were heavily criticized because of their western biases. Rather than illuminating the cultures they studied, critics claimed they confirmed stereotypes and imposed western hegemonic concepts on nonwestern cultures, thus legitimating neocolonialism and racism. Disturbed by such criticism, many anthropologists turned their attention to "thick descriptions" of culture, postponing efforts to relate culture to personality until they had a better understanding of its complexity, or perhaps until the political culture changed.

But other social scientists chose not to abandon the effort to find linkages between culture and personality, many of them focusing on "national culture" and "national character." Political scientists Gabriel Almond and Sidney Verba, for example, argued that a civic culture is the essential element for stable democracies, while Christopher Lasch indicted Americans for promoting a "narcissistic" culture. Yet autonomy and equality, says Richard Wilson, are basic American cultural values. More recently, the study of the relationship between personality and culture is once again emerging as a systematic field of inquiry, largely justified in its potential usefulness for resolving international and intercultural conflicts. Understanding culture is indispensable, write Stanley Renshon and John Duckitt, arguing that international politics, bargaining, and conflict theory can be understood best when they are related to differences of "perception and understanding rooted in distinctive cultural frames and historical experiences."[16]

These social scientists show little interest in material culture, but they are vitally interested in nonmaterial culture, more often called "subjective culture." Their definitions of culture focus on mental constructs, and while they tend to agree on many points, their emphases often differ. Geert Hofstede, for example, calls culture "the collective programming of the mind," and he emphasizes its patterned way of "thinking, feeling, and acting." Lucien Pye defines it similarly, but emphasizes its strong emotional character; culture, he proposes, "can be thought of as being the 'mental map' which provides the knowledge that guides behavior" and whose "strong affective claims" help explain why the " 'clash of cultures' can be so intense." Cultural meaning is the center of Clifford Geertz's work; participants in the same culture are more likely to attribute similar meanings to objects and events, and more often in ways quite different from participants in another culture.[17]

Are the above researchers implying that all individuals in a culture share the same pattern of beliefs and values, and to the same degree of intensity? Not at all—agreement on this point is unanimous. Patterns reflect strong and sometimes dominant orientations; that is, participants in a culture have a "broad tendency to prefer certain states of affairs over others," as Hofstede puts it, or as Ann Swidler suggests, use their culture as a "tool kit" or filter through which they interpret situations. But most scholars allow for considerable latitude in attitudes and behavior. Some beliefs are widely shared among members of a social group and remain quite stable over generations; others are less widely shared and more subject to change, despite the fact that cultural change tends to be slow. All these points may help explain why Fiske and Tetlock define culture as "a *more or less* shared system of models and meaning."[18]

More difficult to resolve are the boundaries of a culture. Where does one culture end and another begin? Do people sharing a culture have to speak the same language? Do they need to be able to meet each other "face-to-face?" Answers vary. Harry Triandis, for example, appears to believe they do. Subjective culture, he agrees, includes "shared beliefs, attitudes, norms, roles, and values" but he adds that they are "found among speakers of a particular language who live during the same historical period in a specified geographic region." Hofstede doesn't quite agree and makes a subtle distinction between the cultures of groups and categories. Culture, he says, "does distinguish the members of one group or category of people from another," where a group of people do have contact, but a category of people does not necessarily require contact to feel they share something in common."[19]

"Groups" and "categories" allow for cultural variations among people sharing the same language and geography, as well as cultural similarities among people who share neither. Minority ethnic groups, for example, living in the same country and speaking the same language as the majority ethnic culture often perceive themselves as unique and distinct. And people who have the same occupation, for example, whether agriculture or engineering, or those who occupy a similar economic status, whether rich or poor, may live in different countries across the world and speak different languages yet still feel they share many things in common. Complicating the matter still further, individuals share overlapping cultural identities based on different criteria: gender, age, occupational and leisure interests, ethnic or political identification, and religion, among others.

Each country has many cultures within its geographical boundaries, and some cultures (for example, ethnic, political, and religious) transcend national boundaries. A religious denomination is sometimes a subcultural group within a nation, and often it is a nationally transcendent cultural group. Catholics and Protestants fall into both categories. As one cultural group within some particular national boundaries, each is likely to be influenced by the national and political culture so that its particular manifestation will be not quite the same as the very same denomination in another country. Catholics living in western Europe, for example, might find some Catholic Latin American theological conceptions and rituals somewhat different from their own, and the same applies to Lutherans. This suggests that there are hundreds if not thousands of cultures throughout the world (Hofstede suggests as many as ten thousand), and many of them overlap.[20] This makes it particularly difficult to determine the exact boundaries of a culture. Yet while cultural boundaries are admittedly inexact and permeable, it seems safe to conclude that they are real.

The above considerations have led to the definition of culture adopted here as the more or less shared beliefs, attitudes, norms, and values found among a group of people who may or may not have contact with each other but who nonetheless share a sense of common identity which makes them distinct from others. In this sense, Protestants and Catholics constitute cultures, while very religious and moderately religious Christians as well as the irreligious do so only arguably. Some might prefer to call the latter "subcultures," that is, segments of the larger Christian population, but even this might not be entirely satisfactory since the irreligious reject a Christian identity. With these caveats in mind but with due consideration for simplification, I henceforth refer to each of them as cultures or groups. In any case, we would not expect members of any of these groups to share identical beliefs, attitudes, norms, and values, but we might expect each to have a core of identifiable patterns that distinguishes them from others.

The concept "religion" also defies simple definition and poses several difficult substantive and measurement issues. Over the years, many social scientists and theologians have struggled to define it, some ultimately refusing to offer formal or theoretical definitions. Accepting the idea that any definition offered is likely to please only its author, psychologists of religion Ralph Hood, Bernard Spilka, Bruce Hunsburger, and Richard Gorsuch, for example, refrain from doing so in their most recent book about the psychology of religion.[21]

To some substantial degree, the lack of a generally accepted meaning of "religion" can be attributed to the concept's long history. Citing Wilfred Cantwell Smith, David Wulff, author of one of the most comprehensive works on the psychology of religion, offers a synopsis of the term's evolution over several distinct periods of time. Its original meaning derives from the Latin *religio*, referring generally to the idea of bonding with a greater-than-human power. During Roman times, it was often used to designate condemned ritual practices generally performed by enemies. During the Renaissance and Protestant Reformation, it was regarded as a feeling of inner piety. During the Enlightenment, it became an impersonal and abstract concept, the name for a system of ideas. Eventually, probably during the nineteenth century, it underwent a process of reification — that is, it was made a "fixed, objective unchanging entity." Smith sees the whole process as one of reification, not just the nineteenth-century portion of it, and proposes that the latter is utterly at odds with the dynamic, evolving quality of religions. To avoid all these negative associations, Smith advocates the concepts of *cumulative tradition* and *faith* as substitutes for "religion." Faith, according to Smith, reflects the human capacity to perceive meaning beyond the mundane and to act in terms of a transcendent dimension, and a cumulative tradition implies a changing and dynamic history nourished by faith.[22]

The above concepts are gaining ground among many people who are beginning to talk of "faith traditions" rather than "religions." Yet many social scientists continue to use the better-known term "religion," tending to define it in terms of its function and its substance, a manner of treatment developed particularly by sociologists.

Functional definitions focus on what religion *does* for a group. Religion, most social scientists agree, is a source of identity, social support, and integration, providing a group of people with answers to many questions ranging from the profound — such the meaning of life and the purpose of suffering and death — to prosaic matters — such as proper dress and diet. It thus allays anxiety and provides a feeling of comfort and security to its adherents, assuring them that the society in which they live is generally sound and that life is meaningful. Anthropologist Clifford Geertz sees religion's function as particularly important in three pressing problem areas: at the limits of comprehension, that is, where confusion reigns and chaos threatens; at the limits of endurance with respect to suffering; and at the limits of moral understanding with respect to perceived injustice.[23]

Substantive definitions, on the other hand, focus on a religion's content. Despite the highly varied nature within and among religions, the content of all religions does share some major substantive elements in common. Notions about who is "religious" have largely emerged from these commonalities.

At least four elements are commonly associated with religion's content: (1) a reference to god, gods, or some transcendent being; (2) a set of beliefs about the sacred; (3) rituals and practices; and (4) a moral code, that is, views about right and wrong. While these are often identified as common elements, not all of them are necessarily endorsed as essential. Writing almost one hundred years ago, Émile Durkheim, among the most eminent sociologists of religion of any century, excluded a reference to God in his definition. Religion, he said, is "a unified system of beliefs and practices relative to sacred things, that is to say, things set apart and forbidden — beliefs and practices which unite into one single moral community called a Church, all those who adhere to them." Sociologist Lester Kurtz's more recent definition also excludes reference to a god, and also omits the word "moral" while including the idea of a "religious tradition." Religion, he says, is a social phenomenon, consisting "of the beliefs, practices (rituals), the sacred, and the community or social organization of people who are drawn together by a religious tradition." Beyond being just a social phenomenon, says Keith Roberts, religion has to do with that "assortment of phenomena that communicates, celebrates, internalizes, interprets, and extrapolates a faith." Taking a less common approach, Daniel Batson, Patricia Schoenrade, and Larry Ventis define religion as a "quest": a process whereby "individuals . . . come to grips personally with the questions that confront us because we are aware that we and others like us are alive and that we will die."[24]

On a popular level, the term "religious" often refers to individuals who accept core denominational beliefs and practice rituals, but a higher standard is generally invoked to merit the label "very religious." In that case, some might insist, people need to manifest all four elements in their lives: not only accepting core beliefs and practicing rituals, but also feeling a strong relationship to something transcendent as well as manifesting behavior consistent with the denomination's moral code. Others might propose that the term "very religious" should be reserved only for those who do these things with exceptional commitment, while still others might suggest that even one of these elements might suffice, provided that it was done intensely. Linguistic conventions which describe these different forms of religiosity include words such as "spiritual," having "faith," "observant" (orthopraxy), and "orthodox."

In light of the above, it is not surprising that measuring religiosity in a scientific way has proved a formidable task. Efforts were already evident at the beginning of the twentieth century, but the most systematic measures did not emerge until the 1960s. Probably the best-known and most frequently used scale, the Intrinsic/Extrinsic Scale, measures concepts developed by Gordon

Allport. But the most commonly used measure today is church attendance: those who attend more often are ranked as more religious.[25]

The measure used here was equally simple but less conventional: respondents were asked to categorize themselves as very, somewhat, not very, or not at all religious. Self-identification is a subjective measure, depending on the respondent's own definition of religiosity, and criteria are thus likely to vary greatly from person to person. Yet it probably is not any more or less indicative of religiosity than is church attendance: a ritual that can be performed regularly but without necessarily reflecting particular meaning or strong religious feelings. Respondents were also asked to identify their denominational affiliation, Catholic or Protestant, during their growing up years.

The answers to the broad question guiding this study — How do levels of religiosity (very religious, moderately religious, and irreligious) and religious denomination (Protestant and Catholic, specifically) influence rescue? — center on value and attitudinal orientations often associated with altruistic behaviors generally and outgroup altruistic behaviors in particular. They focus on five major summary factors, each of which includes several associated measures. The summary factors, and their associated measures, constitute the core of the study and serve as the organizational framework for comparisons within each chapter, although not necessarily in the same order as listed below. Construction of each of the summary factors and their associated variables is given in Appendix B.

The Mastery Orientation summary factor and its seven associated measures assess the means the culture encourages to achieve power and control. It includes an External Mastery Orientation and an Internal Mastery Orientation. An External Mastery Orientation reflects a tendency to achieve mastery through compliance with external criteria. An Internal Mastery Orientation reflects a tendency to achieve mastery through reliance on one's internal resources. Altruism is often associated with a rejection of an external orientation in favor of an internal one.

The Sharing summary factor and its ten associated measures assess the degree to which respondents in each group supported values encouraging the distribution of resources — social and material — for others' welfare. Feelings of empathy, particularly toward others' pain, as well as a sense of care, social responsibility, and personal integrity, are commonly associated with altruism.

The Primary Relationships summary factor and its eleven associated measures concentrate primarily on assessing respondents' feelings about their families of origin. Good relationships with families of origin are also often associated with altruism.

The fourth summary factor, Secondary Relationships, and its eight associated measures assess the types of secondary relationships that the group encouraged. It includes respondents' religious and secular ties, the latter including affiliations with political parties and resistance groups, as well as identification with the national community. The influence of supportive secondary institutions on altruistic behavior, including outgroup altruism, has not been investigated by social scientists as often as other variables.

An Internal Mastery orientation, Sharing predispositions, and solid Primary Relationships are associated with altruism generally, but they do not necessarily imply altruism toward outsiders. The fifth major summary factor, Outgroup Relationships and its sixteen associated measures, are intended to assess the types of relationships with outsider groups that the culture tolerated or encouraged. It includes attitudes toward and relationships with outgroup members, where outgroups include others having a different religious or ethnic status, and particularly focused on Jews.

Chapters 2 through 4 focus on degree of religiosity. Chapter 2 concentrates on the very religious, Chapter 3 on the irreligious, and Chapter 4 on the moderately religious. Chapters 5 and 6 focus on religious denomination: Chapter 5 looks at Protestants; Chapter 6 concentrates on Catholics. Methodology and supportive statistical data are included in the appendixes.

Chapters 2 through 6 are divided into three sections. The first begins with a brief study of two individual rescuers from different national contexts, illustrative in some important ways of participants in that religious group generally and rescuers particularly. The second section focuses on intergroup differences, that is, how the group as a whole compares with other groups. The third section focuses on intragroup comparisons, that is, how rescuers compare with nonrescuers or bystanders within the same group.

Although statistics inform all the following analyses and conclusions, individual case studies are also a major focus of this work. Individuals translate statistics into compelling portraits, yet rarely do they conform to what might be considered "ideal types." Each person conveys not only the tenor of the times and some of the characteristics of their referent group, but also the idiosyncratic perceptions and thinking that mark them as individuals. Intergroup and intragroup discussions emanate primarily from statistical comparisons but also include considerations of what others have said about similar points. In some cases these sources support my findings, and they often also provide a deeper and broader view of the cultural group under discussion.

The word "significant" has a particular statistical meaning in this book: it means that the probability of finding a particular difference between groups if there were no true differences among the larger populations of compared cultural groups is no greater than five times in a hundred samples. Although I've omitted the word "significant" from the narrative in order to avoid repetition, reported differences are indeed statistically significant and can be checked in the tables that appear in Appendix B.

Chapter 7 highlights outstanding factors among cultural groups, including rescuers, nonrescuers, and bystanders, and suggests attitudes and beliefs that might constitute a core group of values reflective of an outgroup altruistic culture. Based on a discriminant analysis function, it also distinguishes among those attributes that appear to contribute most from those that contribute less. Chapter 8 offers some final thoughts on the relationships between culture generally and outgroup altruism.

Appendix A should be of particular interest to those who want to understand the methodological basis upon which all the foregoing is based. Appendix B includes tables and figures.

Despite the passage of years and a different historical context, the people described here probably resemble most of us. While a few will inspire us, and others disappoint us because of their all too common human frailties, some may trouble us deeply. By sharing their wartime lives, they offer us the opportunity for self-reflection, not only about the past but also about a present that continues to be marked by trauma and difficult choices.

The Very Religious

ALICE

In November 1942, I received a letter from the Secretariat of the Catholic Society of the region of Toulouse. The Archbishop of Toulouse, Monsignor Saliège, had proclaimed to all the churches of the area that he was the defender and firm supporter of all the oppressed victims of the war. He had done so by having all the local priests read his letter to the parishioners of the region.

A month later, in December 1942, and with the permission of the Bishop of Rodez, I made the decision to help rescue the persecuted. Only three other nuns and I were aware of the undertaking; the other eleven nuns at the convent, we decided, would not participate: we judged it safer that the whole group not know and we didn't want to put them in jeopardy.

Six months later, the first six children (between five and fifteen years old) arrived at the convent. One child had come from Paris; the other five were from Nancy. They were all Jewish children, all from a camp at Bruyère near Toulouse. All had just been separated from their parents. Right after that, about sixty more children came. By the beginning of the year 1944, a grand total of seventy-eight to eighty-four children from seven nationalities lived at the school. Seven adults, mothers of some children, were hidden in the basement of the convent.

The sisters were very worried and concerned for the safety of the children; it was their job to teach them how to act in accordance with their new civil status. We gave all of them different last names. The sisters had to constantly drill them so that they would answer correctly if questioned by outsiders. They also had to learn the Catholic prayers. All went well for them; all were returned to their own families three or four months after liberation.

My reasons for involvement were human sensibility, Christian sensibility, love for children and young people, patriotism, retaliation and resistance against the Nazis.

Sister Alice, the nun quoted above, belonged to the "very religious category"; like all the others, self-identified as such. Thirty years old and busily engaged as a teacher when she received the archbishop's pastoral letter, she was then living, along with her convent sisters, in a small French town of some 4,000 people. Despite her cloistered circumstances, she represents several attributes of very religious Christians generally, rescuers and nonrescuers, as well as the particular characteristics and circumstances that aroused some very religious rescuers to action.

The archbishop sent his letter in the latter part of 1942, but persecutions against Jews had begun much earlier. Almost immediately after the German victory in June 1940, Jews were deprived of any opportunity to lead a normal existence, the result of a series of publicly proclaimed laws that had progressively deprived them of civil, economic, and legal rights. Roundups in the Occupied Northern Zone and Unoccupied Southern Zone (Vichy) continued throughout that year, and by September some forty thousand Jews were interned in the thirty-one camps in the southern zone alone: most of them refugees escaping from Germany and occupied countries but also including French Jews.[1] Conditions at some camps were horrendous: death by starvation, exposure, and disease were common. Roundups became more frequent, and by the summer of 1942, say historians Michael Marrus and Robert Paxton, "the intensity of Jewish suffering was apparent to anyone who would look." But few in French society were really looking, including the ranks of the Catholic hierarchy. In fact, with the exception of some individual Catholics, observe Marrus and Paxton, "no public utterance by any member of the Catholic hierarchy had troubled the apparently solid front between Church and State" for the first two years of the Vichy regime.[2]

July 1942, however, marked a turning point, when the roundups in Paris made the barbarity highly visible. The Germans had pushed to have 28,000 Jews arrested in the Paris region within two days; 22,000 of them were to be deported "to the east." Concentrating on stateless and foreign Jews, the French municipal police began carrying out the arrests on July 16, assembling the prisoners first at the Vélodrome d'hiver—a large indoor sports arena—

before taking them to the designated camps. Some 13,000 people, including over 4,000 children, were packed into the "Vél'd'hiv'," confined there for five days with neither food nor water nor sanitary provisions, not even enough space to lie down. What had heretofore been invisible to the Parisian public became starkly obvious — the cries of children separated from parents, the stench, the overall despair and terror impressed a population largely indifferent until this point. French public opinion changed — it became clear to a large number that Jews were indeed suffering more than others. And for the first time, as well as the last, some religious figures in positions of power protested.[3]

In this context, Monsignor Jules-Gerard Saliège, the archbishop of Toulouse, sent a pastoral letter to all the parishes of his diocese asking them to read it to their congregants on Sunday, August 23, 1942. It was that letter which Sister Alice received. It read as follows:

My dear brothers:

There is a Christian morality and a humane morality that imposes some actions and recognizes some rights. Those actions, those rights, belong to the "nature of man." They come from God. One may not violate them. No mortal has the power to abolish them.

When children, women, men, fathers and mothers are treated like a vile herd, when members of the same family have to be separated from one another and dispatched to an unknown destination, such a sad spectacle was reserved for our time in history.

Why don't the Churches offer refuge? Why doesn't this right exist any longer? Why are we defeated? Lord, have mercy on us. Our Lady, pray for us.

In our diocese, scenes of terror took place in the Noé and Recedebou camps. Jews are men, Jewesses are women. All is not permitted against them, against those men, those women, those fathers, those mothers. They all belong to the human race. They are our brothers just like any other. A Christian cannot forget this.

France, beloved country, France who brings to the mind and heart of all her children the tradition of respect for the human person! Generous France, I don't doubt it! You are not responsible! Receive, my brothers, the assurance of my affectionate devotion.

Until the moment she read the archbishop's letter, Sister Alice was unaware of what was happening — Jews simply had no relevance for her until that point. Having entered the convent when she was only nineteen, after attending a Catholic elementary school and lycée, she had had minimal contact with non-Catholics and none with Jews. She had not known any in her youth or even as an adult; none had lived in her neighborhood, and her parents had never spoken about them. That the archbishop had noted the injustice perpetrated by the Nazi regime was a noteworthy act given the potential costs under a tyrannical regime. By mentioning "Jews" specifically, rather than alluding to them under the rubric of the generally suffering or maltreated as was more commonly the case, the archbishop had singled them out as particularly abused victims meriting Christian intervention as a top priority.[4] The letter's impact on Sister Alice was dramatic: the sheltered and oblivious person she had been was replaced by a defiant, risk-taking subversive — a particular irony, since one of the major values she recalled learning from her parents was honesty.

ALEXANDER

Living in a different country and under quite different circumstances, Alexander, a Dutch Protestant male, is another example of a very religious rescuer, resembling Sister Alice in many ways. Unlike Sister Alice, however, Alexander was very familiar with Jews, but in a manner that was at best ambivalent and potentially hostile. As in Alice's case, religious leadership was a critical factor in his decision to rescue.

In 1942, Alexander, then thirty-eight years old, was living with his family in Leidsche Dam, a small city of approximately ten thousand people located in northern Friesland, Holland. The family, which included his wife and seven children, ages two to thirteen, had moved there from Rijssen so that Alexander could accept a job promotion. As the director of a gas factory, he earned a generous salary and owned a comfortable seven-room house. Like Sister Alice, Alexander began his rescue activities in 1942:

> When we moved to Leidsche Dam, the Jews were not bothered yet. But within a year we received a letter from my brother-in law that the Jews in Rijssen were having trouble: a doctor and a teacher had been arrested, and others too. We thought immediately of the Levin family. A few days later at the dinner table, we were reading as our daily Bible reading the passage in Isaiah 58 that talks about fasting, sharing your bread with the hungry, bringing the poor and persecuted to your house, clothing the naked and so on. The children were at the table, but my wife and I looked at each other and we knew what we had to do: this was our way. So I wrote to Heindrik Levin that we knew they were in trouble and that our house was open to him. He answered right away and said that he was very happy and thankful, but that he would not make use of our invitation, but maybe his son, Jacob, or his brother would.
>
> Half a year later, early 1942, we got a letter from Jacob that things were getting hard for him. I went to Amsterdam immediately; I didn't dare write.

He was in the Jewish neighborhood. I rang the bell: there was one door for two or three apartments. A woman opened the door. I asked: "Does Jacob Levin live here?" "Levin? Levin?" she said. But then I heard somebody call out: "It's Alexander Donat, Alexander Donat!" Jacob had already hidden under a bed; they were so frightened. He said it wasn't urgent anymore since his wife had a doctor's declaration that she was too sick to travel. But one or two weeks later, I was sitting in my office at the gas factory when I spotted someone with red hair. Jacob! There had been so many raids by then that he had brought along a suitcase with clothes and wanted to make arrangements. I asked the boatsman who went to and from Amsterdam all the time to bring Jacob's family. The next day the lady who had opened the door for me came to fetch the suitcase back. "It wasn't necessary any more," she said. They had gotten a permanent *Ausweiss,* so they felt quite safe.[5]

When I told my wife, she became furious. "Do you believe that," she said. "They should come here now! I'll come with you to tell them to come right now!" When we got there, Jacob's wife said she was ill and couldn't come, but we tried to convince her. By this time, she had gotten to know us and felt more comfortable with us. After a week they came. We gave Jacob and his wife the larger room and moved our eldest sons into the room with their other brothers.

Jacob and his wife, along with their two children born during the war, stayed with the Donats until 1945. Two of Jacob's relatives also stayed for a few weeks.

Given Alexander's persistence and concern, it might appear that Heindrik Levin and his family were close friends. This was not the case. Although Jews lived in his neighborhood, suggesting the possibility of friendships, neither he nor his wife had Jewish friends before the war. He had met Levin the way he usually met Jews: as his mother before him, he called on them in an effort to convert them. What made Heindrik memorable to Alexander was the fact that of all the people he called on, only Heindrik had invited him into his home. Heindrik rejected Alexander's religious message — "He sent me home and told me to read Psalm 147" — but Alexander did not forget him.

As with Sister Alice, religion and church were the organizing motifs of Alexander's life. The same had been true of his parents. His father taught at a denominational school, and Alexander himself attended a sectarian elementary school and gymnasium. Daily Bible readings, church attendance, rituals, and activities with co-religionists shaped his routine life. Not a very social type, Alexander regarded his religious community as a major source of meaningful associations and beliefs. For Alexander, as for his parents, that community was the Reformed Church (*Gereformeerde Kerken*). Not to be confused with the dominant Dutch Reformed Church, the Reformed Church was an orthodox, conservative Calvinist minority denomination.

Unlike the French Catholic hierarchy, the leaders of the Reformed Church in Holland had protested anti-Jewish measures early. As historian Lawrence Baron points out, the synod of the Reformed Church had taken strong anti-Nazi positions even before the war, and lodged official protests with the Reich commissioner as soon as exclusionary measures against Jews were taken in 1940. They condemned antisemitism and had pastors read from their pulpits an ecumenical denunciation of the deportations of Jews when they began in 1942. But religious officials were not united about the appropriate strategy to deal with their tyrannical occupiers: some advocated rapprochement, urging negotiation rather than repudiation and defiance. Notably, although they constituted only 9 percent of the Dutch population, members of the Reformed Church accounted for an estimated 25 percent of rescued Jews in Holland.[6]

Based on an analysis of their transcripts in the Altruistic Personality Project data base, Baron concluded that this religious community's immersion in the Hebrew and Christian Testaments evoked a strong feeling of religious kinship with Jews. While they harbored many conventional social, economic, and religiously based prejudices toward Jews, they also regarded them as "God's special people"; having made a covenant with them, God would keep his word. "These beliefs," says Baron, "predominated over contradictory economic resentments and theological prejudices against Jews."[7] Once the war started, strong anti-German sentiments, coupled with an ethical obligation to help the needy, reinforced their readiness to act. Their religious, social, and political insularity facilitated covert rescue activities; like Alice, they could depend on a strong network of co-religionists who were unlikely to betray them even if they did not actively help.

Alexander represents many of the characteristics Baron notes. He had heard and read about Jewish persecution in Germany before the invasion of his country but not without anti-Jewish prejudices, or perhaps more inclined to credit fellow-Protestants, he tended to trust Germans and dismissed the accounts as "exaggerated." His view was not changed even when Jewish refugees with whom he had business dealings told him about their personal experiences. But once the Germans invaded Holland, he regarded them as enemies not only of his country but also of his religion: "children of Satan," he called them.

Alexander does not say he heard the ecumenical letter that the pastors read; most likely he did. More immediate was the influence and help of his minister. He knew his minister was hiding Jews and consulted with him often on the matter. Asked why he helped, Alexander answered: "Through my upbringing I was sure I could trust God. And just when we had heard about their problems, we read that passage in the Bible." Strongly grounded in the Jewish and

Christian Bible, which his family read daily to seek guidance, and already disposed toward some type of action, he and his wife interpreted the reading from Isaiah about helping the needy as applying to them.

The fact that Alice and Alexander became rescuers only when aroused by their religious leaders gives apparent credence to the hypothesis that if the church had taken a clear stand, the Holocaust might never have happened. Does this then mean that religious leadership was *the* determining agent, that is, that the very religious became rescuers only when supported by their leadership? If that were the case, why then did others belonging to the same community, subject to similar messages and ostensibly sharing a similar degree of religious passion, do nothing? Religious leadership had a strong influence, but other factors also mattered.

The Very Religious and the Less Religious

In this section, I describe some of the characteristics of very religious culture generally, highlighting those attributes that significantly distinguish them from the less religious. In the following section, I compare very religious rescuers with equally religious nonrescuers. The five summary factors (Mastery Orientation, External/Internal; Sharing; Primary Relationships; Secondary Relationships; and Outgroup Relationships), and particularly their associated measures, serve as the organizing framework for these comparisons, although not necessarily in the above order.

How do very religious Christians, rescuers and nonrescuers, compare with those who were less religious? Our data suggest that they share several cultural characteristics that distinguish them from the less religious, some of which suggest a tendency toward altruism and are sometimes alleged to be particularly "Christian."

Christian culture allegedly minimizes materialistic concerns while encouraging adherents to place their own needs second to the needs of others. Alice and Alexander manifested such attributes, and there appears to be a measure of truth to this assertion in a more general way. Part of the evidence emerges from comparisons among religiosity groups with respect to External and Internal Mastery measures, particularly as they related to their associated measures of economic competence and willingness to stand up for their beliefs.

Economic competence, parental focus on matters relating to work and money, ranked significantly lower among the very religious generally as compared with the somewhat religious generally, a distinction that also marked very religious rescuers as compared with somewhat religious rescuers. While achievement and industriousness mattered, the very religious, as compared with the somewhat religious, often regarded asserting their convictions as more important. Asked if they had ever done anything before the war to stand up for their beliefs, the very religious were significantly more likely than the somewhat religious to say they had. It was a quality they shared with the irreligious (see Appendix B, Table 2bV).

As in the case of Alice and Alexander, internal convictions, rather than economic considerations, often motivated the very religious to act before the war, even when such behaviors meant taking up unpopular causes. When they were asked what kinds of beliefs they defended, their answers included political and personal issues, but religious themes constituted more than a third (35 percent) of their claimed assertive postures before the war.

Religious themes included doctrine: "I fought for my faith, against infant baptism and for abstinence from alcohol," said a Dutch Reformed Protestant woman rescuer, while a German male nonrescuer joined the *Bekennenden Kirche* because they held religious views "opposed to the mainstream." In fact, their religious beliefs sometimes cost them valued relationships. Unwilling to convert, for example, a French Catholic woman nonrescuer rejected marriage to both a Jew and a Protestant. A Dutch couple became estranged from close relatives: "I lost family members because my wife and I had different religious ideas from them. We were not dogmatic, but we were critical of them." Merely identifying themselves publicly as members of a particular religious community sometimes had negative consequences. "In 1936," said a French respondent, " I was a member of Juniors for Christ. The math teacher at the school was a member of the Communist Party. Because I was wearing my group pin, I was unjustly punished but I spoke out for my rights." A Lutheran man experienced something similar in the dominantly Calvinist school he had attended: "The Calvinist teacher was putting Lutherans down. So I raised my hand and said, 'I'm a Lutheran.' As a consequence my grades went down."

The fact that a relatively high percentage of the very religious were willing to assert their beliefs publicly, even when such positions might mean social rejection or worse, suggests something about the quality of this group. Unwilling to be as accommodating or as flexible as their more moderate co-religionists, they were often regarded as eccentric, even somewhat "deviant" by comparison.[8] Nourished and sustained by their co-religionists in a way that is often lacking in the larger society, and persuaded of the virtue of their behaviors, the very religious can be a formidable acting force.

Asserting one's beliefs can be construed as a means for expressing distinctiveness and difference from others, a matter of choosing one's own goals rather than those of others. But it may have consequences that transcend individual purpose: bringing the needs and interests of the religious group to the attention of the larger society can enhance the welfare of the group. More intentionally and clearly related to altruism is the quality we call "Sharing." Rather than seeking differentiation or distinction, a Sharing culture is more inclined toward joining with others and committing resources for others' welfare. *Christian religious culture has a strong Sharing predisposition,* a proposition that our data also tend to support.

The very religious scored significantly higher than either the somewhat religious or irreligious on the summary Sharing factor. They evidenced their strong Sharing propensities in several of the associated Sharing measures. More than the somewhat religious, they valued involvement with rather than detachment from others, a difference that also distinguished very religious rescuers from somewhat religious rescuers. Conjoined with this was their sense of social responsibility, which was significantly stronger than that of the somewhat religious and the irreligious. This, coupled with the fact that significantly more of them, as compared with the irreligious, perceived themselves as persons of integrity who possessed a strong sense of empathy for those in distress (a prosocial action orientation), enhanced their Sharing propensities. Even very religious nonrescuers, as compared with other nonrescuers, evidenced a somewhat similar pattern, scoring significantly higher than somewhat religious nonrescuers on empathy measures, and significantly higher than irreligious nonrescuers on prosocial inclinations and personal integrity (see Table 2bIV).[9]

Sharing attitudes and values have been significantly and repeatedly associated with altruism.[10] But herein lies an apparent paradox. Given their strong Sharing impulses, consistency suggests that the very religious in particular might support what Barnea and Schwartz call "economic egalitarianism." Economic egalitarianism supports income redistribution based on equity, equality, and need.[11] But as with their current North American counterparts, the party affiliations of the very religious tended to reflect a rejection or limited acceptance of government-administered economic egalitarianism in favor of pro-capitalistic views (see Table 2aI).

Very few of the very religious or their parents belonged to leftist parties (12 percent and 13 percent, respectively); none were Communists but a few were Socialists.[12] A somewhat larger group, 19 percent, belonged to the economic right: parties advocating general noninterference by government in economic matters relating to private enterprise and free trade, and rejection of social welfare measures. The majority belonged to political parties that took a middle position, endorsing capitalist enterprise but also supporting social welfare policies to varying degrees (67 percent and 58 percent, respectively). In short, the economic politics of respondents, their parents, and their spouses as reflected in their political affiliations was basically centrist with an inclination toward the right.[13]

Yet in economic matters, as in many other matters, religious institutions played a dominant role. The political groups to which many of the very religious respondents or their parents belonged were associated with or directly linked to their churches. The economic policies the very religious endorsed by virtue of their political affiliations thus appeared often to converge with the interests of their religious denominational institutions.[14]

A striking aspect of very religious culture is the degree to which participants felt integrated into the social institutions of their society — religious, political, national, and family — that largely shared overlapping values, many of them reflecting their religious orientations. On the one hand, this strengthened their assertive capacities; on the other it tended to insulate them from outsiders, that is, from neighbors who were unlike them. To illustrate these points, we begin first with family relationships and values (Primary Relationships), go on to values learned from and relationships with religious institutions as well as involvements with and sentiments toward politics and country (Secondary Relationships), and conclude with attitudes toward outsiders (Outgroup Relationships).

Family is where many value orientations are forged, and very religious families are no exception. The very religious were significantly more likely than the mildly religious and/or irreligious to describe their family relationships as close and to speak about their parents and families generally in warm terms (see Table 2bIII).[15] Solid positive family relationships are often linked to altruism by virtue of their propensity to encourage trust in others and model the value of care.

Very religious respondents were significantly more likely than others to have very religious parents, and they reported hearing about religion often in their homes. Parents, far more than church or religious leaders, appeared to influence their attitudes toward religion, doing so explicitly as well as implicitly.[16]

While parents were more successful in imparting the value of religion to their children, neither parents nor religious leaders appeared often to link religion *explicitly* with caring for others. Asked what they learned from their parents, more than a fourth of respondents (28 percent) identified some aspect of religion. Some said parents taught them to pray or encouraged them to study the Bible, to respect the church, or simply to be a good Christian. Parents sometimes emphasized having a special relationship to God: "to love the Lord," "to trust and serve Him," and "to have faith." Faith, their children learned, was a source of comfort; knowing they had chosen the "right" path provided them with a reliable guide for living and a comforting contract. If they did what God wanted, He would reward them. All the same, they needed to be careful: the rest of the world might judge matters by external appearances. But as one respondent learned from her father: "People see things on the outside but the Lord sees the inside. That is the same way you have to live. People must see that you are not only clean on the outside but also the inside."

Religion instructors taught much the same things. Approximately a third of respondents (31 percent) said they focused on items similar to those of parents: religious ritual, Bible studies, and/or appropriate attitudes to the Church and God (e.g., "I learned Catholic rules and to obey these rules," "Church dogma and prayers," "to believe in Christ"). As with their parents, love and trust in God was sometimes expressed as a comforting contract — God would not abandon you if you obeyed Him. Failure to believe, in contrast, could mean damnation. "You had to love God the Lord and believe that Christ died for us, was buried and survived for us," said a Protestant woman, "and pleads for us sinners with our Lord. That way we'll be saved." Some 20 percent of respondents simply said that they heard the same things from their religion teachers as they did from their parents.

While family and church values largely converged, the influence of church teachers during children's developing years appeared to be relatively weaker. It was simply indistinct for approximately a third: around 10 percent said they learned nothing from these teachers, another 20 percent couldn't recall anything concrete. A few recalled negative experiences. One man objected to the shallow quality of what he was taught: "They demanded too much conformity to outward forms . . . prayer, reading, ritual; I found it false and wearisome." Another objected to the fear his religious teachers imposed: "Teachers sometimes tried to teach religion through fear rather than joy. I had very strict religious teachers but they were not very good psychologists; they mainly spread fear while teaching the Catholic faith." A Protestant man had a similar recollection: "They always said you are not sure if you will be saved. You have to pray every day and night. They make you feel guilty." Sometimes teachers could be cruel. An experience with nuns in Mexico, where his parents had sent him for a short period as a young boy, had a devastating effect on one Dane: "They put you in a dark room with a frosted white glass with a light behind it. Nuns would create shadows. There was a red velvet altar and a crucifix. You were supposed to kneel down and pray for your sins." He overcame this trauma, however, when he returned to Denmark and to more kindly instructors. Some learned to distinguish between Church and what they regarded as authentic Christian values: "I learned to respect Christ but had bad luck with priests," said one respondent. Unwilling to make such a distinction, a German rescuer decided she had had enough and left the Church entirely when her minister appeared one day wearing a swastika.

For many more, however, religious instruction was simply neutral. And sometimes it was deeply favorable. Only a few said they learned to be caring and compassionate and to serve others, some even claiming that such obligations extended not only to the faith community but to all of humankind. Yet regardless of the quality of their experiences with religious leaders — whether indistinct, negative, or profoundly positive — the very religious remained strongly attached to their faith communities, identifying with them strongly (see Table 2aII). They suppressed what they might not have liked, preferring on the whole to concentrate on the positive, and when necessary, they made a sharp distinction between religion and religious leadership.

Parents, generally regarded as more effective than religion teachers, also rarely linked religion explicitly with caring for others. Asked how parents taught them religious values, respondents often replied that parents modeled religious behavior rather than giving explicit instructions. "My mother was a saint," said a French woman. "On the first of January she didn't want to wish us a happy New Year before she went to church. She climbed a big mountain by foot, a basilica, to say happy New Year to God. Then she came down and wished us the same." Some parents linked Christianity with joy: "My mother influenced us with her cheerful Christianity," said one respondent, while another said of his very religious mother, "She showed me how to enjoy life. She loved her own little garden and geese, she loved nature." Cheerfulness and playfulness helped, but laxity with respect to religious observance was not necessarily required. "My father was very strict and we had to obey him," said one respondent, "but he played with us too; he really helped instill my religious beliefs." And sometimes, admiration came later, as people matured. As one person put it, "My father was a very devotedly religious person. As I child I didn't get along with him because he was very strict. But my father influenced us greatly without us knowing it with his very genuine religion. He was not hypocritical. He was enormously strict for himself and enormously liberal towards other people." It took many years for another respondent to understand the nature of her father's belief: "I learned to have profound admiration for something I could not name or completely understand," she said. "It was not until much later that I realized that my father was a rather mystical person and I had such admiration for him because of that."

Many very religious respondents learned from their parents not only to respect religion, but also that politics often was a means for implementing family and church values. They were far more likely than the somewhat religious to affiliate politically (see Table 2aII), and the political groups to which many of the very religious belonged were directly or indirectly linked to their churches. Politics, after all, was often simply an extension of family and church, made up largely of overlapping interests, attitudes, and values.

What is perhaps surprising is the strong *patriotism* of the very religious, significantly stronger than the mildly religious and the irreligious even in their youth (see Table 2aII). Many people became more patriotic during the war, either because they suffered the tyranny of the German occupation or because the condition of war demanded taking sides: to choose anything less than total allegiance to one's country risked being branded a traitor. On a deeper level, when the fate of each individual matters little, people are more likely to affirm their kinship ties if only as a way of experiencing some sense of meaning in the brutalities and deaths that are war's constant companions.[17] In times of terror, observes social psychologist Janusz Reykowski, individuation decreases and identification increases.[18] But in times of peace, allegiance to country suggests a competing and potentially rival authority to religion; yet the very religious by and large saw no dissonance between religious and political loyalties. God, church and country were part of a seamless web of overlapping interests and intermeshing loyalties, requiring no conflicting choices but rather harmonious compatibility.

Of course, the churches they represented were most often favored national churches, well protected by government; affirming one meant also affirming the other. Minority religious groups — such as Catholics in Germany or in Holland, or Protestants in France or Poland — often exaggerated their patriotic fervor in order to protect their more vulnerable status. On another level, patriotism and religion serve similar functions, thus perhaps appealing to similar groups. Like religion, patriotism can allay anxiety and provide emotional and social support, impart a sense of truth and righteousness, and reassure people they live in an ordered and meaningful universe under legitimated power arrangements. By becoming part of a greater collectivity, one that has greater endurance and importance than any single person, individuals can feel enhanced, almost immortal. Losing oneself in the group can thus be experienced as gaining oneself; a phenomenon that tyrants have exploited to great advantage. And just as religion can justify all kinds of atrocities by invoking God, so can patriotism by invoking love of country. But like religion, it can also elicit high levels of selfless behavior on behalf of the group.

Yet implied in the notions of religiosity and patriotism is the idea that selfless behavior may be confined to the ingroup alone while those outside are viewed as distant at best or even objects of hostility. The very existence of outgroups can be construed as a challenge to the group, observes Reykowski, requiring its members to overpower them.[19] But as he and others have suggested, patriotism does not necessarily mean nationalism. Patriotism of the kind Ervin Staub calls "constructive" concentrates on love for country that includes critical consciousness and loyalty; nationalism, which he calls "blind patriotism," seeks national domination over others and is strongly associated with bigotry.[20] Their attitudes toward outgroups suggests that the very religious, as compared with the moderately religious, inclined somewhat more to the love of country type of patriotism rather than the blind nationalistic variety. Evidence of this is the nature of their political party affiliations and those of their parents and/or spouse. Although the very religious were not inclined toward promoting equality toward outsiders, the political parties with which they affiliated generally favored forbearance and tolerance (see Table 2aI). Yet while largely centrist in their views, endorsing democracy and reasonably accepting of outsiders, they did not regard Jews as central to their concerns: at best, they were simply peripheral.

Strongly integrated into their own groups, the very religious tended to be somewhat more insulated than the less religious and less likely to interact with or be interested in Jews. As compared with all other groups, they were least likely to meet them at school, a matter not entirely surprising since they tended to attend sectarian schools. And along with the somewhat religious, they reported having learned about Nazi intentions toward the Jews later than did the irreligious. Such distance even appeared to characterize very religious rescuers as compared with other rescuers. Very religious rescuers were also significantly least likely to attend school with Jews as compared with all other rescuers, learned about Nazi intentions toward Jews later than did irreligious rescuers, and were less likely to have Jewish friends or even acquaintances as compared with mildly religious rescuers (see Table 2aI). As a consequence, they may well have been more likely than other groups to regard Jews as an abstraction — attitudes toward them learned more from their parents and churches than from personal contacts.

What they learned was likely to cover a broad spectrum: at one end churches often taught a virulent antisemitism and at the other end and, more rarely, a particular philo-Semitism. Religious groups who taught the latter, observes Christian ethicist David Gushee, felt a sense of kinship with Jews based on their veneration for the Hebrew Bible.[21]

Interest in and respect for the Hebrew Bible clearly influenced Alexander's church; it also influenced the father of a French rescuer. "My father was very liberal," she said, "and this was unusual in Poitiers, which was mostly antisemitic. I think my father was interested in Jewish people because he was interested in the Bible and the Psalms." But interest in and respect for the Bible did not necessarily spare even philo-Semites from conversion efforts, as Alexander demonstrated.[22] Nor did it necessarily mean particular interest in their present fate — which helps explain why the very religious tended to learn about Nazi intentions later than others. Finally, it did not inure them to conventional prejudices, for even as the Bible might provide them with a positive lens through which to view Jews, it could also provoke strong anti-Jewish sentiments.[23]

How prejudiced were the very religious? To be sure, many did express particularistic and exclusivist attitudes: their own religion, they believed, was uniquely true and superior to others. "God's word" meant for them not only exclusion of non-Christian beliefs, but exclusive loyalty to a particular denomination and its official beliefs. As some respondents put it, what they learned from their church leaders was "loyalty to *the* Church," "that Catholicism was the *only right way*," "to serve *the true God*," "to learn *Catholic* rules and to obey them," "*Christian* morality" and "to be concerned that people follow the *Christian* moral laws." Particularism of this sort tends to be accompanied by antipathy toward outsiders, a finding reported by sociologists Charles Glock and Rodney Stark more than forty years ago.[24] In fact, most studies done before 1960 in the United States echoed a similar theme: a positive linear relationship existed between religiosity and prejudice. The greater the level of religiosity, the greater the level of bigotry, concluded many researchers.[25] This link was strongly associated with specific forms of prejudice, especially against Jews and African Americans.[26]

Faced with all this evidence, as well as mounting indications of Christian culpability in the Holocaust, some Christian theologians and historians began to explore the degree to which Christian beliefs contribute to antisemitism. They found strong anti-Jewish sentiment in the Gospels, in Christian theology, and in a long and checkered history of Christian leadership that had at different times and places endorsed and promoted it.[27] One of the earliest Christian investigators of this genre was Malcolm Hay, who concluded that Christian "pride, arrogance and hate" among some of the most learned and pious over centuries prepared the world for the Holocaust, a charge subsequently supported by others as well.[28]

Less interested in theological bases for prejudice, social scientists approached the matter of religiosity and prejudice differently. As methodology became more sophisticated, social scientists began to question earlier studies, concentrating particularly on the measures they used to assess religiosity. Church membership was a frequently used measure, a standard that some social scientists found not entirely satisfactory since it can imply conformity rather than authentic commitment. When they added church attendance to membership, a curious finding emerged. Church members continued to evidence more prejudice than did nonmembers, but those who attended church most frequently and were most active were less prejudiced than other church members. Rather than a linear relationship, this implied a curvilinear relationship between religion and prejudice; that is, the very religious and least religious were less prejudiced as compared with those in the middle, the most prejudiced group. The irreligious continued to remain the least prejudiced.[29]

A curvilinear relationship between religiosity and prejudice characterizes the present study as well, but only among nonrescuers. Very religious rescuers were like all other rescuers in that they did not differ significantly on stereotypic thinking. But among nonrescuers, very religious and irreligious nonrescuers, as compared with somewhat religious nonrescuers, were significantly less oriented toward stereotypic thinking and negative stereotypes in particular. Consistent with the curvilinear finding noted above, somewhat religious nonrescuers scored significantly higher than all other groups on these attitudes (see Table 2aI and Chapter 4 for more on this point).

But with respect to economic and general policy concerns, the welfare of the church and that of ingroup members generally came first. At best, outsiders were marginal. Thus it is not entirely surprising that religious officials all too often supported the principle of discrimination against Jews, even as they may have simultaneously urged "charity." A clearly articulated example of priorities of care was a letter J. M. Étienne Dupy wrote to all the heads of the religious houses in his order in Toulouse in 1941 following a series of publicly distributed anti-Jewish edicts:

> While accepting the legitimacy of the measures taken, we have the charitable duty to help out with the individual suffering that results. The common good of the nation comes before that of the Jews alone, and a baptized Jew, son of the Church, before him who is not, and spiritual goods before temporal goods. . . . The Jews, according to an often well-deserved reputation, require us to exercise extreme prudence.[30]

Those who read this message may well have interpreted it as historian Yaffa Eliach believed the parishioners in Eishyshok, Lithuania, did when following the massacre of some five thousand Jews over the two preceding days, they heard what their priest said on September 28, 1941:

> While the freshly covered graves were still moving and spouting blood, the parishioners listened to their priest explain to them that the Jews had at last been called to account for the killing of Christ. The priest himself had not advocated killing them; nor did he approve of the looting of Jewish homes. In fact, at least one account says that he asked anyone in the congregation wearing stolen Jewish clothes to leave (though no one did). But he seemed to feel that the murder was understandable. Even if it was wrong, a kind of justice had been done.[31]

Rescuers obviously regarded the matter differently.

Very Religious Rescuers and Very Religious Nonrescuers

The above discussion presents cultural pulls among the very religious as a whole. *But how did very religious rescuers differ from very religious non-rescuers?* As with Alice and Alexander, one of the important differences between them may have been the posture of their religious leaders.[32] But was there more, something that a predisposed some to hear the benevolent message if religious leaders delivered it while others hearing the same message remained unmoved? Our data confirm the importance of religious leadership, but they also point to the weight of other contributing factors that in some circumstances allowed rescuers to respond to positive leadership, and even to act despite the silence or even hostility of their religious leaders. There were no significant differences between very religious rescuers and nonrescuers on Mastery measures: Internal or External (see Table 2bV). With one exception, very religious rescuers and nonrescuers similarly endorsed several Sharing values, but rescuers more often emphasized "care" (see Table 2bIV). Rescuers reported learning the value of care from their parents, who expressed it both abstractly and practically — a way of talking and behaving.

Rescuers used caring language frequently to describe the most important things they learned from their parents. Words like "love," "generosity," " hospitality," "humaneness," and "helping others" appear significantly more often among very religious rescuers as compared with equally religious non-rescuers. Many times, parents conveyed caring sentiments with great intensity and expansiveness (e.g., "always be helpful," "help others with pleasure," "love everything that lives") and without attention to reciprocity (e.g., "make sacrifices for others and don't expect anything in return"). Helping the poor and the disadvantaged was a particular focus for some, expressed by the father of one rescuer as "paying a lot of attention for all that is oppressed in life." For others it was a keen sense of empathy and egalitarianism: "Be aware of what it feels like to be a worker in a factory and never look down on anybody," cautioned the affluent father of one rescuer. Not content with language that might suggest limited boundaries, the parents of several rescuers made caring sentiments pointedly inclusive: "to have strong feelings for the family and for humankind"; "all people are equal — all are children of God." A similar sentiment was expressed by an Italian rescuer who reported learning it from his church: "I learned to devote myself to my fellow men and to moral ideals. This led to my attitude toward the Jewish question; devotion to ideals included Jews." Most persuasive was caring action: being hospitable, sharing food, taking care of the sick. For one French rescuer's father, "liberality" and "open-mindedness" meant extending unsolicited help to outsiders.

There were Italian bricklayers at the building sites, many of them poor refugees. My father knew how to speak Italian and he would stop and talk with them. He would ask them if they needed something and say: "Here is my address and my phone number if you need anything." We had lots of these people coming to my home asking for something, and my father helped. After he became an official translator, he helped people who wanted to become naturalized French citizens by filling out their applications free.

Behaviors of this sort and words of such generosity, conviction, and inclusiveness occurred significantly less frequently among very religious nonrescuers as they recalled what they had learned from their parents. Significantly more often, nonrescuers associated Christianity with equity values learned from their religious teachers (see Table 2bIV). Being fair, honest, truthful, and respectful toward elders was far more often the focus of what they remembered. Among very religious nonrescuers, Christian behavior was more frequently confined to what one woman expressed as "the essence of spirituality": prayer, faith, love of God, study of Bible, sexual abstinence, avoidance of alcohol, and observance of religious ritual. Political inaction, social minimalism outside the arena of family and religious community, and restricted boundaries of moral obligation were quite compatible with this view of a religious life.[33]

In this bounded Christian community context, outsiders who were not disliked were often largely irrelevant. Very religious nonrescuers, as compared with their rescuer counterparts, felt far less similar to either Jews or Gypsies, and their parents, they said, spoke about them less often (see Table 2aI). And some very religious nonrescuers who claimed their parents had not spoken to them about Jews could not suppress strongly negative feelings or complete indifference that often surfaced in other contexts. The daughter of a devout French Royalist and staunchly feminist mother, for example, who said she heard nothing at home about Jews, claimed in another context to have learned "not to care for Jews" and not to associate with them. "Matters of antisemitism were of no concern to me," said a Polish respondent, "I had no feeling about the segregation of Jewish students at the university but I did get upset when fights erupted because of it." One of the harshest judgments was rendered by a French woman who took considerable pride in "helping sick and poor people" at St. Vincent de Paul (a volunteer Catholic organization servicing the needy) but who said of her former Jewish co-workers: "I thought they were aggressive, that they were nervy, and they were dirty too." All these very religious respondents had claimed parental silence on the matter of Jews, perhaps suggesting suppressed memories, or that silence can communicate as much as words, and that silence alone was not sufficient to counter the temper of the times.

By way of contrast, Jews were very relevant to rescuers' parents, who spoke about them more often than any other group. Apparently, their comments were of such a nature that very religious rescuers, as compared with very religious nonrescuers, grew up feeling significantly more similar to both Gypsies and Jews (see Table 2aI).

When economic interests were served by excluding Jews, anti-Jewish sentiments posed less conflict with nonrescuers' sense of religiosity; very religious nonrescuers more often accommodated the authoritarian right. Accommodation not only converged with anti-left positions, but also protected economic privilege. Jacques, a young French male bystander, is a good example.

JACQUES

In 1942, Jacques, twenty-four years old and newly married, was living in Paris with his in-laws. Born to a wealthy Catholic family, his parents-in-law were equally financially comfortable. Except for a brief period in the military service, he appeared untouched by the war: he lived well, had a good job, and enjoyed his family. Insulated before the war, Jacques was equally so during the war. It was an insulation he shared with many others of similar class and religious style. Here's how he describes the war years:

> I was in the military between 1939 to 1940. Then I was a student at engineering school at the Ponts et Chaussées from 1940 to 1942. Then I became an engineer, working at public highways and bridges, building roads at Nevers. I was also involved in building the channel there. Afterwards, I worked in the Department of the Seine, in the division of motor fuel and public transportation. My wife was home, busy raising the children.

Religion, family and patriotism — characteristic motifs among the very religious generally — dominated Jacques' life, and their influence began early. He attended a Catholic elementary school, and while going to a nonsectarian lyceum he lived at a Catholic college. After graduating from the university with a degree in engineering in 1939, he married a Catholic student, and together they lived with her affluent Catholic parents until 1942, when he moved to his new job. Although not politically affiliated himself (significantly fewer very religious nonrescuers were), he was nonetheless influenced by a religious and political culture primarily concerned with its own privilege. His father-in-law, he said, "very much favored" the rightist French Action group — a royalist, economically conservative, politically autocratic party, exclusionary with respect to minorities and Jews. A somewhat introverted young man — his major interests were mountain climbing and classical music — he had a few close friends, all of them Catholics from the same social class.

From his mother, with whom he felt especially close, Jacques learned "religion and the importance of family life." From his more distant father, he learned "love of country and work well done, honor and integrity." He described himself as a fervent patriot. Of all wartime figures, he admired Marshal Henri Pétain most because of his "patriotism" and "nationalism." But this sentiment did not require any particular action during the war. He joined no resistance group, and neither did any member of his family. In fact, he did nothing that caused him or his family any mistreatment by the Germans. Like Pétain himself, all that was required was cooperation with the German occupiers.

Yet Jacques' religious leaders had impressed him with what he calls the "leading characteristics of Catholicism," namely "respect for life and love of neighbor." He took this injunction very seriously, but the perimeters were very narrow. Appropriate sexual behavior was critical: he tried to dissuade his friends from frequenting what he tactfully described as "certain kinds of facilities having to do with entertainment and women." More important was his work on behalf of St. Vincent de Paul, where he "visited the poor and gave them sustenance."

"Neighbor," however, did not include Jews or any other outsiders. Both parents, he acknowledged, reflected "the prevailing sentiments of those times"; they "mistrusted Jews and Free Masons." Separated from much of life outside his particular interests and social reference group, he had no awareness of antisemitism in his country. Some Jews had lived in his neighborhood and attended the same schools; he even had two "distant" Jewish cousins. "But I did not really know them," he said, "because I lived in different surroundings." It might well be described as "a different world," as real a cultural ghetto—a ghetto of perception and mind—as one surrounded by impenetrable physical walls.

Inhabitants of the cultural ghetto in which Jacques lived saw little of what was happening around them; if they saw it, they did not perceive it as relevant to them. Jacques was in Paris in 1942, the place and year of the notorious roundups that galvanized Monsignor Saliège and Sister Alice into action. Yet he knew nothing about these events: he had never witnessed or heard about mistreatment of Jews or anybody else, he said, nor had anyone asked him for help, for that matter. Yet at some level, Jacques was aware and even empathic. Asked about the time he learned about Nazi intentions toward Jews, he said "1942 or early 1943." And he had seen Jews wearing the yellow star, a requirement he considered a "hostile" act, "unjust, and very much against human dignity." So accustomed had he become to this sight that he could not retrieve this memory of mistreatment until specifically asked whether he had seen Jews wearing the star.

Would Jacques then have behaved differently had his church leaders encouraged it? Perhaps. That religious influence might have modified his views about Jews, however, is suggested by his changed attitudes after the war. In 1985, the year we interviewed him, he was serving as a representative to the Dominican-led French Biblical Archaeological School in Jerusalem, and he visited Jerusalem twice yearly in order to study there. Encouraged by the work of Notre Dame de Lyon, with whom he was associated in Paris, he had become very much interested in the relations between Christians and Jews and participated in the creation of the Christian Institute for Jewish Studies in Jerusalem. He had made Jewish friends in Jerusalem, visiting them regularly, and interacted more with Jews at his workplace. All of this, he says, had "eliminated the unfavorable feelings of my former education." While "favorable feelings" might not have been enough to promote rescue, they might have removed the comfort of indifference.

JÜRGEN

Jacques does not mention the attitude of his church; whatever it may have been, it apparently did not challenge his views. The church played a more obvious and critical role in the decision of a German nonrescuer, whom we call Jürgen. In fact, Jürgen was a minister in this church, known as the *Bekennenden Kirche* in German and the Confessing Church in English, and although a very benevolent man and not at all indifferent to the fate of the Jews, he did nothing on their behalf. He did take considerable risks on behalf of converted Jews ("non-Aryan Christians") however. Jürgen's story begins in the early thirties, shortly before Hitler's accession to power:

> I was a parish minister in Weisswasser/Oberlausitz in 1932, and led the brotherhood of the *Bekennenden Kirche* in my area. I was already in the Minister's Relief Association and after that, along with my wife, I was part of a special church group that opposed the regular mainstream church. There I had friends who were non-Aryan Christians.
>
> One of the risks I took before the war was to use forbidden words in the pulpit: words for which others were arrested. The special police came to search my house 30 times, but I was never arrested. In 1934, after appropriate instruction, I baptized Mrs. S.; surprisingly, I suffered no ill consequences as a result. In early 1936 I came in contact with the non-Aryan minister D. D., who had then been removed from office by the church leadership in Breslau on the basis of the Nuremberg laws. He was then living with his wife who was born in Denmark and because of this fact his residence was not destroyed but he was taken into custody at the concentration camp at Oranienburg. After a

few weeks he was released and he and his wife were frequent guests at our parsonage. Before he emigrated — we helped him to emigrate — he appeared in my pulpit.

Between 1940 and 1943 I was involved in organizing hiding places for non-Aryan Christians. Several parsonages were involved and people stayed for only a few weeks, concealed as visitors. Mrs. B., for example, stayed at our house for a few weeks without food ration stamps, posing as a seamstress. In the middle of 1943, I was inducted into the military and my wife remained alone with our five children and her old parents in our parsonage.

All the people I helped were baptized Jews.

Asked the reason he helped, Jürgen replied with some surprise: "The reasons are obvious: turning to those who suffer, are in pain, tortured — direct reaching out to humans." Why then did he limit his help to converted Jews only? Given that Jews who had not converted had suffered at least as much and more, why did he not "reach out" to them as well? It was not a lack of sympathy: he felt "very saddened," he said, when he saw them wearing the yellow star, and felt "nothing but disgust" when the Nazis rose to power. Unlike many of the very religious, Jürgen knew what was happening and knew it very early. "As a student in 1929," he said, "I was already aware of what the Nazis intended to do to Jews. We knew we did not belong to those who claimed not to know. A minister gave a lecture then trying to convince us that St. Paul was antisemitic. It all became clear to us." He also had firsthand reports from members of his own family: "Our eldest son experienced mistreatment of Jews at the railroad several times — he was very disturbed. Our other son also saw transports of Jews." Yet this astute and humane man not only remained passive in the face of their travails, but did not even consider helping them. How could this occur?

What Jürgen did or did not do was entirely congruent with the policies of the Confessing Church of which he was a leading member. Enveloped as he was within the culture of his group, he accepted its values as axiomatic and could not even envision an alternative response. *And in some limited respects, the policies of his church were quite bold given the context of the times.*

By 1934, the Nazi regime had already succeeded in subordinating and controlling the administration of most churches in Germany. Some twenty-eight provincial churches had complied readily with this effort, becoming part of the mainstream "German Christians" whose bishops wholeheartedly supported the Nazi state.[34] A Protestant minority, however, dissented and some two thousand of this group met on April 22, 1934, to consider an alternative Church governance structure. The Confessing Church emerged from this event.

What did the Church oppose? Administrative control was an essential matter. Rather than accepting the new state central administration, the Confessing Church appointed their own Reich Council of Brethren, most of whose members had already been involved in the Pastors' Emergency League.[35] But much more than administration was at stake. Unlike the dominant group of Lutheran officials, the German Christians, who argued that Nazi ideology was as sacred as Scripture, the Confessional Church insisted on the absolute supremacy of Scripture and their right to control religious education and the Christian future. Only the Church, they insisted, had the right and the duty to preserve the integrity of the Gospel, and the state could not abrogate it. Holding the Church to its "Christian mission," and repudiating what it called "false doctrine," the Confessing Church leadership rejected the idea that the State could become the "single and totalitarian order of human life."

The Prussian Confessional synod went even further. After the passage of the 1935 Nuremberg Laws, which defined Jews as a race, they boldly rejected the view that "race, blood or Volk" could determine church membership, thus reaffirming their traditional right to baptize Jews on the basis of belief. The "forbidden words" that Jürgen read from his pulpit probably refers to the "Word to the Parishes," which the Prussian Confessing synod sent to its ministers in March 1935 and which essentially enunciated these principles. The synod asked that it be read from the ministers' pulpits, and some seven hundred Prussian pastors who complied were arrested (Jürgen was not one of them) but subsequently released because of parishioners' protests.[36]

The Confessing Church was not ready to yield total authority to the State, but their protest had little to do with political issues. The Church accepted the government's responsibility for political education, said nothing with respect to concentration camps, and raised no objections to discriminatory civil measures against Jews, arguing instead that they were needed to correct past "injustices."[37] Neither Church clergy nor laity professed objection to Hitler throughout the war, some of them believing until the end that a compromise between Church and State was possible. So totally divorced were they from any political stand, observes historian John Weiss, that even Pastor Niemöller — jailed by Hitler in the 1930s for opposing the Nazi takeover of the Church and famed after the war for his eloquent articulation of moral failure toward outsiders — voted for Hitler in 1933, welcomed uniformed SA members (storm troopers) in his church, and preached with swastikas decorating the altar while the congregation gave the Nazi salute.[38]

The Confessing Church did nothing official for Jews, but their stand on behalf of converts encouraged some ministers, including Jürgen, to intervene actively but clandestinely on their behalf. Yet such interventions had their limitations. Although they did not contest the claims of those already converted by 1934, many officials voiced difficulty with Jews newly seeking Christian status. So as to assure others that they were acting out of Christian integrity and scrupulous adherence to doctrine, rather than mere concern with saving Jewish lives, ministers sometimes raised their standards for conversion to be sure of the "sincerity" of those seeking escape in this manner. Jürgen, for example, did convert a Jewish woman in the mid-1930s, "surprisingly without consequences" as he observes, but was careful to note that he did so only after "appropriate instruction."

Jürgen was willing to court considerable risks on behalf of his religious principles. Asked how much risk he thought he was putting on members of his family for helping converts, he replied "extreme." But he had limited boundaries. Not inclusive enough to include those outside the church, *they were in fact the boundaries set by the Confessional Church itself.* That sense of limited responsibility was compellingly captured when he explained why he refused a Jewish woman who asked him for help:

> We did have to refuse help to Mrs. L. (a nonbaptized Jew) when she asked us to be taken in. We were simply not set up to help non-Aryan Christians. With every new person we accepted, the whole was threatened. Jews were not accepted: the risk was too great. The danger to my family, my wife and children, would have been disproportionately great. It took us hours to figure out what to say to her.

Troubled by the forthcoming rejection, the family agonized over a way to explain it to Mrs. L. It is indeed difficult to explain. Since he had acknowledged to us that the risk to his family in helping converted Jews was "extreme," it was not obviously clear how the risk in helping Jews was any greater. But of course whereas he had the support of his church network (the "we" to which he refers above) concerning converted Jews, the family could not count on his group to support them in helping Jews. Totally submerged in his church, Jürgen apparently never thought to criticize or even to question this policy. A sincerely committed Christian, his stance demonstrates that it is possible to be a true adherent to Christian faith without necessarily concluding that it requires helping persecuted outgroup members. It all depends on the substantive doctrines one decides are critical and of the highest priority.

ERICH

Sometimes, however, individuals were able to transcend the limits of their religious leadership. Erich was one of them. Eight years older than Jürgen, he too was a pastor, married and helped several baptized Jews. Like Jürgen, he too was a member of the Confessing Church.

> In 1941, I helped a half-Jewish schoolmate immigrate to Canada. I also sup-ported his Jewish mother who stayed behind. Through various connections with retired officers, I helped her find shelter in several estates in the country. I did the same thing with other original Jews who by that time had been bap-tized and were members of the Confessing Church. I also procured falsified papers, sheltered them for up to three weeks at a time (it would have been too dangerous any longer especially during bombing attacks when everybody had to go down in the cellar and if they looked like Jews) and then found other places for them to stay, gave them falsified foodstamps, and lied to the Ges-tapo.

> I was severely injured at the front and came to a hospital in Berlin in 1941. I had a good relationship with the chief physician (who had divorced his Jewish wife and sent her to the United States, and re-united with her after the war was over), who gave me lots of "recovery" vacation that allowed me to go home. He was promoted to Corporal with the help of a Communist general. I got an official job with the Army in Potsdam distributing already signed papers to people who got bombed out. I took the chance to declare many Jews as bombed out; they were then free of all hassles since the Army had issued their papers.

The categories invented by the Reich created a linguistic jungle from which many who lived in Germany during that time have not yet escaped. Erich sometimes used the word "half-Jews" to mean having one Jewish parent or to refer to assimilated Jews as they might have been in his schooldays, and some-times to mean baptized Jews. It is clear, however, that he did not restrict his help to baptized Jews only, including among others his schoolmate's Jewish mother.

Erich's reference to his half-Jewish schoolmate suggests a strong personal relationship with an outsider. And the pointedly positive context in which he refers to a "Communist," unusual among the very religious, suggests a broader political acceptance than was common among this group. Both these themes — close and broad friendships, as well as a broader political stance — occur re-peatedly through his life, beginning with his parents.

Erich had attended a nonsectarian elementary school, gymnasium, and uni-versity, where he studied journalism and German and finally theology. A very social person, he had many close friends. Even in his youth, they included those of lower economic status (his own family was wealthy) as well as Jews. He had close Jewish friends before the war, even when such contacts became very dangerous, and he helped several of his Jewish schoolmates, including four families with children, as well as some Jewish strangers. Asked why he became involved initially in these activities, he responded, "I wanted to follow up on the fate of my Jewish schoolmates." This type of concern for school friends, especially Jewish friends, suggests a strong capacity for enduring emotional attachments.

Erich's capacity to form such personal relationships with Jews appears to be largely attributable to his mother. Religion was as important to Erich as to Jürgen, and he credits his mother, also a Confessing Church member, with teaching him about its importance. What Erich also learned from her was the special status Judaism had within her Christian view: "Christianity," she told him, "is the sister religion of Judaism." A "sister" implies not only an intimate connection, but also equal status. Equally important, he also learned from her that "social commitment" is part of a religious view of life. Social commitment implies action rather than withdrawal from the world.

His "not very religious" and very strict father, with whom he did not feel very close, extended this broader point of view into the political arena. Like most of the very religious, his father belonged to a middle-class moderate political party, the German People's Party (economically centrist, democratic, and tolerant of minorities and Jews). Yet he was very sympathetic to those less privileged, making Erich keenly aware of the life of the ordinary worker. Strongly anti-Hitler, his father refused to join the Nazi Party (Die Nationalsozialistische Partei Deutschland, often referred to by the acronym NSDAP) and was forced to retire early from his lucrative position.

Religious leaders who influenced Erich most promoted similar ideas. One of them, a Confessing Church parson with political tendencies similar to those of his father, led a youth group to which he belonged. He learned from him not only to value the Bible but also "to assess the political situation." From other religious leaders, he acquired a theological view of the world and "ecumenical thinking." Ecumenical thinking contributed to his admiration for the Bündische Jugend — in this case a socialist youth group that he describes as advocating "world citizenship." Strongly rejecting the nationalistic sentiments that prevailed in Germany at the time of the war, he lacked even a sense of the conventional patriotism that marked many of the very religious; in fact, he described himself as "not at all" patriotic.

All this left Erich feeling very much like an "outsider"; different "politically, socially and in religious beliefs." Already provocatively active before the war, making speeches and helping foreign workers, he provoked the wrath of his neighbors who reported him to the authorities. He wound up in a German court, forced to defend himself. Angered by colleagues from abroad, who painted rosy pictures of Hitler's Germany in 1937, he made them listen to his reports of persecution and concentration camps. It also made him strongly judgmental about the role of the Confessing Church and churches generally during the war:

> There were concentration camps, persecution of Christians and Jews, and for Christians, an unbearable opinion among Nazis with respect to race questions. The official church had been led astray by accepting the idea that Judaism is not a question of religion but of race only. They still supported baptized Jews, but that was it. It was apparent that this question of Judaism would be the crucial test for the church — neither the official nor the Confessing Church passed the test. The only question left for the individual was if he wanted to play the role of the benevolent Samaritan. That was the role I chose.

Very religious nonrescuers rarely mention religious leaders, but religious officials helping Jews appear often in the accounts of very religious rescuers, either as rescuers themselves or as indirect facilitators. In their different ways — through words and/or actions — these leaders made clear what the members of their congregations were obligated to do.

The advantage of a committed religious leadership was not only moral but also practical. Religious leaders could galvanize already existing natural helping networks into subversive trustworthy ones. Like Alice, the initiators of rescue activities in Catholic orders were often individuals in the order; like Alice, they were particularly responsive to children. A single person could mobilize the group, and even if all could not be counted on to help in equal measure, colleagues were unlikely to betray them. Male and female Catholic orders often played this role in countries throughout Europe (in Poland, for example, says historian Eva Kurek-Lesik, 189 Polish convents sheltered Jewish children and managed to save as many as 1,200).[39] But natural religious networks also existed outside the cloistered walls of Catholic religious orders. The Reformed Church to which Alexander belonged was one of several such,[40] but Le Chambon is probably the best-known example.[41] Prompted by their leadership, local churches sometimes also engaged in collective rescue. A Protestant pastor, for example, living in a Catholic community in Rodez, says he received help from his entire parish of fifty families who, between 1942 and August 1944, helped forge or steal identification papers for Jewish victims and found hiding places for them.[42]

Sometimes religious officials initiated help as a consequence of a superior's request, as did Alice, and sometimes they acted independently. Sometimes they responded to requests from the victims themselves or from other Jews acting on their behalf, or from religious representatives of other denominations. The brothers in one teaching Catholic order, for example, responded to an entreaty from a Jewish representative to take some children, while a Polish nun said she began hiding Jewish children as a result of a plea from an irreligious formerly Catholic couple. While approval from their superiors might be sought before or after the deed, subordinates would often be content if they simply refrained from disapproval. At the request of a fellow priest in a different town, a Polish priest kept a very gifted Jewish adolescent between November 1942 through the summer of 1943, presenting him publicly as his cousin. Although he had helped several other Jews for short periods without seeking permission from his religious superior, in this case he sought it. "You are old enough to make up your own mind," the prior told him. He interpreted the response as tacit approval. Tacit approval was also conveyed in other cases where a known minister, priest, nun, or other religious official was rumored to be helping Jews, supplying baptismal certificates, or even hiding Jews. In such cases, respected religious officials modeled appropriate behavior even if they did not actively recruit help themselves.

While the encouragement of religious leadership was neither sufficient nor necessarily essential for rescue to occur, it often made the critical difference. A hostile religious leadership legitimized discrimination and persecution; an indifferent or unconcerned religious leadership had the same effect. A moral and courageous Church leader, on the other hand, could inspire others to follow. Those who had learned values conducive to outgroup altruism from families and Church figures could hear the message and respond; sometimes they could also lead.

The Irreligious

ANDRZEJ

Obviously, what helping we did had to be focused on Jews. It began almost spontaneously with my colleagues before the war, the Jewish Socialists, who hid themselves in my apartment. They simply had my address and they would come to me. Most of them wanted to leave Poland and their transfer had to be arranged. Some of them would be directed to Hungary and from there elsewhere; others would be transferred eastwards, to Japan, through the Soviet Union. They would stay in our place until we could arrange passage. That was at the beginning, right after our defeat; later it became much more difficult.

After the Ghetto was walled in, we had to deal with other problems. Taking care of people who found themselves there became our main line of activity. I worked with the Jewish Socialist Organization as well as with the Korczak Orphanage. My wife and I were assigned to work in a German firm and we used our official jobs to get passes to enter the Ghetto, even a car pass. I used to carry food in the car either for the orphanage or for the comrades from the Bund, the Jewish Youth Organization. I went to the Ghetto almost every week. Our organization was blown and I was arrested in the late autumn of 1941 and spent a couple of months at the Pawiak prison, where I was rather meticulously beaten up.[1] Owing to our German comrades who worked with us, and my own organization that helped me, I was released. My jaws were broken but I was free.

I had to vanish from Warsaw and left for Lvov, where I organized help for Jews working on demolition of oil-refineries. Because of my family connections, I had a lot of experience dealing with Germans and I spoke perfect German. When I put on my German outfit—a jacket, breeches, boots, a Tyrolian hat—it seemed to suit me perfectly. After some three months the Gestapo caught on and we—my wife and I—had to run for our lives.

We then found ourselves in the Wojewodztwo Kieleckie Voyvodie, in the Swietokrzyskie Forest, in the area of Kielce. We organized and later participated in Socialist political and guerrilla activities. At first we were a part of the Underground Army but after the rupture with them and the Domestic Government, we were on our own. There were Jewish comrades in our partisan troops and I was mostly concerned with military operations. We also hid Jews who turned to us for help. Unfortunately, we were not always successful. This activity continued until the end of the war.

Several items mark Andrzej's amazing story: extraordinary bravado and bravery, absolute self-assurance that he was doing the right thing, and uninterrupted persistence for six long years in the face of constant threats. Already prepared for Poland's defeat, which occurred five days after the Germans invaded on September 1, 1939, he and his wife began a stream of activities that focused initially almost exclusively on Jews. While it was not exactly a common story among irreligious rescuers, it had features far more representative of them as compared with very religious rescuers. The cultural milieu in which Andrzej made his decision was significantly different from that which characterized the very religious in several distinctive ways.

Those who called themselves "not at all religious" included people who were hostile to religion or simply indifferent to it; a few called themselves "spiritual." Andrzej was more antireligious than indifferent, but he was not aggressively so. While acknowledging that he did not like the Church, neither did he express the antipathy toward it that some others did.

A medical student and married, twenty-year-old Andrzej was living quite comfortably in Warsaw in 1939. His wife, a Jewish convert to Catholicism who like Andrzej also considered herself "not at all religious," was working in a commercial bank at the time. The only child of a successful and loving father, an architect, Andrzej nonetheless endured a somewhat turbulent family life until age ten because of his mother's mental illness. After his father's second marriage to a Jewish woman, who "practically brought me up," life became more stable and harmonious.

Andrzej admired and felt particularly close to his father, whom he describes as "a very honorable man." "I learned from him to do well—to do your job as best you could—to be responsible, and honorable. I also learned not to jump to conclusions about people but to observe them and be close only with those who deserve it." Yet, he acknowledged his father was "very authoritarian," although disciplining him rarely because he was very "obedient." "I was punished once," he said, "but I don't remember how. My father told me what he thought and I just listened." Irreligious like his son, Andrzej's father was nonetheless an affiliated Catholic and sent his son to a Catholic elementary school. Andrzej claims he learned nothing from the Church, but he does credit a high-ranking Church official, an uncle, with teaching him something very similar to his father: "to respect people; not only for what they are saying, or believe in, but also for what they do with their lives."

Both father and son had strong views about Jews. "In no way was my father an antisemite or racist; he equated antisemitism with racism," Andrzej asserted. Andrzej shared similar sentiments. Confronted with people who "took certain political stands or talked about minority groups in a negative way," Andrzej would raise strong objections. Asked which categories of people he was most like, he ranked Jews along with the poor highest of all. Both father and son had many close Jewish friends.

Father and son shared many similar political views. Both were ardent antifascists and had the strongest contempt for the nationalistic right: "I intensely disliked a fascist organization called ORN, and the National Party because of their nationalistic stands and fascist views," Andrzej said. Such political beliefs often led to his feeling of being an outsider. "Before the war," he said, "I was in a student dorm where many of my acquaintances were country gentry who belonged to a fascistic type of Polish party. This led to conflict. We had many arguments that often ended in fistfights. They were stronger, and I got beat up a lot. But I didn't stop challenging them." While he objected to the chauvinistic stands represented by the extreme right, Andrzej nonetheless considered himself "very patriotic," but his conception of patriotism was quite different from the conventional view.

As father and son saw it, antisemitic attitudes intersected with nationalistic views and both were antithetical to Socialist values. Andrzej's father considered antisemitism a "nationalistic phobia" and, although never himself a member of the Socialist Party, sympathized with them, took part in several of their activities, and even contributed money to the cause occasionally. Andrzej became a strongly committed Socialist, participating in street demonstrations often. In fact, politics became an organizing core of Andrzej's identity; those he felt closest to shared his political perspective. In addition to Polish Socialists, they included "democrats and people who were sympathetic with communism."

He shared yet one other sentiment with his father: a particular affection for young people, and most particularly those less privileged than he. His father, he said, spent some time "teaching at a school called ORT." The Organization for Rehabilitation and Training is a Jewish institution designed to help uneducated youngsters develop vocational skills. "My father," he said, "was the only non-Jew teaching there." Andrzej's political work also involved him in teaching the young; not vocational skills, however, but "history and Marxism." He not only enjoyed doing this, but also regarded it as a way of expressing his patriotism and "defending my country." He also did volunteer work at one of the orphanages supervised by Dr. Janusz Korczak, a Polish Jewish pediatrician and educator renowned for his progressive educational ideas and work with orphans.[2] His work on behalf of the orphanage continued even after its occupants were forced into the Warsaw Ghetto. Korczak's ideas stayed with Andrzej long after Korczak perished alongside his Jewish orphans, indeed, influencing him throughout his life.[3]

In view of his uncommonly close connections with Jews, it is not entirely surprising that it seemed "obvious" to Andrzej from the start that they, above all, needed him. He estimates that before the war ended, he had helped approximately one hundred people: some close friends but most of them strangers, and most of them Jews. Asked his main reason for first becoming involved, he replied: "The basic, the primordial reason, was the desire to fight the Nazis. But I believe I did it out of feelings of solidarity with those who were weaker and therefore needed me." It was a theme that also characterized his life after the war. Although more involved in politics than medicine at that time, he helped open a sanitarium for patients with tuberculosis and was involved in the International Korczak Movement for the protection of disabled persons and children. Overcoming his antipathy for the Church, he also participated in the activities of the Catholic Church's Relief Committee. "I am not a churchgoer nor do I even like them," he said, but he could not resist their efforts on behalf of the destitute.

NELLIE

Nellie, a Dutch irreligious rescuer who together with her husband hid several Jewish people throughout the war, shared much in common with Andrzej. Her war story began on May 10, 1940:

> The war started all of a sudden with parachuting and shooting in the streets. In the afternoon my husband went with an ambulance looking for the wounded and dead. At night I was in the cellar and a very good Jewish friend, a high school teacher, was with us. I said to him, "Don't go home," and so he stayed with us for four days.

At the end of the first year people from the Resistance asked us to hide a Jewish woman — a woman of about forty-five from Amsterdam — she came at the beginning of 1941. She stayed with us two and one half years. She couldn't go out and she couldn't even stand in front of the window — it would be too dangerous. She was very lonely and it was hard on all of us because our place was small and eating at the same table all the time and being together got on everybody's nerves. When she was there for about a year someone came and said, "Perhaps you can hide Professor S." He was an outstanding law professor and we thought, "If only we could have him!" And there you are weighing people — a very moral conflict. People are people and it seems awful to give priority to an interesting and marvelous professor above a simple and not very interesting woman. But we couldn't have the professor — we had this woman.

We got to know some very nice Jewish people who were hiding. When the moon was dark, we had them over to visit and had a good time together. In the middle of one such night, the house where they were staying was bombed and there we were, in the middle of the street, not knowing what to do. We found a place for the couple and invited the sister-in-law to stay with us; by then the other Jewish woman had left. Toward the end of the war — February or March — she asked if we could help locate her daughter and we did. Such joy when we brought her to our house!

We had a third person; a Jewish young woman we sort of adopted as a foster daughter after the war — not really adopted because she was too old by then but we considered her a foster daughter and her children are my grandchildren now. My husband brought her home one day. She was sixteen, a wonderful, wild and adventurous girl. She stayed with us too, and helped my husband in his medical practice.

It was natural to do it. You wanted to resist — to fight those people and their frightful occupation: to harm them as much as possible. Small acts of resistance happened all the time; any German soldier who asked his way was always shown the wrong way by any little boy.

In 1939, thirty-one-year-old Nellie was living in Dordrecht with her husband, a physician. A social worker by profession, she was then unemployed. The daughter of parents she called "progressive," Nellie grew up with strong moral principles and very high expectations of herself. Her father, a physics teacher, "was concerned about moral questions, human relations," she said, and would reason with her. "When I would come home from school angry with some friend, he would bring up both sides. 'Look at it this way,' he would say. 'You are wrong if you consider it that way.'" High self-expectations led her to question whether she was really an honest person: "What is honesty? It's not so easy to know yourself. Honesty in terms of moral issues, of course. But if you are a closed character like I was — and still am — is it honesty or not?

And if you don't talk about things, then what's honesty?" High self-expectations are also reflected in her self-evaluation as a rescuer; in comparison to others' activities, she assessed her own as not very substantial. "I know that what we did was risky — but if you compare it with the real Resistance, what they did was much more important and risky. And they lost a lot of people — a lot of people. Thousands perished in the Resistance. You did what you could."[4]

Like her parents and Andrzej, Nellie was a strongly identified Socialist, and she was the spouse of an equally committed Socialist. Like Andrzej, she worked with young people in the party (as well as a woman's group) and shared his fierce concern about fascists: "There was a group of fascists in Holland three or four years before the war. They were represented in Parliament and very 'anti' our ideas. I never had direct contact with them but I was very angry and worried about what was going on."

Like Andrzej, too, Nellie had what she described as "a special affinity for Jews": she had Jewish friends, her closest lifetime friend was Jewish, and Jews were simply a natural part of her life. It was thus no accident that a Jewish friend was with her on the very first day of the war. Like Andrzej, she was aware of what was happening to Jews in Germany even before the war and relied on similar trusted sources for information: Jews in her own country, Jewish refugees from Germany, and Socialist newspapers and colleagues who were non-Jews as well as Jews. "We heard a lot," she said, "but it was piecemeal. One of the most unforgettable things I heard was from a good Jewish friend who was the president of a Socialist group in another city. One evening he was sitting in my living room and said, 'Listen, I have information from Germany. We are all going to be exterminated.' I said 'My God, you can't believe that,' but as it turned out, he was right."

Yet she differed from Andrzej on two important points: she did not feel politics made her an "outsider," and she ranked herself as "not at all patriotic:" "Loving your country?" she said, "Oh my dear! Being patriotic was completely indifferent to me. Patriotism was something you didn't talk about. In my father's view you had to be an internationalist. Holland is a nice little country but what's so special about it?" Here Andrzej and Nellie perhaps reflected quite different national realities.

In the late 1930s, Poland was drifting toward a dictatorship, and the forces of extreme nationalism and antisemitism, long strong Polish realities, were gaining power. Partitioned three times during the eighteenth century, at the end of which time it lost most of its territories, Poland did not regain its land or real independence until after World War I, in 1923. Barely fifteen years had passed before it was threatened once again by the same external enemies.

Feelings of heightened vulnerability to external threats, coupled with a weakening economy, led to magnified suspicions of internal "deviants": minority groups who did not claim an identical national and religious identity but who were perceived as economic competitors, and political leftists who might ally themselves with the imperialistic and atheistic Soviet Union. In response to these perceived external and internal threats, the country started to shift increasingly toward autocratic rule, expanding its anti-minority and particularly anti-Jewish discriminatory policies, and failing to inhibit zealous nationalists from venting their anger toward them in the universities and on the streets. With a population of approximately three million Jews constituted almost 10 percent of the total population and thus were a particularly visible group. In this political context, Andrzej was doubly suspect, as a Socialist and as a "Jew lover." And whereas Andrzej claimed to have strong patriotic feelings, they were not the typical kind. Rather than being identified with mainstream Polish culture, which included being a Catholic and a strong defender of the country and its dominant values, Andrzej saw his Socialist activities as patriotic: a view that would only have confirmed the worst suspicions of his nationalistic compatriots.

By comparison, Holland had been a stable democracy for many years and by the late 1930s was becoming more so. In 1939 and for the first time in its history the coalition government, normally limited to conservatives only, included representatives of the Social Democratic Party. Although Socialists were not too happy with the Queen, they did regard her as an increasingly important unifying force in the face of mounting external threats. Not without its indigenous fascists and anti-minority tendencies, including antisemitism, Holland was nonetheless a comparatively tolerant society where Jews, who constituted only 1.5 percent of the population, lived comfortably. Whereas in Holland it was possible to declare as Nellie did without fear of reprisals that religious, social, or national categories were "simply irrelevant," religious and national boundaries were sharp in Poland and dissenters from conventional views risked varied forms of retaliation. In the political context of this more relaxed society, one not facing any realistic threat from the Soviet Union, it was more possible to be a public Socialist and an internationalist without feeling completely "different."

Yet Andrzej's and Nellie's similarities appear to override their differences. Both were irreligious, rescuers, and Socialists; and politics and Jews played central roles in their lives. Was this the case with all the irreligious or only with irreligious rescuers? What was the cultural milieu in which the irreligious made their decisions and how did it compare with those more religious? And how did irreligious rescuers compare with irreligious nonrescuers? I begin by comparing the irreligious with the moderately and very religious, focusing first on several measures associated with an Internal Mastery Orientation.

The Irreligious and the More Religious

How did the irreligious compare with those more religious? Although the irreligious differed from the more religious in many important ways, interestingly enough they shared some characteristics in common with the very religious.

One of the attributes the irreligious and the very religious more commonly shared as compared with the somewhat religious was their greater readiness to assert their beliefs through public action (see Appendix B, Table 2bV). Given their inclination toward less mainstream views, they, along with the very religious, might also well have been considered to be somewhat deviant by their more moderate peers. But unlike the very religious, who more often focused on their religious values, *the irreligious more often focused on their political values*.

Despite the strong anti-religious or anti-Church views that some shared, the irreligious rarely took public action that was overtly anti-religious or anti-Church. More often than the very religious, their public stands focused on political matters. Some of their political behaviors converged with those of the very religious: they distanced themselves from friends and colleagues as their political views began to diverge, and they too helped Jews. But the irreligious report doing these things earlier and considerably more often, and they also undertook more diverse activities, several of them quite risky. They report boycotting German goods, pilfering pro-German newspapers from newsstands, and participating in anti-fascist and anti-nationalist street demonstrations, sometimes doing so repeatedly. The men more often found themselves in physical fights with these same groups.

Yet even though the subjects that aroused their passions frequently differed, the irreligious and very religious appeared to possess a degree of uncommon ardor, not generally shared by more moderate groups. More oriented than moderates toward their internal beliefs, both groups appeared to act more often on the basis of internalized principles, so that public action flowed more naturally and spontaneously from a more clearly defined sense of right and wrong. Unwilling to be as accommodating or flexible as those in the middle, both may have felt somewhat marginal to mainstream society and thus challenged to make their views known. What they felt passionate about overlapped to some degree, but unlike the very religious, among whom religious issues played a prominent role, the irreligious considered politics central — and sometimes their only — concern.

But willingness to assert their beliefs was accompanied by a much weaker Sharing disposition; as compared with the very religious, they were significantly less characterized by tendencies frequently associated with altruism. They scored lowest of all groups on the prosocial factor (empathy for the distressed and personal standards for persistence) and lower than the very religious on social responsibility. As compared with the very religious, they were thus not a "tender-hearted" culture, making judgments on "soft" sentiments. But neither did they credit themselves with too much virtue: they scored significantly lower than the very religious and the somewhat religious on personal integrity (see Table 2bIV).

Was this lower self-attribution of uprightness among the irreligious a more honest self-evaluation or did it reflect particularly high self-expectations, as was apparently the case with Nellie? Or perhaps the irreligious were simply more candid, with little need to project a positive self-image to impress themselves or others. It may even be that they did not regard such characteristics as desirable. It does seem likely that a combination of family experiences and their personal characteristics interacted in a particular way to produce something akin to disdain for conventional thinking and commonly accepted views of "virtue."

Their comparatively weaker Sharing propensities probably began to evolve in their families of origin. Family ties among the irreligious were the weakest of all groups. They felt significantly more distant from their mothers and families generally than either the very or somewhat religious, and least close of all groups to their fathers (see Table 2bIII). Some evidence suggests that the development of empathy is highly influenced by fathers' involvement with children — that is, the degree to which fathers spend time with them — and mothers' tolerance of dependent behavior — that is, the degree to which mothers respond to children's dependent behavior.[5] Did something occur between parents and children, and particularly fathers that might explain such distance?

Was it due perhaps to harsher discipline? Our data do not suggest this — the parents of the irreligious were neither more nor less likely to discipline them, and if they did, they were significantly more likely than the very religious to depend on reasoning and significantly less likely than the mildly religious to use physical punishment (see Table 2bIII). Asked the reasons they were disciplined, some accused their parents of having unreasonable expectations and behaviors. Yet for many, parental expectations appeared to be no more than routine: not coming home on time, messing up their clothes, breaking things. Several complained of "poor communication," parental failure to understand and support them. But more often than the very religious, they admitted to what might be called youthful rebelliousness, resistance to external control or a drive for independence.

Several acknowledged they were "sassy" and "not easy to raise." "I was fresh as dirt," said one woman, while another described herself as "what today would be called a juvenile delinquent: I always defended myself against rowdy boys," she said, "I would beat them up; I also became the leader of a group of thieves." "I asked too many questions," said another respondent, while yet another, who described herself as "always vehemently and openly objecting to the untrue aspects of the Dutch Reformed Church," said she was "kicked out of the house for a short time" because she "cut her own hair." Several emphasized their desire for freedom, independence, and disengagement. "My mother disciplined me for disobedience mostly and bad manners," said one man, "and always made up for it by giving me a huge amount of toys, but I would rather have had the freedom." Another described himself as "completely independent and relatively invulnerable to the opinion of others." And in one case it was a desire to escape overbearing parents who expected adult behavior too early in life. "I went to work when I was about ten or eleven," he said, "and had little time for pranks or mischief but I resented my mother involving me in her family's arguments." As psychologists might explain it, their conflicts with parents often reflected a drive for independence.

Yet despite less intimate familial relationships and their more frequently expressed desire to control their own lives, the irreligious, like the very religious, nonetheless tended to adopt the same political stance as their parents. And while they were as likely as the very religious to be politically affiliated, their politics were very different. It was in their politics that the Sharing orientation of many of the irreligious resonated best.

Very much unlike very religious respondents and their parents, who tended toward the center/conservative end of the political spectrum, irreligious respondents and their parents gravitated significantly more toward the liberal/ left end of the spectrum (see Table 2aII). Given that the irreligious tended, as did the very religious, to follow the political inclinations of their parents, it appears that rather than rebelling against their parents, many of the irreligious were in fact emulating them. Even their ostensible efforts to distance themselves from their families might be explained as imitation rather than variation. Given that conservatives controlled governments in all European governments of the time, embracing leftist ideologies required some independence from the centers of power and authority. If parents were able to withstand dominant social authorities, why not their children, even when the authorities were their own fathers and mothers?

The liberal/left parties with which the irreligious affiliated strongly favored the weak. If they were liberal labor or Socialists, they favored economic policies supporting the less privileged, rights for minorities and Jews, and democracy and reform through democratic procedures.[6] If they were Communists, they were avid anti-capitalists, advocates for the poor, minorities, and Jews, but they were not democrats, promoting instead reform through revolution. What Communist and Socialist ideology largely did share was an international and classless vision for humankind and a belief that nationalism was basically an unhealthy and artificial social organizational principle, responsible for much of the world's violence. In this context, and in light of the growing xenophobic nationalist politics that preceded World War II, it is not surprising that the irreligious regarded themselves as the *least patriotic* of all groups even while growing up (see Table 2aII). While the very religious considered their particular country's interests among their highest values, the irreligious more often looked to what they regarded as the welfare of the world.

Not all the irreligious were politically affiliated, nor was it equally important even to those who were. But as with Andrzej, politics often became a central issue among the irreligious, sometimes their paramount concern. Political identification for the irreligious served much the same function as religion did for the very religious. It bestowed a distinct identity and a community that shared many similar values. As illustrated in the accounts of both Andrzej and Nellie, political parties often served the same function for the irreligious as religious institutions did for the very religious, providing members a sense of identity through parallel social and educational activities as well as a trusted network of colleagues. As the very religious felt themselves most similar to those of their religious community, so the irreligious felt themselves most similar to their political communities. Despite the fact that the very religious and the irreligious were similarly likely to belong to political parties, politics for the very religious was more the handmaiden to religious convictions, whereas the primary concerns of the irreligious tended to be political convictions regarding economics and justice for the excluded.

Given their broad and intense political interests as well as their greater sensitivity to minority concerns, it is not surprising that the irreligious scored higher than other groups on several measures of Outgroup Relationships. As compared with the somewhat religious, they scored significantly higher on the Outgroup Relationships Factor and early awareness of Nazi intentions, as well as significantly lower in accepting any sense of similarity with Nazis. Given that they were more likely than the very religious to attend school with Jews, they were more likely to know Jews as concrete realities. And as compared with all other groups, they were significantly more likely to belong to political parties endorsing inclusive views. Irreligious rescuers, as compared with other rescuers, reflected some similar distinctions (see Table 2aI).[7]

In comparison, then, with others more religious, the irreligious emerge as a culture with a strong pull toward ideas in which religious, national, and ethnic differences mattered less. (This did not mean that they did not harbor routine prejudices — "latent antisemitism was normal" as several put it.) And despite weaker Sharing propensities, as expressed in commonly identified altruistic attitudes and emotions, the irreligious subscribed to a politics that manifested major concern with those on the economic margins of society. Concerned with society's dispossessed and less constrained by limited notions of "us," the irreligious should have been a rich source of large numbers of rescuers. Indeed, while their actual numbers in the population are unlikely ever to be known, in our sample at least, the irreligious, along with the very religious, constituted a disproportionately large percentage of rescuers.

Irreligious Rescuers and Irreligious Nonrescuers

But large numbers of the irreligious also were nonrescuers who differed significantly from irreligious rescuers in several ways. *How did irreligious rescuers differ from irreligious nonrescuers?* They differed on at least one associated measure in all summary factors, and many more on Outgroup Relationships.

Irreligious rescuers were more fortunate in their family relationships; as compared with irreligious nonrescuers, they had a much better start in life. They had better family relationships generally, and they were far less likely to perceive their parents as authoritarian (see Table 2bIII). They emerged from this experience with significantly higher self-esteem and a stronger sense of personal integrity (see Tables 2bV and 2bIV). And while no more likely than nonrescuers to identify and affiliate with secular secondary institutions, they had significantly better relationships with and attitudes toward outgroups. Their parents had made them conscious of Jews in positive ways, sometimes as a positive stereotype such as "intelligent," "hardworking," and "taking care of their own," and sometimes about individuals they knew: someone who was particularly generous, told good jokes, was a good student or just a good friend. They claimed knowing about Nazi intentions earlier and they were far more empathic toward them. Unlike many irreligious nonrescuers, who claimed no emotion in reaction to Jews wearing the Yellow Star, irreligious rescuers in significantly larger percentages, said they felt "intense pain," "became very angry," or just "couldn't bear it." They were also significantly more likely to belong to left leaning political parties, whereas nonrescuers were significantly more likely to belong to centrist or right leaning ones (see Table 2bI).

Conversely, irreligious nonrescuers had poorer relationships with their families of origin (including their parents), thought less well of themselves, and had more negative view of outsiders.

The stories of two irreligious nonrescuers, Gosha from Poland and Jules from France, highlight several of the above characteristics. For Annette, a French Communist nonrescuer, priorities other than rescue were more important. We begin with Gosha's story.

GOSHA

We left our flat in Warsaw and went to our summer place — we rented rooms there. And I helped the local people a lot. Just to give you one example. A woman I knew died leaving a husband and nine children. The priest refused to bury her because the family could not afford a coffin or pay him. I said to him: "What are you saying? Aren't you ashamed?" So I went from house to house collecting money but didn't get enough. The priest wanted them to sell their cow but I said to him: "You'll have the payment you'll never forget! You won't be able to sit on your behind. You better forget the money." And what do you think? He buried her. I frightened him.

My first contact with the partisans was in our summer place. My husband became friends with the local schoolteacher but it was not his real profession. He was really an Army man and he was in hiding because the Germans were after him. He suggested that we join the partisans but that was too much for me: "I won't make it," I told him. Then he told me that he was going to establish a station here and suggested that I distribute (illegal) papers. Although my baby was still small, not yet one year old and I had to carry her in my arms, I agreed. My husband did not join the Resistance — he was too much of a coward.

I also worked at a first-aid station in 1944 where different people came: Poles and Russians. My whole training amounted to a three-month first-aid course. I always took my baby along. I thought it better to die together than to leave her an orphan.

I did it to help Poland — that was the most important thing, to help Poland.

Gosha, her husband, and their infant daughter left Warsaw in search of safety shortly after the war began. She had not anticipated becoming involved in any illicit activities, and courted considerable danger in circulating illegal papers. The reason she gives for agreeing to do so — "I did it to help Poland" — is a central theme in her story. But Polish patriotism meant something very different for her than it did for Andrzej.

Orphaned when she was ten years old, Gosha hardly remembered her parents, but she did not think they had been close. She and her two older sisters were then placed in a Catholic orphanage, an apparently bad experience resulting in a strong rejection of religion even when very young. In addition to projecting her self-image as a caring person on behalf of the poor, the story she tells about the greedy priest reflects her ongoing hostility toward the Church.

Gosha's relationships with others mirrored similar feelings of disaffection. She belonged to no political party and claimed no interest in politics. Asked how she felt about the Nazis taking power in her country, she said: "I wasn't interested in that subject but when war broke out I was sure that the Nazis were going to lose." In 1935, when she was twenty-eight years old, she married an equally irreligious but affiliated Catholic, a printer by trade, who lost his job immediately before the war. Unlike Gosha, her husband was an active Communist.[8] Gosha appeared not to respect her husband very much; probably as much for the fact that he was unable to provide for the family as for his "cowardice." Except for her infant daughter, she had few if any close relationships, even with the one teacher in the orphanage whom she liked. Abandoned by her parents at a very early age and seemingly deprived of any intimate relationship in the orphanage, Gosha remained distrustful of others.

The type of emotional distance that Gosha describes was particularly grievous, suggesting a strong sense of alienation. Emotional distance from parents and nuclear families is often accompanied by a lack of self-confidence and trust, particularly when subsequent life experiences tend to be constricted: Gosha had few opportunities for expanded choices with respect to education, occupation, and friendships. She socialized almost exclusively with those of her own social class and nationality. It is thus not entirely surprising that the one quality Gosha claimed to have none of was a "willingness to take chances." In the context of an uncertain and difficult life, it was better to be as invisible as possible, and when it was necessary to take stands, it was best to make sure they were popular ones. This helps explain her nationalistic type of patriotism: it was an identification that could gain her a measure of general approval as well as physical security. It may also help explain in part her attitudes toward Jews.

Warsaw, the city where Gosha grew up and lived in before and during the war, numbered approximately one million people, among whom approximately one-third were Jews. Yet Gosha reported knowing no Jews while growing up, "didn't know" whether Jews lived in her neighborhood before the war but thought "quite a lot did," and of course had no Jewish friends. Poland suffered one of the most brutal German occupations, and the Warsaw Ghetto was right in the middle of the city. Yet with the exception of one instance — where Nazis shot a Jew and a child born of a union with a Polish woman — she claimed that she had never witnessed or heard about any German mistreatment of Jews. She did, however, witness Nazis shooting Poles: "I was walking to my sister and trenches full of prisoners were passing by. The Nazis took them out and shot them and made people stop and watch. I also saw a young girl and two other people shot."

But Gosha had in fact seen German brutality toward Jews on several occasions. Asked when she became aware of Nazi intentions toward Jews, she said: "I could see Jews transported from France and Italy to Auschwitz; I knew they were not going for a vacation but to die." Asked how she felt the first time she saw a Jew wearing the yellow Star of David, she said: "I thought what everyone else did; that Jews as well as Poles were going to die." Unwilling to grant Jews any special status because of their persecution, Gosha often quickly referenced questions about Jewish suffering to Polish suffering. Even when she admitted that "I don't like Jews; I didn't like them before and I don't like them now," she conjoined it with an erstwhile patriotic motif: "They did a lot of harm; they say Poles didn't help them during the war," a bit of irony that escapes her in view of her own inaction. In fact, she also "doesn't like Gypsies" and felt "not at all like" rich people or Catholics.

The absence of any strong attachments during the early formative years frequently has long-term consequences. Parents often provide the prototype for future connections — children raised without warmth and deprived of emotional comfort frequently find it difficult to develop empathy for and attachments to others later in life.

JULES

Gosha is an extreme example; the lack of *any* close relationships was not common, even among irreligious nonrescuers. Jules, a Frenchman who was thirty-four years of age in 1939, began life in more advantageous circumstances, but he wound up with similarly strong hostile feelings toward outsiders generally and Jews particularly. Like Gosha, he claimed to be very patriotic, but unlike her he did not interpret this to mean supporting resistance of any kind. Unlike Gosha, he remained passive throughout the war.

> In September 1939, my regiment entered Germany and reentered France two days later. Between the eighth and the tenth we retreated further and stayed in the vicinity of Lorraine and Forbach where we experienced no further attacks until May 11, 1940. On May 12, the German troops attacked and I was severely wounded on my right arm. I became a prisoner of war and my arm was amputated. A Red Cross train took me to Sagan and to Stalag 8, a prisoner's camp. In June 1940, the Germans put me in charge of my fellow French prisoners. I escaped and arrived in France on March 19, 1941. When I came to Toulouse, General Sciard sent me to Foix, where he appointed me "Attaché of the Censorship Services." I had to examine all mail addressed to the Prefecture of the Police and the Ministry of the Interior and report my findings to the prefect of the police.

Having enlisted in the army in 1932, Jules, a professional soldier and married, was not with his wife and three children when the war began and did not see them again until 1941.

The only child of parents of modest means — his father was a carpenter and his mother a maid — Jules felt estranged from his father but close to his mother. He and his wife, as well as his parents, all of them not at all religious, belonged to no political party. He became a professional soldier in 1932, and during the war worked for the Vichy Government as a postal censor, charged with examining all types of mail that might be inimical to the regime's interests and reporting his findings to the prefect of police. It was a reasonably high-status position, particularly in view of the fact that his education did not exceed elementary school. His good fortune lasted for some time after the war, after which he lost his job and returned to the blue-collar craft he had apparently learned from his father, earning his living first as a carpenter and then as a craftsman in a furniture factory.

Despite his limited education, Jules thought well of himself, ranking himself very able to take responsibility and make decisions, very helpful, adventurous and willing to take chances, and very patriotic. But nowhere does he express any support for the French Resistance; acting as a censor on behalf of the Vichy government, a German puppet government, did not apparently violate his sense of "love for country." Yet portentously he saw himself as very weak on one measure, admitting that he was "not at all" willing to stand up for his beliefs. Some of those beliefs were about Jews.

Like Gosha, Jules had little to say about Jews initially. His parents never spoke of them, he knew none growing up, none lived in his neighborhood, and he knew none in the military. Like other irreligious nonrescuers, he learned about Nazi intentions toward Jews only in 1942, well after the start of the war and significantly later than irreligious rescuers. During the war, he was never personally mistreated by Nazis, never witnessed or even heard about Nazi mistreatment of Jews or anyone else for that matter. He claimed not having seen Jews wearing the telltale star until 1943, and his only thought at the time was, "Oh, another one is wearing the star." It was not only a nonempathic response but also a confusing one: if this was "another one," it would appear he had seen at least one such previously. Only toward the end of the interview did he acknowledge his intense feelings: "I detest politics," he said, "politics and politicians who do nothing. France is dying because of politics and anti-French racism is increasing. France is being invaded by foreigners and Jews are taking over the country." It is perhaps these beliefs he feared making too public, preferring to project an outward affability even while scolding himself internally for his weakness. Although ostensibly self-confident, Jules may have been afraid of the economic competition outsiders posed.

Gosha and Jules were not politically affiliated but their political sentiments veered toward the nationalistic right; the type Ervin Staub calls "blind patriotism."[9] Without allegiance or affiliation to any other secondary institution — whether religious or secular — that might counter such ideas with more constructive views, one attachment that could provide some sense of belonging and security was a type of patriotism that absolutely excluded outsiders.

ANNETTE

Choices sometimes depended on circumstances, and sometimes they were the consequence of distinctly different values. In the case of Annette, a French Communist nonrescuer, personal circumstances, combined with a political view very unlike that of either Gosha or Jules but not quite representative of rescuers either, appeared to make the difference.

> A week before the war started, I took a group of children from my school to the Château de Tremblé in the region of Vièvre. Paris had prepared this evacuation plan so as to protect the children in the event of war. While I was gone, the Germans arrested all the people who lived at the New City at Chatenay because of their leftist ideology, but released them very soon afterwards.
>
> In September 1939, I went to the Loire-et-Cher district to rejoin my husband. He was then the director of a children center serving some 100 children and I was to assume the title of "Supervisor." I left on June 13, 1940, for my parents' home in the Department of Haute-Loire, taking my three-year-old son with me. I was pregnant at the time with my second child. I left because I learned that my husband had been unfaithful to me with a teacher at the center, and because I was concerned about safety.
>
> After the birth of my second child in September 1940, I returned to the New City where I had lived since 1933. Some four or five people had left to join the Resistance; others, who were Polish Jews and not naturalized French citizens, had also left. My brother-in-law, who had a Jewish wife, also left to join the Resistance. Only about fifteen people remained.
>
> My two children and I stayed there until the end of the war. The Germans never disturbed us, although we were under supervision at all times. I continued to teach school while my mother took care of the children. No one asked me to join the Resistance, but if they had I would have refused because I was an abandoned mother of two. In 1945, I was able to get back my official Communist Party membership card and I have remained a party member ever since.

Born in a small village of some nine hundred inhabitants in the Haute-Loire in 1910, twenty-nine-year-old bystander Annette tells a war story that largely speaks for itself. A single mother with two young children, the oldest already showing signs of emotional problems, she understandably put her children's interests above all else. But more than these circumstances alone distinguish Annette from rescuers.

Annette's life had never been easy. Her father, a miller, earned scarcely enough to feed his family. Having just begun her first job as a teacher in 1932 and newly married she was hopeful about the future. But her husband became ill almost immediately thereafter and her parents' financial situation worsened, requiring her help. In 1933 she and her husband, both strongly committed Communists, moved to New City, a communal housing project composed of twenty-four people who shared similar political views and pooled domestic labor. As Annette explained: "They were not Communists but were very much against fascism. The women did the housework and we all ate very little meat."

Several of New City's inhabitants were Jews, and it was in this context that Annette began to befriend them. Like many irreligious rescuers, she knew about German intentions early and empathized with their victims. "I was aware of what the Nazis intended for Jews as soon as Hitler came to power," she said, and "felt uneasiness, pain and solidarity with them." But there was nothing that made Jews special for her, nothing that gave them particular merit or weight. She had known no Jews in her youth, none had lived in her neighborhood or attended the same school; neither she nor her husband knew them as co-workers, and her parents never spoke of them. While her parents — "decent, simple, and loving people" — said nothing negative about Jews, neither did they say anything positive. She had Jewish friends in New City, but none were particularly close.

By way of contrast, irreligious rescuers often did ascribe particular merit to Jews, and such associations tended to begin with their own parents. As compared with irreligious nonrescuers' parents, they were significantly more inclined to say positive things about Jews, thus suggesting a very early exposure to favorable impressions. Simple as they appear, such comments suggested a shared humanity not always evident in societies marked by "normal" levels of anti-Jewish sentiment; they were particularly important indicators in very hostile environments. Rescue required a particularly positive evaluation, one that made this group appear to be especially worthy, and if positive attitudes did not begin early, they needed to develop later. For very religious rescuers, it often emerged in a Biblical or religious context, and was often conjoined with their notions of patriotism. Among the irreligious it was more likely to be because of alleged admirable group characteristics, a strong sense of cultural kinship, or powerful personal friendships — none of which appeared to characterize Annette.

Annette also reflects another characteristic of irreligious nonrescuers, one that despite their more egalitarian views as compared with the very and somewhat religious, also inhibited rescue. Had her circumstances been different, Annette implies, she might have joined the Resistance. Like many on the left, including Nellie, military goals — espionage and sabotage — rather than saving lives appeared to be the most efficacious means of defeating the Nazis. Resistance, in their view, required destroying the system; saving lives did little toward ensuring that goal. In fact, saving lives, and particularly the lives of Jews, who were the most relentlessly hunted, was often perceived as a liability, for it diverted resources and magnified the danger. Willing to courageously risk death and torture, Resistance fighters — many of whom included Jews themselves — did not abandon prudence nor did they seek martyrdom. They were unwilling to be diverted from their hopes for an ultimate and quicker victory; the destruction of any one particular group was very unfortunate, but basically less important than the major goal.[10]

One other quality distinguished Annette significantly from rescuers. As she recounts her story, she projects a sense of personal strength and assuredness despite her difficulties. Yet she characterized herself as not being particularly able to take responsibility or make decisions, as neither adventurous nor willing to stand up for her beliefs. And she described herself as neither self-confident nor independent. Such qualities distinguished her from many irreligious rescuers who scored significantly higher on self-esteem than did irreligious nonrescuers. Some sense of heightened mastery over events was required for resistance of any kind. Yet a sense of impotence could be overcome given the support of a trusted network and a culture of rescue. Andrzej, for example, had Jewish as well as non-Jewish Socialists with whom he worked, and Nellie's first rescue move came in response to a request from "people from the Resistance." Without the support of her husband or her New City group — many of whom had also "abandoned" her — Annette had no trusted network with whom to work even had she been so inclined.

Political and personal associations with like-minded people were the networks irreligious rescuers largely depended on to do their work. As with Andrzej, their political contacts were largely Democrats, Socialists, and Communists, all of them including disproportionate numbers of Jews who also participated and frequently initiated rescue activities: finding hiding places, forging papers, bringing messages, recruiting other rescuers, and performing all other activities as might have been possible.[11] Personal associations, often formed in the context of such political associations, included non-Jewish and Jewish colleagues and friends. Politics and personal attachments frequently overlapped, allowing networks to cohere and tighten.

Personal and political inclinations, as well as the absence of a supportive network, contributed to Annette's decision. For Gosha and Jules, it was a matter of distinctly different values. Blind nationalism did not overcome either Gosha's or Jules's sense of bitterness, nor did Annette's wartime passivity lead to subsequent satisfaction.

By way of contrast, Maartje, a left-leaning but politically unaffiliated rescuer, did emerge with an entirely different feeling. I conclude with her story because in a reversal of what might have been the more ordinary pattern, she began as a member of the Resistance, only to become a rescuer subsequently. As she describes it, being a rescuer was far more satisfying.

MAARTJE

Twenty-five years old when the war started and living in Groningen, Maartje was then a student, managing to eke out a living by tutoring English and writing children's stories, tourist articles, and the like. Banned from attending university and doing her job because of her refusal to sign a declaration of allegiance to the German occupiers, a move that also threatened her with deportation, she became involved in Resistance work. Along with other university students, she became a member of the Englandspiel group. Organized by the British, Englandspiel (the "English Game") was a network of intelligence agents from England who parachuted into the Netherlands to conduct and coordinate espionage and sabotage.[12] The group had a short life; they were betrayed and many were arrested. Fortunately, Maartje was not among them. Her sense of outrage at the German occupation and the apparently serendipitous way she became involved in rescue is reflected in the following excerpts from her story:

> Right after the Dutch surrendered, Germans were spreading stories that the bombing of Rotterdam had been absolutely necessary and was our own fault. Incredible lies of course! Then General Winkelman, who was the authority since the government was gone, gave us the real facts.[13] Since the newspapers couldn't print it, we typed it and distributed it, along with a letter about the treatment of the mentally ill. I ended up with the Englandspiel, a network of intelligence and agents who came here by parachute or otherwise. But after the Englandspiel ended, I was out of work and the thing with the children started.
>
> I saw what was happening and talked with friends, fellow students, and others. By chance, a farmer's son once said to me: "If expenses were paid, some farm workers would be willing to hide a child." I thought to myself what a great idea. So I went to talk to some of the farm workers, and some of my

friends agreed to supply the money. So suddenly I had three addresses but no children. So I went to Amsterdam to see Joseph Kaplan; that was early 1942. As a child I had been a friend with his children. His daughter worked in a daycare center from which children were routinely taken to a temporary shelter. So I talked to her and some others and told them about my plan. "How many places do you have?" she asked. Proudly I answered "three." "Oh, we have three hundred children," she said, and there I was in the middle of it. From then on I traveled around looking for places and distributing coupons.

I was mostly involved with Jewish children, and some adults. I provided them with coupons, clothes, etcetera. Most important was finding a hiding address of course, but school was also important. I had to find a principal who was willing to put a child with a false name on a class list. I also had a married couple, a nineteen-year-old girl, and strikers from the railway. Of course, there were always different children. When I didn't have an address, I'd shove it on to a colleague or the colleague to me.

I got the coupons through a liaison who is still a good friend. He got them directly from the director at the distribution office, an NSB member.[14] In fact, he had become an NSB member with the purpose of helping and was very valuable to us. We distributed coupons every month and I carried them on my body because there were often inspections on the trains. I had all kinds of individual contacts. It was all a matter of personal trust.

As with Andrezj and Nellie, Maartje knew many Jews; she had grown up in a family with positive feelings toward Jews, and she herself had several close Jewish friends. The network she relied on was diverse and multi-branched, including even an ostensible Dutch Nazi, the NSB individual she talks about. As she points out, "It was all a matter of trust."

Maartje found great satisfaction in her rescue work, a feeling not always shared by her colleagues active in the Resistance. "I had a friend," she said, "another student who did espionage work and once he told me in despair: 'I doubt if anything I do has any value. I don't know whether my messages arrive or not.'" Maartje tried offering him some encouraging words but he would not accept them. "It's easy for you," he said, and Maartje agreed. "He was right," she said, "it was easier for me. I saw positive results." Maartje did in fact see many positive results. Through her informal network of trusted allies (a student who was the son of a farmer, two farm worker families, a Jewish couple, a friend in Utrecht where she could stay overnight and leave a child for a few days if necessary) she calculated that she had helped some fifty people stay alive.

The Moderately Religious:
The Mildly and Somewhat Religious

RENATO

I was parachuted into France in the middle of the war where I began to organize two resistance groups. My area of operation was the southeast of France in the Alps region. One of my jobs was to gather intelligence. By chance, I ran into a friend, a major, who was stationed in Aix-en-Provence. He told me that the Germans had gathered about a hundred and five Jews in the castle of the town, and that they were planning to send them to concentration camps. I got in touch with a woman in the French Resistance — her nickname was "Chère mitraillette" because she had killed many SS officers. Together we worked to prepare a plan to free them. She put me in touch with a doctor who was a friend of the Venezuelan Consul. We succeeded in obtaining one hundred and two Venezuelan passports and then managed to save the whole group by claiming that they were in fact Venezuelans living in France. First we went to Marseilles and then to the Spanish border by train. We got off at a small country station and began walking toward the border. German soldiers were guarding the border, but with the help of French and Spanish partisans, we managed to get the group (they included older people, pregnant women, and children) into Spain. In Spain we ran into a border patrol and we told them that "You are under Franco and we are not against Franco but for humanity. Save these people." They took them away. Later I learned that they were sheltered and protected.

Italian-born Renato, self-described as only mildly religious, was thirty years old and married when he parachuted into France in November of 1942. Having immigrated with his family to Canada some twenty years earlier, he joined the Canadian Air Force in the late 1930s, becoming a captain pilot. Subsequently recruited into the Allied Secret Service, he was sent as their secret agent to Milan and then to southeastern France where his assignment was to organize resistance groups and gather intelligence. A chance meeting with a friend altered his course: acting on his own initiative, he successfully carried out the rescue of more than one hundred imprisoned Jews destined for deportation to extermination camps.

Aix-en-Provence was only Renato's first successful rescue effort. His second venture occurred in the south of France where he led another group to Switzerland using Italian military trucks as transport vehicles. Eventually, he managed more than 100 such escort trips, most of them launched from northern Lombardy, which he entered clandestinely in 1943. There, he formed yet another resistance group, consisting of pilots, assorted other volunteers, and former "smugglers" — that is, people who had experience crossing borders illegally. Before the war was over, Renato and his colleagues succeeded in taking to Switzerland 3,303 persons: 1,550 Jews, 930 individuals who were trying to escape the draft, 300 political dissidents, 165 wounded partisans, and 358 Allied prisoner escapees.

A very determined man, Renato was able to do what seemed at times like the impossible. Having begun his rescue work on his own initiative, he was pleased to receive General Mark Clark's encouragement to continue helping political dissidents and Jews (Clark was in charge of Allied General Headquarters in southern Europe). Although gratified to receive an official blessing, he did not necessarily require it: "I would have carried on even without it," he said. But he interpreted Clark's message as allowing him to focus primarily on Jews, and immediately formed patrols whose exclusive duty it was to accompany Jews to the Swiss border. Quite surprisingly and unlike the experiences of other Jews who were overwhelmingly refused entry, the Swiss accepted all whom Renato brought. The reason, Renato explained, was an extraordinary agreement his group had negotiated with the Swiss government with the help of an "influential general," one of his relatives. The agreement provided that "in the event of a German attack on Switzerland, we would help the Swiss provided that they allowed Jews into the country."

Renato's achievements were exceptional by any measure: resourcefulness, persistence, success or courage. Yet on the surface, Renato appeared to be a moderate man, more inclined toward aloofness rather than engagement. In many of these ways *he resembled moderates generally.* Asked if he had ever stood up for his beliefs before the war, he replied, "Never." He had never joined any political party. And although he rejected the self-description "irreligious," preferring instead to call himself "not very religious," he never belonged to any church. Even in intimate relationships, Renato maintained some distance: he described the relationship with his mother as "somewhat close" and with his father as "not at all close." But his wartime activities belie such reserve. He was in fact a very passionate man, but his passions were not attached to political parties, religion, or even family.

Renato's passions appeared to be largely shaped by his family's experiences and Socialist values, and those of a Catholic elementary teacher, also a Socialist. Strongly anti-fascist and faced with immanent arrest, his parents, along with his uncle and five cousins, fled Mussolini's regime in 1922 when Renato was only ten years old. They settled in Canada, joining Renato's grandfather who had preceded them. Renato's Italian roots remained strong in this new country — he attended an Italian public school during his junior high school and high school years and retained fluency in his native tongue. He entered medical school, eventually becoming a biopathologist who specialized in tropical diseases. Before completing his medical studies, he assumed the directorship of a mobile hospital in Africa, primarily serving areas in Kenya, Uganda, and Ethiopia. He and his wife returned to Africa after the war, eventually resettling in Milan in 1958 where he developed programs to assist the poor and the arthritic, as well as disabled veterans.

The above activities suggest a particular readiness to serve the needy, and it was indeed a dominant theme of Renato's life. His early years provided him with an unusually congruent set of values along these lines. Despite his distant relationship with his parents, he did value what he learned from them. From his father, a university professor in veterinary science, Renato claimed to have learned "self-discipline" and "love for other people." From his mother, a university professor of music, he says he learned not only to play and to sing, but also "how to be compassionate and to be willing to help those who suffer." And the person who most influenced him during his early years, a Catholic elementary teacher to whom he felt closest, taught him similar views: "to respect others, not to use violence when defending my own ideas, and to help those who suffer." He proved very susceptible to all these sentiments; even as a schoolboy he recalled strongly objecting to any activities that might hurt others physically or emotionally ("like calling them nicknames," he said). And despite the fact that he never joined the Socialist Party, he apparently internalized egalitarian ideas, one small example of which was his refusal to consider himself a leader or follower among his friends, describing himself instead as a "brother" to all.

Did he have a particular passion for helping Jews? He was more than or-
dinarily interested in and sensitive to them. "My father always spoke well of
Jews," he said. "He had many Jewish friends in Milan, and many more in
Canada." His mother shared similar sentiments and friendships. Renato too
knew many Jews, had close Jewish friends, and ranked Jews generally among
the three groups he felt most like. But it is his beloved elementary teacher who
may have contributed most to his particular alertness to Jewish oppression.
"She would talk to us about Jews in our history classes," he said, referring to
them as "the people of Israel" rather than "the Jews." "She told us about their
religion and described how they had been historically persecuted." He learned
about the Nuremberg Laws early, and in 1939 readily believed the Jewish
escapee from Hamburg whom he met in Africa who said that extermination
camps for Jews and anti-Nazis already existed in Germany. He also heard
about the roundups from a former Nazi who fled to Italy where he joined
Renato's resistance group, and in 1942 he heard similar reports from Alsace-
Lorraine refugees. With his already intense anti-fascist experience, coupled
with his powerful sympathetic predispositions, he did not doubt what they
said.

Whatever moderation Renato expressed as he talked about his life disappeared when asked the reasons for his activity. "I hate fascists, Nazis, and
Spanish fascists. I wished I could have killed them all. I hated those animals."
Careful about aligning himself too closely with any group or any ideology and
thus limiting his scope of action, Renato preferred to carve out his own path,
guided by his deepest feelings. Rather than rejecting family, church or politics,
he selectively chose from all these groups the values that most resonated with
his own deeply empathic nature, reserving his fierce anger only for those who
violated the most basic of humane principles.

STEFANIA

Stefania, a somewhat religious rescuer from Poland, shares several characteristics in common with Renato. Like Renato, she reserved her passion for
something other than religion or politics. But the object of her passion was
something very different from Renato's, although like his, it facilitated her
rescue activity.

> In 1940, when I became aware that they were persecuting Jews, I immediately
> contacted my friend and said: "Ewa, you cannot become an outcast; I will
> look after you. I'll register you at my place and you'll stay with me." And so I
> did, and she stayed with me for two and one half years. She didn't want me to

support her and so she got a job at a photographer's studio. One day a fifteen-year-old Polish boy said to her, "You're Jewish; give me money or you won't get away." She gave him money and he came back several times. Finally, she had no more money and he said to the first German that passed, "She's Jewish," and they took her to Pawiak and from there to Palmiry — the forest near Warsaw — where she was shot.

In 1943, I saw the vice president of our club — the sports club Skra [a Socialist sports club] — and he had the Star on him. "Doctor," I said, "why are you wearing the star?" "I have to," he said, and when I asked him where he was living, he answered, "In the ghetto." I offered him a separate room in my apartment to live but he refused. "My place is with my wife and baby in the ghetto," he said. He and his wife were murdered but his daughter somehow survived.

I had been a member of the sports club Skra since April 21, 1926, and I knew all the girls in the Jewish Workers' Sports Club: Makabi, Gwiazda, Gwardia, Jutrznia. The bourgeois clubs, Polonia and Warszawianka, didn't accept Jews. Anyway, we had sports matches and I got to know all the girls. So if anyone came for help, I arranged Kennkarte [identification papers — in this case, false identification papers] for them. I had access to documents because I worked in the Citizen Registration Department. My brother was in charge of the registration books in two apartment buildings and we needed to have two photographs, sometimes three, stamped by the person in charge of the books. So I would select from the archives original birth certificates of someone who had died, and tell people to go to the parish church, and then when the certification was complete, my brother put the photographs on their identity cards and registered them in the book. Word got around about what I was doing and the girls came to me — girls I knew and girls I didn't know. Of course, they had to say who sent them. I did this for almost two hundred people.

Unmarried and living alone in Boernerowa at the start of the war, thirty-two-year-old Stefania earned her living as a clerk in the Registry Office at the City Hall. In 1944 she married a man who worked as a cashier at a railway station. Unfortunately, her marriage with him was short-lived; he died in a prison camp in 1945. Although she subsequently remarried, she had no children.

Stefania described herself throughout her life as "somewhat religious," implying a stronger sense of religious commitment than that of the mildly religious Renato, but like him moderation characterized many of her attitudes. Rather than "not joining," however, she preferred a middle course — one that kept her affiliated with those around her but that was slippery on issues. Like her parents, brother, and friends, she was a member of the Socialist Party, but she appeared to be one in name only. She spent little time talking about or even considering political beliefs: "I didn't think about ideas," she said; "I don't think I had any." She was equally noncommittal about patriotism: "I don't know if I thought of myself as patriotic while growing up." As for religion, she kept her identification with the Catholic Church throughout her life, even refusing "to get into any discussion that would be critical of the Catholic religion." Rather than taking sides, she preferred an evasive course that kept her among many different groups: among the Socialists but unwilling to reflect on their ideology, reluctant to declare herself on patriotic issues, and among the religiously affiliated but not too strongly so, while preferring to avoid challenging discussions.

Yet despite Stefania's generally temperate orientation toward religion, politics, and nation, she did have one passion and it is in the context of this passion that her rescue activities occurred. She was an avid sportsperson. It was an interest that was already very strong at age nineteen, when she joined Skra. By the time she was twenty-three, she had won many athletic awards: second and third place in discus throwing, and third place in high jumping and shot put. At age seventy-eight, the year we interviewed her, she was in ill health (she suffered a "nervous breakdown" after the war, she said) but was still active in a sports club where she registered new members, collected membership fees, and did other paperwork. "In fact," she said, "the only activity I do is the sports club." As the interviewer observed: "Stefania was most excited when she talked about her volunteer work for the Sports Club. It seems like the most important thing for her — more important than her husband's illness or anything else that happened in her life."

A Socialist sports network that included many Jews provided the means whereby Stefania overcame her feelings of isolation and developed a sense of belonging. Speaking of the neighborhood in which she lived, she said: "I felt like an outsider in my community." She attributed her estrangement to her family's leftist politics, one consequence of which was that her father was exiled to Siberia before World War I. "That became a reason for the neighbors to stay away from my family," she explained. "They were neither friendly nor willing to help us although we were very poor." As a result, she claimed, she lost all interest in them. "I spent my time working and devoted myself to sports," she said.

Helping Jews was no oddity for Stefania; her Socialist family, whom she loved, was similarly involved. At the time she made her initial offer of help, she felt particularly isolated, for her mother was in prison and her father already dead. Offering to help her good friend Ewa — a fellow sportswoman — seemed a very natural thing to do. "I liked her very much. I knew it meant death if I was discovered — everyone knew that. But I thought to myself that I have no mother and no father — my mother was then in prison and my father had by then died in Pawiak and life had no value for me. I didn't know if I would survive, but I felt it was my holy duty to help as many as possible if I did." Friendship, despair, and a sense of abandonment no doubt contributed to her rescue decisions. But this was also part of a lifestyle she shared with her family, who were similarly engaged in rescue and other underground activities. Thus it was that this courageous woman — who described herself as "not at all" adventurous, decisive, or independent or inclined toward risk taking, and who tended toward moderation in most things — became involved in life-threatening tasks for some four years, ending only with the Warsaw Uprising in 1944.

The Moderately Religious and the More and Less Religious

The largest group in our sample is the moderately religious, a not entirely surprising fact given the likelihood that they also constitute the largest group in society at large. They included 296 respondents (188 rescuers and 108 nonrescuers). The *mildly* religious among them — that is, those who described themselves as "not very religious" — are the smaller group: 106 respondents (71 rescuers and 35 nonrescuers). Renato belonged to the mildly religious. The *somewhat* religious — that is, those who described themselves as "somewhat religious," — are the larger group: 190 respondents (117 rescuers and 73 nonrescuers). Stefania belonged to this group. While rescuers and nonrescuers within all groups differed significantly from one another, somewhat religious nonrescuers stand out: significant differences between them and somewhat religious rescuers are the most numerous as compared with rescuers and nonrescuers in all other religiosity groups.

The concept "moderate" has different value connotations. On the one hand, it implies prudent, judicious, careful, and reasonable: characteristics deemed admirable in many contexts. On the other, it implies compromise, conservatism, and "fence sitting": terms connoting unprincipled, wedded to the status quo, and vacillating. In either case, moderation implies distance from entangling involvements. Whether "moderate" is regarded as a positive or negative attribute, neither view suggests passion or a readiness to act, particularly when it involves self-sacrifice. If the moderately religious were inclined toward moderation generally, rather than confining it to religion alone, it would help explain the fact that while they constituted the largest group in our sample (as compared with the very religious and the irreligious), they included a disproportionately low percentage of rescuers and a disproportionately high percentage of nonrescuers. Evidence suggests that as compared with the very religious and the irreligious, they appeared to be more inclined toward moderation in at least one way: their family relationships were cooler than the very religious but not quite as cool as among the irreligious. If moderation implies keeping careful distance from involvements, the somewhat religious in particular exhibited this characteristic.

We begin with a description of the somewhat religious as compared with other religiosity groups, followed by a description of the mildly religious.

THE SOMEWHAT RELIGIOUS

One way moderation manifested itself among the somewhat religious in particular was in their greater reluctance to challenge others. They were significantly less likely than either the very religious or the irreligious to assert their beliefs publicly, perhaps because like Stefania, they had none, they were undecided about them, or they preferred not calling attention to themselves (see Appendix B, Table 2bV).[1] They were also less inclined than either group to get involved generally, preferring instead to distance themselves from other persons and events. They scored significantly higher than the very religious on detachment and significantly lower on social responsibility (see Table 2bIV). They were also significantly less likely to affiliate politically, as compared with the very religious and the irreligious, possibly out of their preference to avoid conflict and controversy, as well as their general distaste for public action that might distract them from higher-priority goals (see Table 2aII).

Concern with economic matters may well have been one of the high-priority goals for the somewhat religious, keeping them from involvements in other matters. "Industry," "hard work," "be a go-getter," "thrifty," and "careful with dispensing money" were among the words the somewhat religious heard more frequently from their parents as compared with the parents of the very religious. More oriented toward external authorities for success than the very religious or the irreligious, the somewhat religious scored significantly higher than either on the External Mastery factor (see Table 2bV). Such emphasis did not necessarily keep them from having kindly impulses: they were as likely as all other groups to feel empathy for others and more likely than the irreligious to regard themselves as honest, helpful, and responsible. But as compared with the very religious, they had much weaker Sharing impulses, including a stronger inclination toward detachment and a weaker sense of social responsibility (see Table 2bIV).

Yet as compared with the irreligious, the somewhat religious generally were reasonably well integrated into the conventional dominant institutions of their society. They had closer relationships with their families of origin (see Table 2bIII), rated themselves as more patriotic (see Table 2bII), and of course, unlike the irreligious, kept their religious ties.

Given the paradox of their inclination toward disengagement yet their careful maintenance of reasonable ties with family, country, and church, the somewhat religious appear to be largely conformists. Conformists are willing to take on the outward forms that dominant social institutions demand, but without any necessary internal commitment to their values: they neither challenge them nor necessarily embrace them. Unwilling to take imprudent risks, socially or politically, they prefer "going along" to provocation. Their religious commitment may be of a similar kind; that is, more oriented toward using religion for enhancing sociability and status (Gordon Allport calls this "extrinsic" religiosity), rather than as an end point for defining principles and living by them (Allport labels this "intrinsic" religiosity).[2] The somewhat religious, in other words, may be more inclined to be bystanders than either the very religious or irreligious by virtue of a general predisposition rather than in the context of a crisis only.

This interpretation may also help explain yet another orientation more characteristic of the somewhat religious. As compared with the irreligious particularly, the somewhat religious were significantly *less open to outsiders* with respect to several measures associated with Outgroup Relationships, including the distinction of claiming a greater sense of similarity to Nazis (see Table 2aI).

THE MILDLY RELIGIOUS

How similar were the mildly religious to the somewhat religious? On the whole they were less Externally Oriented than the somewhat religious, and not quite as weak on Sharing (see Tables 2bV and 2bIV). Their family relationships were largely similar, although relationships with mothers may have been somewhat weaker. More than the somewhat religious, however, they complained of being *physically disciplined*. They also deemed themselves less patriotic (see Tables 2bIII and 2aII). And they were not quite as weak with respect to Outgroup Relationships—claiming more empathy for Jews and no particularly strong similarity to Nazis (see Table 2aI). In short, they appeared closer to the very religious in some ways and more similar to the irreligious in others. More important, as compared with the very religious and the irreligious, they tended *not* to evidence strong positive orientations in any of the summary factors or individual measures associated with altruism generally or outgroup altruism particularly.

Moderately Religious Rescuers and Moderately Religious Nonrescuers

How did moderately religious rescuers compare with moderately religious nonrescuers? Moderately religious rescuers, as compared with their nonrescuer counterparts, were more consistently focused on their attachments to and affirmation of others. A more psychologically fortified group, clearer about their identity and their values, they more often emphasized their connections to others, including outsiders.

Some of the sharpest differences occurred between somewhat religious nonrescuers and somewhat religious rescuers. Many of the differences between them appeared to begin with their families of origin, where acquired negative attitudes among nonrescuers appeared to persist into adulthood. They began life in far less advantaged circumstances and developed their views in a context more often marked by emotional deprivation. Their family relationships generally were less positive, and more of them felt estranged from their fathers, who in more cases relied on physical punishment to discipline them (see Table 2bIII).[3] Apparently having learned early that obedience was the way to avoid punishment, they were far more oriented toward complying with external authorities — in fact scoring highest of all groups on External Mastery (see Table 2bV). Their Sharing orientation was significantly lower, and they were far less concerned with matters pertaining to personal integrity (see Table 2bIV). Their family culture, as compared with rescuers, was less egalitarian and more exclusionary. Their parents inclined heavily toward stereotyping generally, and particularly negative stereotyping about Jews; their own posture duplicated and sometimes exceeded that of their parents. They were significantly less likely to have Jewish friends (lowest of all the groups), claimed learning about Nazi intentions toward Jews later, felt significantly less similar to outsiders generally, including Jews and Gypsies, and were less likely to have friends different from themselves in any way — vertically (economically) or horizontally (ethnicity or religion) (see Table 2aI).[4] Given all the above and their stronger identification with Nazis as compared with very religious nonrescuers — a distinction they also shared with mildly religious nonrescuers — it is not surprising that they were less likely even to have family members who participated in resistance activities (see Table 2aI).

Mildly religious nonrescuers shared with somewhat religious nonrescuers many similar outgroup sentiments, but they are particularly noteworthy for their strong identification with Nazis.[5] Whereas the heightened susceptibility to outgroup prejudices among somewhat religious nonrescuers appeared to be associated with their stronger sense of vulnerability, probably largely due to harsher family experiences, the susceptibility of mildly religious nonrescuers was not attributable to a similar source. And whereas somewhat religious nonrescuers differed significantly from their rescuer counterparts on many measures, mildly religious nonrescuers differed significantly from their rescuer counterparts on Outgroup Relationships measures primarily and most particularly as they related to Jews specifically. Their family relationships as compared with mildly religious rescuers were not significantly different, nor did their Sharing or Mastery orientations differ. Their susceptibility to Nazis appeared to be more associated with their pre-war political culture — mildly religious nonrescuers and their parents were significantly more likely to belong to conservative and rightist parties before the war (see Table 2aI). As societies became more polarized in the immediate pre-war environment, a democratic parental orientation sometimes favored a stronger liberal position whereas an autocratic parental orientation often encouraged a pronounced move toward the right, including Nazi totalitarianism.

Ideological preference, opportunism, submission to the historical circumstances, or simply survival may have prompted both somewhat religious and mildly religious nonrescuer groups to assume the stands they did. Some chose to withdraw from events, hoping to resist the tide, or to comply with the powers of the time. In some cases they chose to join what looked like the victors, hoping to take advantage of possible opportunities. The nonrescuer stories below illustrate several of these themes, including other inclinations described above. Marc, the first of these respondents, chose withdrawal. After a short stint as an active resister, Louis chose the same. Hans and Rudolf became Nazi supporters, although not quite in the same way or for exactly the same reasons.

MARC

French-born Catholic Marc, a moderately religious nonrescuer, can best be characterized here by a series of things he did not know, feel, or do. Born in 1922 in Montraux (Seine and Marne) to parents of modest means, Marc grew up in Connante, a small village of some two to three hundred inhabitants. While he described his relationship with his family as "good," he confessed that he had not been very close to either of his parents. All they taught him, he said, was "respect for work." As a young man, he considered himself "not at all" adventurous, independent, or willing to take chances, unable to make decisions or take responsibility, and only somewhat patriotic. But he did consider himself a self-confident person and a helpful one. Consistent with this self-description, he said he had never done anything risky or particularly adventurous before the war, nor asserted his beliefs publicly in any way, but he did help his neighbors and friends and generally had a sense of competence doing so. Like his parents, he had never belonged to any political party.

Only seventeen years old when the war began, and too young to be drafted, he was working as a gardener. He married two years later, and the young couple moved to a small village of twenty-five inhabitants some eleven miles from Romilly. There they lived in a two-room house at the time of the German invasion in September 1939:

> I was expecting the war, but I felt nothing. I continued working at the vegeta-
> ble farm. I saw many refugees from the northern part of France go through the
> town, many families with children, tired and weary. Romilly was bombarded,
> and the nearby airfield was practically unusable. Many homes were also
> destroyed. On June 13, I, along with my parents, took to the road, hoping to
> escape the rapidly advancing German Army. On June 15, the Germans with
> their tanks joined the convoy of refugees and suggested that they should all go
> back to their home. All of us went back and resumed our lives as before.

Entrenched in his immediate surroundings, the only group of people Marc felt similar to were other Catholics. He rejected any sense of likeness to Gypsies, and as for all others — Protestants, Jews, and Nazis — he was evasive; he didn't know if he was like or unlike them. He never was personally mistreated by Nazis, nor had he ever seen anyone else being mistreated by them. He refused to answer questions about what he would tell his children to do should Nazis come to power today. As for Jews, he said his parents had never spoken of them and he had never known any. He claimed that he had not known what the Nazis intended to do to the Jews, and he had never seen a Jew wearing the star. He did not admire any particular leader during the war. No one in his family had been involved in resistance activities, although he thought some people in his village might have been. Events not directly within his vision were largely outside his grasp, and he learned about the end of the war in the same way he learned about most matters. "In 1944," he said, "we saw American tanks at the main street in the town nearby. That is how we found out that the war had ended."

In view of the enormity of the destruction in World War II, it seems inconceivable that Marc knew so little. Was ignorance a path he chose or did it reflect the absence of opportunity to know? Marc acknowledges hearing that some people in his village were in the Resistance, suggesting that opportunities for knowing were present. Marc was hardly alone, however, at least with respect to ignorance about Jews, for even many active resisters claimed not to know their fate. Most assuredly, Jews were irrelevant for Marc, as they also were for many nonrescuers; irrelevance bred unawareness. Like many, he may have opted for apparent safety through accommodation, choosing not to see nor hear, neither to affirm nor to reject. Perceiving might have compelled intervention, a dangerous activity even before the war. Invisibility was the best hope for survival, and it depended on censoring one's awareness appropriately.

LOUIS

Although quite different from Marc in social class and education, Louis, a twenty-two-year-old Dutch Catholic nonrescuer university student, offers another striking example of this strong tendency toward disengagement. Yet for one short period, he actually became involved in some resistance activity. He was an articulate and introspective man, and his reflections about that period evidence some of the attitudes toward Germans and Jews that a number of moderates shared.

Louis's affluent parents, and particularly his father, a film distributor who belonged to the conservative Catholic Party, emphasized "hard work and fair play." Disciplined repeatedly by his father and in a manner that embarrassed him — he "didn't want to say how" — Louis did not feel very close to either of his parents while very young. By age thirteen, his feelings changed; he became quite attached to his father and apparently learned from him some basic attitudes toward Jews:

> My father made a lot of unflattering remarks about Jews and they were largely true. I don't think there was much antisemitism in Holland. There were some remarks — and I still believe Jews do a lot of things that deserve those remarks — not the general population but as individuals. Like I said, I have Jewish friends. But to some extent they have brought the wrath of the world upon themselves — and still do. I am very much opposed to what we are doing right now about the Holocaust. The Jews are not the only ones who suffered during the war. The Jews make themselves too important. The Jews were not that important in Holland.

He did, however, admire scientific achievement and strongly objected when the Germans expelled Jews from the university shortly after the occupation. "At that time I was very much aware that Jews played a very important role in science. It was outrageous to dismiss Jewish professors. In general, I would have been against throwing anyone out for whatever reason." While Louis here may be implying that fairness or perhaps academic freedom dictates his basic attitude, his admiration for science and technological achievement remained a strong theme in his life and helps explain his attitudes toward Germans — considerably more generous than toward Jews despite very trying circumstances, as reflected below.

Louis described himself as "not at all patriotic" before the war, a disposition he attributed to his sense of marginality: "I got along okay, but I have never in my life had any place where I felt I belonged." Outraged at the occupation, however, he grew more patriotic: "Once the war started, I changed." Uncharacteristically prompted toward action, he became a courier for a Dutch underground group for some four months. "I admired Germans before the war," he said, "they do very good work in the technical field—it is related to that. Of course it was a different story after the war started." Apparently quite naïve about politics right before the invasion, he confessed, "Nazis didn't mean anything to me at that time." And he was careful to distinguish between his attitudes toward Germans and Nazis: "Let's talk about Germans," he said, "not Nazis." His general positive attitude toward Germans allowed him to regard them empathically even when he was arrested and tortured:

> I was picked up as a transmitter by the Germans—I was sending information. I was tortured. I still cannot talk about that. I felt that although I hated the SS—the SS did it—I hated them for being in our country—they shouldn't have done that. But I could not blame them too much for torturing me at that time because I would have done the same. They were fighting for their lives at that time—in November of 1944. That was just before the Battle of the Bulge and there was all kinds of information going to England about the German positions. They were obviously very much upset by this and tried to get all the information they could. I don't blame them for that. Some acts of normal soldiers were extremely unpleasant.

His father, who had some political influence, managed to have him released, but the experience augmented his sense of marginality and diminished his self-esteem:

> To be quite honest—I know that at that time I didn't want to be involved with any group because I knew I couldn't trust myself. How much of that was an excuse? I don't know. I was definitely not a hero; I know that. I didn't have the hero mentality—doing something, whatever the consequences. If I am at peace with myself it is because I am convinced I couldn't be trusted and because I really had their welfare at heart. But I see myself in not too favorable a light. But on the other hand, I really wasn't a bad guy; I was just twenty. Things are not black and white. In some cases people are very concerned about somebody else—I had my own problems at the time.

The experience also left Louis with an intensified resistance to engagements of any kind. Politically unaffiliated before the war, he remained so thereafter. Whereas he had some connection with the Church before the war, he severed his religious ties completely. And he subsequently never participated in volunteer activities of any kind: "I don't volunteer," he said.

HANS

Not all nonrescuers shared Louis's preference for disengagement. Another group of moderately religious nonrescuers did become passionately engaged, but in a diametrically opposed direction to that of rescuers. Hans, a somewhat religious Nazi, is one such example.

> Before the war I was a member of the Hitler Youth and did Labor Service. I volunteered for service in the war and became a noncommissioned officer in the Army. Beginning in 1941, I was a reconnaissance patrol leader. I was wounded and sent back home in 1945.
>
> I felt triumphant when Nazis took power. Kristallnacht was quite all right with me. My father told me that Jews don't belong with us. Their religion teaches them that a Jew may commit any wickedness, but not toward another Jew. This is written in their Bible, their Talmud. It was clear to me from the beginning that Jews do not belong to the German nation.
>
> I never saw Nazis mistreat anyone, including Jews. I admired Rudolf Hoess greatly, his charisma, his personality. I am totally unlike Jews, Catholics, Turks, Gypsies, and rich people. I'm only somewhat like other Protestants. The group of people I feel closest to are Nazis; I have the most positive feelings toward National Socialism and am negative about everything else. If a party with goals similar to those of the Nazis came to power today, I would tell young people to support it. But "Fatherland and Nationality," offered to young people then, is not available to the young today. The destruction of Germany is being continued systematically in the moral realm, through foreign influences, racial mix, and destruction of the German spirit.

Born in Leipzig in 1921, Hans was only twelve years old when Hitler was appointed Reich Chancellor of Germany. His years in the Hitler Youth and the army may well have been the high points of his life. The indoctrination he received during these early years has lasted a lifetime; as the above interview indicates, he was clearly an unreconstructed Nazi when we interviewed him in 1986.

With the exception of his father's hatred for Jews, Hans's family appeared to be quite ordinary. Lukewarm Lutherans, and like Hans, only somewhat religious, they were a conventional group with ostensibly standard values. The younger of two children, Hans described his family as "very close." From his mother, to whom he felt only "somewhat close," he learned to value education. His father, whom he admired greatly, taught him to be "sincere, loyal, honest, and industrious," values identical to those he reported learning from his religious leaders. His parents disciplined him, but "with words only."

Hans's family was affluent during his growing years. Despite having a limited education that ended with elementary school, his father earned a very comfortable living as an interior decorator and department manager in a large furniture store. But the family's financial circumstances changed dramatically during the Depression: they were "very poor" before the war, Hans said. The poisonous antisemitic animus of the times and the purges of Jews from all walks of life probably suited the family's altered circumstances: the elimination of occupational rivals, some of them perhaps in the very department store in which his father worked, could only help. Nazi rhetoric that blamed Jews could well have inflated his father's ego while simultaneously advancing his financial aspirations.

Hans himself showed little promise of gaining upward mobility through conventional educational channels. After completing elementary school, he began training as an auto mechanic, a vocation he maintained throughout his life. His cool relationship with his mother might be attributable in part to the emphasis she placed on formal education and at which he apparently had only minimal success. Given the absence of any countervailing values from his parents suggesting care and kindness, the importance of industriousness and hard work loomed large. And given his less than stellar educational performance, and his father's financial reversals, Hans probably did not feel very optimistic about his future.

The Hitler Youth, which Hans joined in the early thirties, redressed some of his concerns. It not only provided him with a network of young people and adults who shared a common ideology, but also gave him a strong sense of belonging, self-esteem, and power. As he acknowledged, others had not thought much of him before, but after he joined the Hitler Youth his sense of power over them grew. It also earned him his father's approval — association with "unsuitable friends," primarily Jews, was the critical thing his father had disciplined him for, and Hans claimed never to have had either Catholic or Jewish friends or any friends different from himself religiously. He developed a very good opinion of his own character, giving himself the highest ranking on honesty, self-confidence, independence, responsibility, and adventurousness during his growing years, and considered himself a leader among friends. He also asserted that he had been very willing to stand up for his beliefs (although he could think of no time when he had actually done so).

In recounting his activities during the war, Hans glossed over the details. Asked if had ever refused help to someone who asked, he replied, "I don't know." He had never witnessed any Nazis mistreating Jews and had only heard about Kristallnacht. Yet when asked, he admitted seeing Jews wearing the yellow star. How did he feel about it? "It was unjust, embarrassing to me." His concern, it appears, was more with himself than with the victims — he did not like to be embarrassed. And his response to the question that came next suggested that his view of injustice was not a conventional one. Asked the occasion on which he had become aware of what the Nazis intended to do to the Jews, he replied: "It was clear to me from the beginning that the Jews do not belong to the German nation." Did "justice" mean getting rid of Jews but doing it in a way that did not embarrass him? He implies he knew nothing about extermination of Jews during the war and "after the war"; he said, "Nobody talked about it." The silence, he suggests, was due to the fact that "Jews were unpopular," thereby perhaps implying that the rest of the country actually approved of the policy. His children, he said, know a great deal about his life during the war but, despite his hopes, do not apparently share his nationalist thinking. He acknowledged that they strongly disapprove of his wartime activities.

Was Hans a perpetrator? He certainly had the opportunity to be one, and there is reason to think he did not resist it. Perpetrators tend to demonize their victims, suppress memories of the horrors they create, reframe them as acts of honor and ideological purity, or try to create the illusion that their victims have simply disappeared as though without cause. Hans probably considered himself an "idealist," a description his referent moral universe probably endorsed. He had shown himself ready to subordinate his own interests to that of his group, most clearly evidenced by volunteering to serve in the army. And according to the values he had learned from father and church, he had remained "loyal" to his Nazi friends, was "sincere" and "honest" about his convictions, and had worked "industriously" on their behalf.

"Denial and delusion are twins," aptly observes Howard J. Ehrlich, editor of *Perspectives,* a publication of The Prejudice Institute, and their twinfold nature reveals itself in Hans's narrative. According to Ehrlich:

> In denial, people refuse to recognize the existence of something "real." In delusion, people make real something that doesn't exist. While denial and delusion can be understood as psychological properties, as the consequence of a closed cognitive structure, they are, in the perspective of a societal frame, best understood as social norms. Every society socializes its members into what is true and what is false knowledge, what is real and what is not. Denials and delusions, like all cultural patterns, are transmitted across families and friends, through parents and teachers, and authorized and maintained by the legitimate authorities in the government, the church, and the mass media.[6]

RUDOLF

Rudolf, another moderately religious German male nonrescuer, might have called Hans an "idealist," but while perhaps not quite as delusional, he nonetheless also failed to see the reality in which he was immersed. "Not all Nazis were alike," he said. "There were idealists and excellent people, as well as sadists and murderers. A man I knew was described as a bad criminal in a pamphlet published by the National Committee of Free Germany in 1944. I didn't want to believe this at first, but later I learned to differentiate." Rudolf did not explain how the behaviors of Nazi "idealists and excellent people" differed from those who did not achieve such high status, but the above suggests that he considered most of them worthy, at least until 1944. In the western context, idealism is more often associated with humanitarian principles; in Hitler's Germany it meant self-sacrifice for the sake of Nazi ideology. Rudolf did not share Hans's intense passion about Nazis—"not very like them," he declared—but neither had he quite managed to disassociate himself from them. Unlike Hans, he preferred to keep some distance but confesses that he "preferred Nazis to Bolsheviks." To some degree the esteem in which he holds them stems from his occupational role and the tight collegial network associated with it.

Four years older than Hans—Rudolf was born in Stuttgart in 1917—he became a military officer in 1936. In 1940, he was sent to France, and in 1941 to Russia. While he never joined the Nazi Party himself, no doubt many of those under his command as well as his fellow officers did. Military culture is a particularly "tight" culture: participants undergo a common harsh training program, share a common set of rules distinct in many ways from those of the rest of society, including unqualified obedience to authority, learn that survival depends on teamwork, and socialize together frequently. Horizontal pressures to conform become very strong. Under conditions of war and privation, bonds intensify. Professionals like Rudolf often idealize their activities and those of their comrades to maintain their self-respect, and out of loyalty to each other they tend to cover up brutal excesses.

Yet Rudolf never completely internalized the expectations of his military culture, perhaps because of his family's political orientation, quite different from that of Hans's family. He suffered a tremendous blow when his mother, whom he described as "very warm and friendly," committed suicide. In contrast, his father, with whom he had a somewhat more distant relationship, "was very strict and beat me with a stick or just slaps in the face." While the values he reported learning from him were similar to those Hans said he learned from his father—"order, obedience to authority, cleanliness, and not to waste money"—the political culture was different. Rudolf's father had been a member of the Social Democrats, the German Socialist party, until 1934, joining the Nazi Party late in 1944, and then, as Rudolf explained it, "only under coercion." As was common among Socialists generally, Jews were disproportionately represented in their ranks, often playing leadership roles.

Perhaps out of such conflicting influences and loyalties—to his kind mother and physically abusive but politically liberal father, to his Nazi comrades, and to his country—Rudolf began to develop characteristic responses. When he described his military activities in Russia, he emphasized his helpfulness to other soldiers and to the population under occupation. Unwilling to accept personal responsibility or to censure those he cared for, he attributes blame to "everybody" and "nobody," to "the times," and finally to the victims themselves. This motif begins to appear in response to the question, "What did your father tell you about Jews?"

> There was a difference between general talk about Jews and specific personally known Jews. Relationships with the latter were normal — similar to other people. My father disliked some and liked others. Around 1933 to 34, "general Jewish topics" came up in conversations: such as unscrupulous Jewish merchants, fight of Nazis against forces beyond the government, like Bolsheviks, the Catholic Church, Free Masons, and Jews.

Hitler became chancellor in 1933, and within a year, Rudolf suggests, a radical cultural change had occurred in Germany. Antisemitic sentiments in fact had been common for at least a decade earlier, but as the Nazi government mounted its cumulatively more virulent antisemitic attacks, Jews became successfully demonized within a few short years, objects of loathing and fear. Although the Nazi apparatus did its part, most of this indoctrination was accomplished through the process of simple social interaction — in routine "conversation" among intimates and strangers. "Stereotypes do not simply exist in individuals' heads," they are "social representations," argue Augoustinos and Walker. They "emerge and proliferate within the particular milieu of a given historical moment."[7] The historical moment penetrated deeply into German consciousness.

In our interview with Rudolf, he also appeared to be making an effort to distinguish between his own attitudes toward Jews and the social climate in which he lived. But despite such valiant attempts, his biases favoring and protecting Nazis as well as himself surfaced consistently. Asked how he felt about Kristallnacht, he said "distressed" — not because of any expression of empathy with the victims, but rather "because one made enemies unnecessarily." The "one" are the perpetrators, and what he objected to is their errant strategy, not their ideology. Again he explained the behavior as an expression of the times: "Jews were looked at as a force beyond government that had to be challenged by antisemitism." He had not seen but conceded hearing rumors about mistreatment of Jews, but he had discounted them. "Enemy propaganda and bathroom talk have always existed in war and because of that nobody believed it," he explained. If "nobody" believed it, Rudolf, too, was relieved of responsibility. He also acknowledges visiting the Warsaw Ghetto in 1941, where he "saw a situation that was unworthy of humans." What did he see? "Jews were beaten by Jewish assistant police," he said. That this was the only item he recalled suggests that he may have been trying to avoid incriminating Germans by implying that Jews themselves had created the horrors.

Rudolf played by the "rules of the game" as defined by the dominant institutions of his society and times and, like Hans, may very well have been a perpetrator — military personnel did participate in genocidal activities. But unlike Hans, he apparently did not totally internalize the values of this culture. Unwilling both to reject his Nazi comrades and to eschew completely his father's early democratic values, and concurrently averse toward assuming personal responsibility and toward attributing blame to his party friends, he consistently interpreted events in such a way so as to absolve both himself and his comrades. Although somewhat more ambivalent about reality than was Hans, Rudolph, too, tended to deny it.

Germans, of course, were subjected to a particularly virulent form of social virus. The cultural norms that had marked society in pre-Hitler times had been decimated: turned "topsy-turvy," as one rescuer put it. A relentlessly hate-filled barrage of propaganda and ideology pounded out by the State and all the social institutions that it controlled had managed to change civil values and behavior in only a matter of years. All forms of dissent had been crushed under a brutal terror, and the civilian population, even when not entirely enculturated into the new ethos, were either coopted by opportunism or coerced by fear. In this context, any form of resistance — physical or even emotional — required more than ordinary countercultural supports — but most of these had almost completely disappeared.

Disregarding particular national and historical circumstances, are the moderately religious nonetheless more likely than the very religious or irreligious to succumb to outgroup attitudes and behaviors of the above sort? Perhaps. Some studies conducted in the United States, for example, found stronger inclinations toward stereotyping and prejudice among the moderately religious as compared with the very religious and the irreligious.[8] But even strongly prejudiced groups, moderates or otherwise, are likely to behave in a reasonable fashion toward outsiders when societal norms insist on tolerance and helpfulness. On the whole, they incline toward conformity, not deviance.

Family culture helped shape attitudes and values among all religiosity groups, but among moderates who were less likely to be strongly associated with supportive secondary institutions, it may have been particularly important. Resisting the poisonous atmosphere permeating the occupied countries of Europe after the Nazi onslaught usually required some type of social support. Among moderates, who were less committed to or affiliated with religious or political institutions, family culture often played the decisive role in determining appropriate action. I conclude this discussion of the moderately religious with the story of Armand, a French male rescuer, who offers a good example of how family dynamics, almost imperceptibly, sometimes worked to effect rescue.

ARMAND

As I told you, it was not me who did it all. My mother was then working in a factory in Ivry as a secretary. Mr. D, who collected metal scraps, came to the factory to borrow a big vat in which to melt them. In 1941, when Jews were having more and more trouble, he asked my mother to look after his sister, who was living in the town. This is how my mother met Mrs. B. She also had a little boy who was five years old. My parents met her and began to take care of her.

During a particularly big raid in July 1942 we had to move her and her son very quickly to hide them. From that point on, they took refuge in my parents' house. But our house was very small, and I was still living at home. So we sent her to one of my aunts who had a little room for her. She stayed there until about the end of 1943.

During that time I asked the Resistance people to try to find a way to rejoin her with her family. In September or August of 1942 I went to Grenoble where some of her cousins lived. But they were not much better off than she and advised me that she should wait before joining them. So she stayed with my aunt, and while I was gone my father had placed her son in a Catholic institution.

In 1944 I came back home from the Resistance and Mrs. B.'s security had worsened. So I took her with me to Montreuil and looked for a place she might hide. A friend's house was the first place I looked, but he was raising rabbits and it was so dirty she couldn't stay there. Eventually I found a place for her in a restaurant, and she hid there until the day of liberation. Her husband, who was in the Foreign Legion, came back after the war.

An only child, Armand was born in 1922 to moderately comfortable French parents in Ivry, a city of approximately thirty-five thousand inhabitants. His mother, a seamstress, and his father, a post office employee, worked many hours, so he spent a good deal of time in the care of a beloved neighbor. While he described his caretaker neighbor as having "no religion," his mother, he said, was "somewhat religious" and his father mildly so. Neither his caretaker nor his parents belonged to a political party.

Armand's relationship with his father was somewhat cool, "only somewhat close" he said; away at work for many hours, his father did not see Armand all that much. From his caretaker neighbor, whom he described as influencing him most, he learned how to appreciate nature. From his mother, with whom he also felt very close, he learned about "religion, morals, and personal integrity." One of the religious and moral lessons he valued greatly he recalls learning from his religious leaders: "People should love one another and people should not hurt others."

Armand regarded himself as "very independent" and began to evidence it early. "I generally did or said the opposite of what my friends told me. At that time specifically it was politics that I was against, and also the economic system. I fought with other students about political beliefs, especially against Communism and royalty."

He also described himself as a fervent patriot, and patriotism for him meant liberating his beloved country from the hated occupiers. Asked how he felt at the Nazi occupation, he answered, "incredibly sad, devastated at the beginning of the occupation." Asked to name the leaders he most admired, he mentioned General Charles de Gaulle first and then two other generals who fought hard against the Germans. In 1942, he left school, where he was studying "electricity and mechanics," and went to Paris, where he worked on behalf of the resistance group known as the Movement for National Liberation (Mouvement de Libération Nationale). He came home periodically thereafter, and it was during those periodic returns that he became involved in his parents' activity.

Did he have any particular feelings of attachment to Jews? It did not appear so. In fact, his world was quite insular. The only group he felt "very like" were Catholics, and he had only one non-Catholic friend: not a Jew, however, but a Protestant. His parents didn't talk about them and he wasn't conscious of them at school. He found out inadvertently that some students in his elementary school were Jewish: "We were in a class on civic instruction and we were talking about religion. I was surprised to learn there were different kinds of groups," he said, but it did not mean much to him then.

Yet, he became aware of Nazi intentions toward Jews reasonably early: "at the end of 1940 — perhaps the beginning of '41. There were noises to the effect that Jews were being killed — there was talk around town like that." When first seeing them wearing the Jewish star, sometime in 1942, he felt "very much against it" and he along with other students protested.

Did he become involved because his mother asked him? "Not really," he said. "She told me about it," and it became an understood family responsibility — "we were all in this together." As it turned out, the "all" included not only his immediate family but also his aunt. Asked why he helped, he replied: "I did it to help people in distress; it is perfectly natural to help people in distress." As it turned out, the family was even more "together" than Armand suspected at the time. As he learned only after the war, his father was also in the Resistance and belonged to the very same group as he, although to a different network. For this family, doing the "right thing" was similarly understood by all, and it did not require much talk or explanation.

Armand married and became a salesman after the war, and he retained the values that marked him and his family during the war. He spent some six hours a month as a volunteer for the Red Cross, and a few hours every week helping his paralyzed mother-in-law. As for what he would tell young people to do should a Nazi-like party come to power today, "I would tell them to avoid Nazism and to prefer democracy — to resist that kind of party and to resist it forcefully. I would tell them to create incidents to overthrow the government."

Protestants

MATHILDE

Solomon Rosen stayed in Berlin after his cousin emigrated. He remained behind because his wife was in the Jewish Hospital there and suffering from cancer. He had promised not to leave until she died. A contact in the Criminal Department always warned him when the Gestapo was coming to arrest him, and he simply moved out and went to another apartment. It dragged on that way for quite a while.[1]

In January 1943, I met with Bertha's cousin. She asked me if my political convictions were the same as they had been and I answered: "Do you think I change them as I would a blouse?" "Can you take someone in?" she asked. "Old or young," I asked. "Old," she said, "about sixty-three; the Gestapo is after him." Of course I had to say yes. I couldn't have done anything different. After all, he was a human being in distress. I had to, even if it cost me my head. I would rather have taken my own life if something had happened to that man because I didn't help.

When he left his apartment to come to me, he didn't have any warning. The Gestapo was already at the front entrance and had broken down the door. He ran down the backstairs and took only a little suitcase with him. What did he have in it? Four pairs of left shoes! It was then thirty degrees below zero. I had to get him everything: a wristwatch, ties, shoes, everything. I dealt in the black market. I sold diamonds. I was well known because I understood something about diamonds. When I ask someone, "How did you survive the war," and the person answers, "Oh, one always had ration cards," I immediately become suspicious. The entire German nation dealt in the black market and if they hadn't done that, they would have starved to death.

He had to stay in the house during air raids. He couldn't go to the big air raid shelter, such as the Pallasbunker, where everybody went because that is where the Kettenhunde were. They were sergeants of some kind. They had big chains on and a big metal emblem on their chests, and they were in charge of checking out the men. As a Jew you couldn't go in there — your number would have been up. They were also checking on soldiers who might have been deserting. The Kettenhunde were always there.

Once a week he met other Taucher for coffee at the Nürnberger Platz: all those who lived without a name were *Taucher* [divers], and I was the *Tauchermutter* [the divers' mother]. Rosen had to give me his word of honor that he would tell no one where he lived. One time I needed a doctor and he had an acquaintance who had been the best doctor on the Kurfurstendam, a very fashionable main thoroughfare of Berlin. He was a Taucher too. He told me there was nothing wrong with me except nerves and I said, "Well, I'll just have to pull myself up by my bootstraps." And afterwards he went to the café at the Nürnberger Platz to meet the other Taucher. Rosen wanted to follow him and for some reason I was very restless and I told him I didn't want to be alone. I was able to hold him back for another three hours and that was his good luck. When he got there, the waitress told him that the Gestapo had come and arrested all the others.

The Gestapo came to my house too. Once, he was sitting in his room, writing away and I was lying on the couch downstairs, waiting for an ambulance to take me to the hospital. It was my husband's day off and he was on the street, waiting for the ambulance to appear. The doorbell rang and my daughter answered the door. "Mother," she said, "there are two SS men here." "Surely, I'm not the first woman they've ever seen in a nightgown," I said, "Ask them to come in." So in came these two boys. "Whom are you looking for," I asked. "There's some cognac over there, good cognac. Help yourselves. My husband brought that back from France." I pushed the carafe in their direction. "We're looking for a Frau Müller because she hasn't been at work." Frau Müller had worked with me but had stopped because she was ill. In any event, they searched every room in the house; the only door they didn't go into was Rosen's.

Neither my husband nor my daughter knew who Rosen really was. I gave him a different name and I told both of them he had been bombed out of his house.

Mathilde, thirty-six years old when her rescue activities began in 1943, was then living with her daughter, age fifteen, in a four-room apartment in Berlin.

Fortunately for her secret activities, her husband was rarely home. A member of the Nazi Party, he had worked as a statistician in the Reich Statistical Office before the war and as soon as the war began he joined the military, where he drove ambulances and escorted medical personnel.

Compared with other Jews, life appeared almost normal for Solomon Rosen. Mathilde provided him with all his basic needs, he had a weekly expedition to the café, and even went to the theater once; he had his own room, in which he spent most of his time writing. But the line dividing life from death was very thin; the Gestapo hunts that almost succeeded were terrifying, but they did not interfere with Mathilde's affection for her "guest." She grew increasingly fond of him, regarding him "almost like a father to the family." Shortly before the war ended, her husband came home and she told him the truth. "He swallowed hard," she said, "looked at me and said: 'Well, Pooleken, we've managed to get through so far with him, we'll get the rest of the way through.' " Rosen stayed with the family until the end of the war and for two years thereafter, after which she helped him find and furnish an apartment of his own. They kept in touch until he died in 1956.

Although she considered herself not at all religious, Mathilde had grown up in a Lutheran home, attended a Lutheran elementary school, and married a man of similar background. One of the characteristics she shared with other Protestants was her sense of personal potency — she viewed herself as a decisive, independent, and adventurous risk taker, responsible, and self-confident. This sense of herself helps explain some of her exceptional behaviors even as a child. When she was ten years old, Mathilde observed a schoolmate whose pants had caught fire as a result of playing with matches. Ignoring the group of children around, she tore off her dress and wrapped him in it. "Everyone laughed at me," she said, "because I was in my slip but I didn't care. I brought the boy home with me and bandaged him." Few youngsters would have known what to do in this situation even if they had felt responsible for doing something, and perhaps fewer still would have risked the derision of their school chums by doing it.

Another school incident that occurred somewhat later revealed not only her powerful sense of responsibility and self-confidence, but also her sense of justice:

> At my elementary school, there was a boy, a skinny little fellow, a Jewish boy. He also wore glasses. The kids let out their anger on him. So I flew into a rage and beat up the boys. I was a feisty little devil and not scared of anything. I went at them, and had there been twenty of them, I would have done the same. I couldn't stand injustice.

The need to remedy injustice recurs often in her story, sometimes unleashing within her an uncontrollable anger. Asked how she felt the first time she saw a Jew wearing the Star, she replied: "That was terrible for me; from my earliest youth on, I couldn't tolerate letting heads roll and the like, or to punish others for religious or political reasons. That was my deepest conviction." Asked her reason for helping, she repeated a similar theme: "I simply couldn't allow a fellow human being to harm another person simply because he had a different religion or political view. That was my highest conviction." She viewed Nazis with horror: "I howled and cried with rage when they took power. My husband kept telling me not to cry because there was nothing I could do." Impotence in the face of cruelty was not a feeling she accepted graciously.

Like many more Protestants as compared with Catholics, including Protestant rescuers as compared with Catholic rescuers, Mathilde became aware of Nazi intentions early. She had read *Mein Kampf* in 1927 or 1928, and "whoever read that," she said, "knew what Adolf Hitler was all about. He was an insane man. One didn't need to have a political opinion to know that." And as a German and a Berliner, she knew about Nazi intentions not only through reading but through direct observation: "I knew it when the S.A. marched through the streets shouting, 'Jews, die!'"

But despite her sense of outrage, determination, and self-confidence, she was no stranger to fear, although she struggled mightily to overcome it. "In my innermost self," she said, "I knew with certainty that I could not allow myself even to think the word 'afraid' because that in itself would attract fear. That was deeply ingrained in me, so I wasn't afraid. Nor did I know the word 'danger.' But try to repress all of that and your body won't cooperate; your nerves refuse to go along with you." The stress wore heavily on her and she became ill quite often during the war, but it never occurred to her to give up. The notion that one should not succumb to fear or even acknowledge it may be part of the overt manifestations of a culture that places a great deal of value on personal potency.

DEREK

Unlike Mathilde, Derek, a Norwegian Lutheran rescuer, was very religious in his youth and continued to be so throughout his life. In that sense he more strongly resembled Protestant rescuers who in significantly higher percentages than Protestant bystanders described themselves as religious (see Table 3aII). Despite their different levels of religious commitment, age, social position, and geography, he nonetheless shared with Mathilde a strong sense of personal potency. A twenty-three-year-old theology student in 1942, Derek began rescue activities as a consequence of a request from one of his professors:

> It started in October 1942, right after a theology lecture. The professor called me to his office and said: "Are you able to take a couple to Sweden? It's a Jewish couple and they are in hiding." I said, "Yes, I know an escape route but I don't know if we can use it right away. I'll have to take them home first."
>
> I knew about one route for people to escape to Sweden; I had learned about it through the Church leadership. As a student, I had contact with the highest secret church authorities. The Bishop of Oslo was arrested, and all the bishops as well as the majority of pastors resigned. They organized an underground church leadership and needed a secret system of messengers and couriers going to Sweden and around Norway. They used young pastors and students for that purpose and since I was involved in this, I knew how to help people get to Sweden. Of course, Jews from Germany and Austria had no citizenship, so they were collected in one city in Sweden called Alingsas; there the Swedish government took care of them.
>
> I met the couple that evening and we took the train to my home. They had left Vienna in the late thirties, and arrived in Norway before the Nazis. After them other Jews contacted us—some from Germany and also some Norwegian Jews. During that fall period, we hid some twenty-five Jews at our home, but not all at the same time. We used the train and bus to escort them, and I always took some of my textbooks with me. We also brought food and information to Jews in hiding.
>
> But one day in December 1942, the Nazi police came to arrest me. Fortunately, I had just left for the university and was not at home. My mother called the university and told a clerk to find me and tell me to pack my suitcase immediately. I disappeared and one week later, we crossed the border to Sweden. The informer responsible for this knew nothing about my activities with Jews; he was a Nazi sympathizer and after pretending to befriend me, denounced me for my anti-Nazi views. My sister was arrested half a year later with the rest of the *Asker* group: seven of them died in prison including my brother-in-law.

Derek made it to Sweden, where undaunted, he continued his underground work; this time his Resistance activities did not include helping Jews. In the spring of 1944, he was recruited to serve in a small Norwegian military group, and after about three months of intensive physical training, agreed to return to Oslo. He became a "jack of all trades": a courier between Norway and Sweden, responsible for organizing military mail on undeveloped film, and the leader of a group of four men who transported weapons to a farm in Norway.

Why did Derek become involved in helping Jews initially? Not because of personal relationships: he had no Jewish friends, not even Jewish acquaintances. "I didn't know any Jews," he explained, "except that once, as a student, I went to a Jewish synagogue in Oslo." He was asked to help by his theology professor, a person he esteemed as a religious teacher and underground participant, and that might have been sufficient. But his reason went beyond mere acquiescence to a request by a respected teacher, and in fact was quite different from that of most other Protestant (as well as Catholic) religious rescuers, including Alexander, the Protestant Dutch rescuer discussed in Chapter 2. As Derek saw it, helping Jews was a way of righting a long historical wrong; a wrong committed by the very same Norwegian Lutheran State Church of which he was a part:

> It was self-evident that I had to help. It was very satisfying because I knew that the Church had treated Jews badly. It was a deep satisfaction because Jesus and his disciples were Jews. It was a special satisfaction to do some good when our Church forefathers had so badly misunderstood our fellow men and women. It was a privilege.

Unlike Mathilde, who depended entirely on her own resources, Derek had a network of people supporting him, most of them connected to the same church as himself. That network included his local church leadership, as well as the Norwegian Lutheran church leadership who had spoken out publicly on behalf of Jews and were also participating in their rescue.[2] But like Mathilde, his strong sense of self-confidence had emerged early in life, and both peers and adults acknowledged his leadership qualities.

> I was usually a leader among my friends, not a follower. I frequently objected to what they were doing and wouldn't go along. I didn't go where there was much alcohol and I never learned to dance—I didn't like to dance, I felt uncomfortable. In many situations, even when I was the youngest, I was asked to lead. I usually had something to say even when others didn't. When we (the Boy Scouts) went to the World Jamboree in London, they would put up the flag every morning and always asked me to lead the ceremony. When I was eight years old I had to lead morning prayers at school. When I was eleven, the Boy Scout leader who was twenty-five would ask me to lead the singing; it was as though it was my responsibility to have everyone do it.

Derek's peers may have valued him as much for his physical skills as for any other attributes he may have possessed. "Skiing, climbing mountains, jumping, swimming, any kind of physical activity—that was my life," he said. He actually enjoyed fighting; not just verbal fights but physical ones: "I liked to use my muscles and in elementary school we would argue about who was strongest, who had the best father, or who was the best automobile driver, and we would fight about that."

With his customary clarity of purpose, Derek decided on his life's career path when he was barely out of childhood. "I was thirteen years old when I decided to be a pastor," he said. His mother approved heartily, but his father had some reservations: he had different career aspirations for his son: "There was a strong military history in my family and he wanted me to be an officer. He had served in the Spanish American war, and my grandfather went to Denmark where he fought against Prussia and was killed." But as matters unfolded, Derek realized both goals to some degree—a courageous adventurer during the war, he became a pastor after it ended. As a pastor his attentions have focused on peace and ecumenical activities, but he has been particularly concerned with the psychologically and physically ill, acting as an advocate and counselor on their behalf. Known for his strong anti-Nazi fervor, he has been threatened by neo-Nazis on several occasions but remains unintimidated.

Protestants and Catholics

How much did Mathilde and Derek share in common with other Protestants and *how did Protestants generally compare with Catholics generally?* I begin by comparing Protestants with Catholics, followed by comparing Protestant rescuers with Protestant bystanders.

Like Mathilde and Derek, Protestants as compared with Catholics were particularly strong on potency measures. All Protestant groups, rescuers and bystanders, as compared with their Catholic counterparts, scored significantly higher on personal potency (see Table 3bV).

Did this imply that Protestants were also more independent and individualistic, as many have suggested, and therefore more likely to make decisions based on values associated with individualism? Not necessarily in the way individualism is often defined.

Beginning with Max Weber's seminal work almost a hundred years ago, Protestant culture, as compared with Catholic culture, has more often been described as individualistic. Despite the fact that Weber's thesis has been heavily critiqued since, this association continues to be strong.[3] Theology is commonly invoked as one explanation for the individualism commonly ascribed to them.

Protestants and Catholics clearly share in common the fact that they are Christians, meaning that both generally accept as core beliefs the idea of the Trinity of God, that God sent his son, Jesus, to earth as proof of his love, and that salvation and eternal life can be attained by faith in Christ. But Roman Catholicism adds to this the requirement that believers must accept the factual truth of the gospel as handed down in the Catholic tradition. This tradition insists on the acceptance of the supremacy of the Pope, who together with the bishops have inherited in varying degrees the spiritual authority of Christ; it also requires acceptance of the Roman Catholic church as the one and only Christian body through which God's grace is conveyed. Protestantism, on the other hand, insists that the Bible is the only source of infallible truth, that the relationship with God is direct and mediated by faith alone, and that all believers constitute a universal priesthood.[4]

Since salvation is viewed as a personal matter between the individual and God and depends on neither Church nor any intermediaries, for that matter, Protestantism implies that only individual conscience, mediated through a direct relationship with God, can ensure proper conduct. Putting the individual at the center in this manner, and permitting him or her considerable discretion in choosing what is right, is consistent with the idea of individualism as well as independence.

The Protestant Reformation, which began as protest against the official Catholic Church, clearly supported a more individualistic view of humanity in relation to moral and spiritual matters. But as frequently understood, Protestant individualism has also extended to economic matters. In fact, Protestant theology itself was strongly connected to an economic view of the world particularly associated with a growing bourgeoisie during the years of the Reformation.

Restrained by a Catholic Church that attempted to control their economic undertakings, the rapidly expanding and ambitious entrepreneurial class found Protestant theology liberating. As individual conscience could guide spiritual matters, they argued, so could it also serve to direct economic matters. Practices commonly frowned upon by the Catholic hierarchy, such as competition and rivalry in the marketplace, became legitimate under the new theology, since individual conscience could guide them as well. The effects were revolutionary, for what this theology also did was encourage "people to break free from bonds of kinship and feudalism," as sociologist Lester Kurtz explains, thus joining individualism with the industrialization of western society.[5]

Although fundamentally liberating, the new ethos had some unintended consequences, one of which was the very reverse of individualism. The idea that each person was responsible for his or her own relationship to God, says Kurtz, and could depend on no one but oneself, also produced a sense of anxiety. Without any guarantees of salvation, assured in Catholicism by works, Protestants sometimes felt a particular "vulnerability to social pressures." This was especially so "within small homogeneous religious communities." In such circles, "personal faith" was of utmost importance, and the way to prove participants had it was by expressing it "in the approved manner that reproduces other believers' equally intense, radical personal encounter with the sacred." In these communities, says Kurtz, "little deviation from the norm was tolerated."[6] In other words, if individuality implies self-differentiation, the reverse occurred in some communities where participants, fearful of damnation, chose a stringent form of conformity.

Several Protestant respondents did in fact belong to such small religious communities, which may help explain why Protestants did not see themselves as any more individualistically inclined than Catholics.[7] Mindful of community standards, their stronger sense of personal potency may have related more to choice of means than to choice of goals. This may well have applied to very religious rescuers in particular; once clear about the community's moral requirement, they often acted largely on their own, creatively inventing how best to achieve their objective.

A sense of potency is also more often associated with masculine attributes than with feminine attributes, and Protestant culture is frequently described as being a "masculine" culture. Some scholars have argued that Christianity generally is devoid of soft-heartedness, while others have insisted that Protestant Christianity is considerably more so than Catholic Christianity. Our data tend to support the latter view.[8]

George Coe and William Sheldon, who studied the relation of temperament to religious experience in the early part of the twentieth century, believed that Christianity generally promoted feminine characteristics.[9] Pointing to the fact that women in disproportionate percentages are attracted to Christianity, they argued that the Christian tradition generally emphasizes typically feminine dispositions such as warmth and feelings rather than traditionally masculine traits, such as intellect, physical adventure, and risk taking. The Christian tradition may well have started off in a humanistic mode, asserted Erik Fromm some sixty years ago, but once it became the religion of the rulers in the Roman Empire, its nature changed. Previously identified with the dispossessed, it became infused with an authoritarian spirit, and a desire to conquer and exploit.[10]

Yet because of their different symbols and rituals, many support the position that Protestantism is more supportive of masculine values while Catholicism inclines toward the feminine. By dethroning the elevated position of the Virgin Mary as the mother of God, said Erikson, Luther eliminated the feminine and ushered in an unmoderated masculine bias in Christianity. The Protestant movement which followed "perpetuated . . . an exclusive emphasis on the divine Father-Son" relationship.[11] The overwhelmingly masculine themes and the elements of identity and roles that Luther provided, he continued, centered on fear, love, and defiance in father-son relationships, and were appropriate chiefly for the Western male. Carl Jung agreed: Protestantism's neglect of the feminine, he said, leaves it with "the odium of being nothing but a man's religion."[12] Jungian analyst Ann Ulanov attributes a number of individual and collective ills to the exclusion of feminine elements from religious symbolism, especially pronounced in the Protestant tradition.[13]

The disposition to share is often associated with softness and femininity. The weaker disposition to share resources for others' welfare among Protestants as compared with Catholics lends some ostensible support to the idea that Protestants more than Catholics have expunged much that is "tenderhearted" from their discursive worldview. They scored significantly lower than Catholics on half of the Sharing measures, a distinction that also characterized Protestant rescuers as compared with Catholic rescuers (see Table 3bIV).

A weaker sense of sharing, as well as the stronger sense of potency, may be associated with parental discipline. While no different from Catholics in relation to family closeness, Protestants were significantly more likely to say that parents had disciplined them (see Table 3bIII).

What might explain the apparently more rigorous and demanding discipline that Protestants received? Historical religious beliefs and economic concerns associated with anxiety again offer a partial explanation.

However onerous Catholic control may have appeared, it did make clear the requirements for salvation and provided a reasonably accessible means for achieving them. While it was quite true that poverty, sexual abstinence, and other forms of self-denial were the marks of the true Catholic, only monks, priests, and nuns were really expected to fulfill such obligations. As for ordinary Catholics, they needed only to adopt some modified form of such virtues and fulfill the sacraments as interpreted by the Church hierarchy to be assured of heaven.

Protestantism, on the other hand, offered no such clear road. The road to salvation lay in personal virtue, and that required knowing God's word as revealed in Scripture. Without the benefit of a mediating and united church to offer a singular interpretation of Scripture, individuals were left largely adrift, guided only by their individual conscience to make righteous choices. Success in worldly endeavors signaled God's grace, but one could never be sure. In this view, God hardly contented himself with this alone; he also required other Christian duties, such as humility, avoidance of conceit and ostentation, and proper sexual feelings and behavior. The laity, as well as religious clerics, were charged with these obligations. As Weber put it, the Reformation put an end to otherworldly asceticism such as that required by monastic ideals, but in fact created an ascetic ethic within the world.[14] In this ambiguous environment, Protestant apprehension regarding their own fate and that of their children mounted, requiring from all strong self-controls.[15]

Religious anxiety about salvation was augmented by worldly concerns. Without the ecclesiastical benefit of the Church's direction, the rules of the social order imposed by Church authority no longer obtained. Unable to depend on external Church authority to maintain order, yet highly dependent on social stability essential for entrepreneurial success, Protestants feared anarchy above all. Order required a population prepared to behave in a predictable fashion, and in the absence of a powerful and legitimated external authority, the family needed to assume this role and assure appropriate behavior by imposing a kind of discipline that guaranteed strong internalization of the required attributes and ethos. In other words, self-discipline needed to replace imposed discipline.

How did children learn this demanding ethic? According to Alice Miller, through harshly punitive discipline and physical as well as emotional abuse.[16] But given the similar sense of family closeness between Protestant rescuers and bystanders, and no reported significant differences between them regarding discipline, this picture may be overdrawn. Although written about a different time and place, Philip Greven's penetrating work, titled *The Protestant Temperament*, offers a more complex and layered view of Protestant discipline; one that suggests a more varied picture.[17]

Greven's work centers on early America, essentially the seventeenth, eighteenth, and early nineteenth centuries. Using historical sources — diaries, letters, biographies — he proposed three characteristic patterns of Protestant child rearing: Evangelical, Moderate, and Genteel. Although each differed substantially from the other in method, all were intended to form what he calls the "Protestant temperament." Duty, self-control over "lurking passions," and restrained intimacy were the temperament's common themes, and the three patterns differed not with respect to these aspirations, but in their means for achieving them.

Believing that avoidance of damnation and salvation required total submission to God, Evangelicals sought to break the will of children. They lived by authoritarian and repressive family rules, and children were subject to daily discipline in all matters — dress, manner, diet, habits. Moderates, on the other hand, sought to "bend" the will of children, molding and shaping them to do their duty through love and reason. Reason was particularly important in controlling all manner of passions, including avarice, ambition, and anger. Children were to respect authority but authority, had its limits and needed to be based on conscience: family relationships were thus authoritative but not authoritarian. While parents were preoccupied with maintaining order in family life, they simultaneously tolerated greater diversities of child behavior. More confident that a benevolent God would grant them salvation, the Genteel, members of the gentry, took religion less seriously. For this group, affectionate family relationships were all-important and punishment was reserved for only the most provocative of circumstances. But family relationships were to be governed simultaneously by decorum and distance; love needed to be accompanied by "reverence": appropriate respect, a sense of awe, and intimate distance. A sense of duty was taken for granted, and for men specifically that included "manliness": learning to assume leadership roles in commerce, trade, and politics.

Greven thus describes a range of disciplinary strategies, from harsh to liberal, from authoritarian to permissive. Our data suggest a similar range. Regardless of type of discipline, Protestant rescuers and bystanders in similar percentages tended to perceive it as merited rather than gratuitous, clearly related to violations of what they regarded as socially accepted behaviors, thus helping to explain why parent relationships tended to be similar in both groups. But even at its most liberal and permissive, and however affectionately expressed, discipline was expected to result in self-control, decorum, and self-discipline: attributes essential for economic success and a stable social order.

Such attributes may help account for the fact that on the whole Protestants appeared to be well-integrated in their societies, in some ways better integrated than their Catholic counterparts. No more religious than their Catholic counterparts, they viewed their neighbors as more friendly and tended to be more involved in political institutions (see Table 3bII).

But their relationships with outgroups were far weaker: Protestants, including Protestant rescuers, scored significantly lower than Catholics on the Outgroup Relationships factor, as well as on several associated measures. While they were more likely than Catholics to affiliate politically, their political affiliations tended more often toward the right. As compared with Catholics, Protestants identified less with Gypsies and more frequently rejected feeling similar to Catholics than Catholics did to Protestants. As for Jews, while many did know them, particularly in the context of their school environments, and some even befriended them, Protestants as compared with Catholics were significantly less likely to have Jewish friends or even acquaintances. But they were no more and no less likely to claim hearing stereotypes about them in their parental homes. They did say they understood Nazi intentions toward them earlier—attributable perhaps in some measure to the fact that many Protestants in our sample lived in Germany—and expressed more empathy for them when seeing them wear the Jewish star (see Table 3aI). As noted in the stories of Hans and Rudolf (see Chapter 4), such sensitivity was not always entirely what it appeared to be, for even Nazi supporters often had objections to the star based on their evaluation of it as poor strategy rather than on empathy for the victims.

Protestant Rescuers and Protestant Bystanders

The section above illustrates differences between Protestants and Catholics generally, but *how did Protestant rescuers differ from Protestant bystanders?* To highlight some attitudinal and value differences, I begin with a very religious Lutheran Dutch bystander, whom I call Knud.

KNUD

Born in Amsterdam in 1922 to very religious Lutheran parents, Knud remembered most vividly his family's poverty. The lack of money is a recurring theme in his life story. It began with his father, a bookkeeper who earned a modest living when he was young but remained unemployed throughout most of the Depression. "He did anything he could to find work," Knud explained; "He was a traveling salesman, a truck driver for a building materials outfit, but money was always a difficult problem. It was pretty tough and we didn't have very good food to eat." The most important values he remembers learning from his parents revolved around money and hard work: "I learned from my parents to be honest and work hard. To save money. Money was always a difficult problem; we never had much of it, but my parents were both honest and hardworking people."

The lack of money meant possessions had to be treated very carefully, and punishment was often associated with damaging them. "My father did not lay a hand on me — he scolded me instead, and for small things. If I broke things in the house, for example. Once he bought me a pair of new shoes, and I played soccer with them in the street and kicked off the soles and he disciplined me for that." Not having money also eliminated life choices; Knud yearned for adventure, for example, but his mother wouldn't allow it, he said, because he needed to help the family. "It was simply a matter of eating. I got my first job when I was fourteen and when I brought home one guilder and fifty cents from my first job I was terribly proud. We needed to eat and have clothes and that was all we thought about. Everybody worked."

Not having money also taught him the importance of obedience. "I was never an independent type of person; you just did what your parents told you." Keeping a job meant obeying your boss. "When you were told to do something, you had to do it right. If you are not responsible and don't do it right, you get fired. During the tail end of the Depression, you did what you were told. If you had a job, it was worth gold. If you didn't have a job it meant that you were not good enough to keep one while others were. So you didn't take any chances."

He had always avoided risk, Knud said: "You never did anything risky because it was dumb. What you did was work hard and save." He had learned the futility of risk taking from his father's experience. His father's one attempt to protest the German occupation had resulted in his being unemployed for the duration of the war. The leadership of the Christian Democratic Union, which Knud described as a "Protestant labor union of German origin," of which his father was treasurer, instructed its members to strike shortly after the Nazi invasion. The net result was that the Nazis brought in strikebreakers who beat and arrested the leaders, and his father could not get a job for many years afterward.

Knud's one attempt at protest during the war also proved futile, almost putting him in a concentration camp:

> I was out of work for a while so I was forced to go to Germany to work. We did anything we could to sabotage the work. I worked in a shipyard, in repair, and we tried to slow things down; I sometimes would take one whole hour to measure a single piece of wood. We were six or seven Dutch young kids in Germany, all about nineteen years old, talking Dutch. We thought nobody understood us but that was not true. One guy had worked in Amsterdam before the war and he reported us so we had to go to the supervisor of the shipyard. He scared the hell out of us. He had written down a long list of our sins — we hadn't built the boat on time, we had sabotaged, it was endless. And we had to sign it. He said, "One more little thing and you guys go to concentration camps." We were pretty good after that for about a week or two and then the supervisor sent for us again. He said, "next week you all go to Holland." It turned out that the chief of the shipyard in Amsterdam was trying to get some boys back and I was lucky to be among them.

The war reinforced Knud's sense that defying authorities was fruitless, and his early experiences with poverty help explain why he felt "very like" poor people and "not at all like" the rich. But it was not all poor people with whom he identified; he felt very similar to poor Protestants only. His attitudes toward others was based on class but far more frequently on ethnic identification; despite his attempts at times to reevaluate his beliefs in light of some new evidence, he rejected any sense of similarity with groups other than Protestants.

His hostility toward the rich began early:

When I was growing up, working people didn't get to share the profits. There were communists and socialists, and I was exposed to communist propaganda about capitalists daily. Fighting for your country was fighting for the capitalists because they ran the country and they were your enemies. So your boss was your enemy — any boss you worked for was automatically your enemy because you knew you were being used and when they didn't need you any more you got a kick in the butt.

His feelings about Catholics also started early:

I hate to bring this up you know, but when I was around ten or so we lived in a Catholic neighborhood, and I was a Lutheran boy and it took a long, long time before those Catholic kids would play with a Lutheran boy. Their parents had told them, "Don't play with that Lutheran kid." The Catholic people, they were different. They bought in Catholic stores, had a Catholic labor union, had Catholic newspapers, and their kids would play with Catholic kids. There was animosity between Catholics and non-Catholics. My grandmother detested Catholics.

He also harbored resentments toward Calvinists:

At elementary school, a Calvinist school, the Calvinists thought themselves superior to Lutherans and so the Calvinist schoolteacher put Luther down. I raised my hand and said, "Sir, I'm Lutheran" and down went my grades. Maybe it was my fault too, but they went down further and further.

Knud knew little about Gypsies: "We didn't see many of them — they were not allowed in town I suppose," he said — but he knew he had "nothing in common with them of course." He knew no Turks before the war but expressed contempt for them nonetheless: "Do you know what they do now, those Turkish people? You give them unemployment money for five years and then they go back to Turkey."

As for Jews, while he denied having any ill feelings toward them, he went on to expose several:

Anytime you deal with a Jew — I hate the word "Jew," it sounds so rotten you know — buying or selling, you knew beforehand you would be cheated because they were smarter than you. Sunday morning was a workday for Jews; there was a big market in Amsterdam and you could buy anything there. It was almost completely Jewish people who sold and bought; they had all the stalls, and if you would buy a shirt, he would say, "Oh, it looks fine," but the shirt wouldn't fit too well.

Asked if he had personally experienced being cheated in this manner, Knud confessed he had not. "But everybody knew this about them, and there was no animosity." Everyone also knew that "Jews wouldn't fight," although he acknowledged that they had proved to be wonderful fighters in Israel. Fighting was important for Knud, perhaps because his father had supported the pacifist position of the Christian Democratic Union and lived to regret this position. But he admitted that he himself had intended not to fight should war begin. "I was proud to be Dutch," he said, "but I had read a lot about wars, and I had promised myself that if I was drafted and had to fight, I would dig a hole and sit in it until the war was over."

Yet despite such sharp divisions between "them" and "us," and the associated negative generalizing, the only group of people Knud expressed actual hatred for was Germans. He had learned to be afraid of poverty and the powerful, and in the context of his life Jews, like he himself, had not deserved their terrible fate but they were not entirely meritorious either. What was very much present in Knud's narrative was his strong sense of vulnerability and estrangement from all outsiders with no sense of obligation to any.

Knud had many fears, but Protestant bystanders generally felt as personally potent as rescuers; no significant distinction exists between Protestant rescuers and bystanders on this measure (Table 3bV). Rescuers sought control of their environment by emphasizing different values while deemphasizing others.

One of their differences centered on a value Knud expressed repeatedly: the importance of economic competence. Protestant rescuers, as compared with Protestant bystanders, grew up in families who placed significantly lower value on work-related virtues. Focus on "hard work," "doing the best on the job," and "industry" occurs far more frequently among bystanders as a learned value; it was an admonition they heard from their parents significantly more often than did rescuers. In fact, they heard it more often than any other group, including Protestant and Catholic rescuers as well as Catholic bystanders (see Table 3bV).

Many if not most people endorse values associated with hard work; many if not most might suggest that bystanders may claim moral superiority in this respect. Max Weber believed hard work was a virtue in its initial development within Protestant culture, but he also argued that it changed later to become something not quite so worthy.

As Weber described it, Protestants in their initial years placed great importance on economic competence, emphasizing hard work and occupational skills. During these early years, such values were instrumental goals rather than terminal ones, serving what he called the Protestant spirit or Protestant ethic. Its ultimate value was not the accumulation of riches but rather the development of a state of mind that applauds the fulfillment of a duty to a calling. "It is an obligation which the individual is supposed to feel and does feel towards the content of his professional activity, no matter in what it consists" said Weber. It was also what he called "the embodiment of the capitalist spirit."[18]

Representatives of the capitalist spirit believe that providing people with material goods is one of the most important purposes of life, serving both God and humanity. But, cautioned Weber, this should not be confused with avarice and greed, or moneymaking as an end in itself—that, said Weber, has existed throughout time and in all cultures. Nor does it imply unscrupulous speculating or daredevil risk taking. On the contrary, says Weber, the individuals who carry out the capitalistic spirit most successfully have "grown up in the hard school of life," are "calculating and daring at the same time, temperate and reliable, shrewd and completely devoted to their business." Since the Protestant spirit proscribes ostentatious consumption, the capitalist imbued with the Protestant spirit gets from his vocation the "irrational sense of having done his job well."[19] The end result of such focused activity is monetary gain. Without indulgence in the excesses that money can buy, capitalists imbued with the Protestant spirit accumulate more capital, and material success is accompanied by the satisfaction of having done their duty to God and community.

But while asceticism and devotion to duty were characteristic of early Protestant devotion to vocation, Weber believed it had degenerated into simple greed and moneymaking in the modern age. Ascetic religiosity no longer exists, Weber wrote some years later, and in the absence of devotion to vocational duty the avaricious impulse has triumphed among all groups in all capitalistic societies.[20]

But avarice alone does not necessarily underlie the current work ethic or the ethic of Protestants during World War II; it can emerge from a variety of values and concerns. A strong work ethic can, for example, be interpreted as a human impulse to achieve something for its own sake; the need to master something difficult and overcome a challenge, as H. Murray proposed.[21] It can also derive from what Kelvin and Jarrett call a "wealth ethic," the goal of which is not greed but rather leisure and independence, that is, liberation from economic constraints or the need to ask others for help.[22] And of course as most people recognize, and as Knud certainly did, hard work may be the only way to keep body and soul together.

Protestant rescuers were not only less concerned with economics, but were also far less focused on those characteristics associated with external success. Success requires a general sense of external propriety; being polite, avoiding obscenities, and knowing how to say the right thing even when feeling angry was something far more bystanders as compared with any group remembered learning. Success is also often predicated on being appropriately compliant, and consistent with this orientation, significantly higher percentages of by-standers, as compared with rescuers, cited "obedience" as a primary value they learned from their parents (see Table 3bV). As Knud had learned in a most forceful manner, doing what the bosses wanted — whether capitalists or German occupiers — appeared to be the only way to ensure survival.

Early Protestant entrepreneurs may well have scoffed at obedience as the means for success; in their economic world, independence and prudent risk taking probably counted far more. But those who seek success in modern bureaucratic structures — whether economic, political, or religious — need to learn to conform to the expectations of their superiors. In rational bureau-cratic organizations, goals and status are arranged hierarchically so that those with less authority are expected to obey those with more in pursuit of those goals. Unlike early Calvinists, who viewed industry as a means of serving an approving God, their western European Protestant counterparts in the twen-tieth century were probably more inclined to see it as a means of self-service via obedience to god-like mortals. It was a lesson that apparently impressed bystanders more than rescuers.

Learning to serve their superiors well may also have accounted for the high self-esteem with which Protestant bystanders regarded themselves. Conven-tional expectations might suggest that Protestant rescuers would score higher on self-esteem; helping Jews, it can be argued, required an exceptionally good opinion of one's abilities. But the reverse occurred: Protestant rescuers had a much lower sense of self-esteem than did bystanders; in fact, Protestant by-standers scored significantly higher on self-esteem as compared with all other groups. Success may have been one source of this positive self-image, where "success" may have meant money, prestige, and power, or just approval by authorities who could bestow psychological as well as material rewards. Prot-estant rescuers appeared to evaluate themselves by different standards. More than any other group, not only rescuers but also Catholic bystanders, Protes-tant bystanders had standards that appeared to be externally oriented (see Table 3bV).

Protestant rescuers had learned to value external matters less, while also learning some competing values regarding obligations to their fellow human beings. Protestants generally as compared with Catholics generally evidenced significantly fewer of those Sharing dispositions associated with altruism, and Protestant rescuers and bystanders were quite similar in this respect. But one exception stands out: rescuers' parents more often had taught them the value of caring for others. On the value of care, Protestant bystanders scored not only lower than rescuers but also lowest of all groups (see Table 3bIV).

Is the weaker emphasis on care in any way associated with the strong emphasis on economic competence among bystanders? Evidence collected more recently on what is called the Protestant Work Ethic (PWE) suggests it may well be.

Social scientists typically describe the PWE as including the endorsement of values such as industriousness, thrift, ambition, wealth, productivity, achievement, and advancement. It has been measured in several ways over the past thirty years: through self-reports, scales, as well as assorted observed behaviors.[23] Researchers using these measures have found that positive support of PWE values tends to be associated with self-satisfaction and with condemnation of idleness, waste, failure, and poverty.[24] Strong supporters of the PWE are more likely than weak supporters to distinguish between the worthy and unworthy poor, commonly believe that the needy are unworthy of help, and are less likely to endorse social welfare measures. Why would this be so?

It may well be that those who possess material resources know that they are morally obliged to help those who need it but, resentful of having to share what they have, prefer instead to designate the helpless as creating their own victimhood and deserving their fate. Individuals who believe that the helpless deserve their fate, says psychologist Melvin Lerner, tend to subscribe to the "just world" hypothesis. The idea that justice rules in the world and that individuals get what they deserve, they say, comforts believers who have accumulated money and material comforts. If the world was capricious and goods randomly distributed, then belief in their own merit would evaporate; the "just world" hypothesis assures them that they are entitled to what they have and that the world is stable and orderly.[25] Bystanders were far more likely to view Jews as deserving their fate, often for very similar reasons. Rather than accepting any obligation to help, many preferred to regard Jews as economic exploiters, meriting their punishment. If they in turn profited from Jewish punishment — by inheriting jobs and possessions — they justly deserved them.

Can some of the above differences between Protestant rescuers and bystanders be attributed to differences in personal relationships while growing up, particularly relationships to parents? None surfaced. To similar degrees both groups claimed to have been close to their families and parents, and were disciplined similarly (see Table 3 bIII).

If family relationships did not appear to distinguish Protestant rescuers from bystanders, relationships with secondary institutions did. Protestant rescuers were significantly more religious — in fact, more so than all other groups — and while they were similarly likely to belong to political parties, their political allegiances, beginning with those of their families, were quite different (see Tables 3aI and 3aII).

The fact that Protestant rescuers were significantly more religious than Protestant bystanders suggests that the religious groups to which they belonged may have modified economic concerns by emphasizing more humanitarian values. Religious rescuers often understood in some way that being Christian implied helping Jews, a sentiment that became more obvious while giving their reasons for rescue. Calvinist rescuers frequently cited Biblical sources while Lutherans, Calvinists, and other Protestants would speak of Christian duty or responsibility. In many cases among religious rescuers, including Alexander (see Chapter 2, "The Very Religious") and Derek (discussed earlier in this chapter), local religious leaders and more rarely national religious leaders had reinforced such interpretations, and sometimes were rescuers themselves.

In addition to religious institutions, family politics reflected different agendas. Parents of Protestant rescuers, as compared with bystanders, were significantly more likely to belong to centrist or leftist political parties supporting democracy and tolerance with respect to minorities and Jews. Rescuers themselves followed similar political patterns. They were also significantly more likely to belong to resistance groups themselves and to have a kinship network resistant to Nazis, albeit not necessarily concerned with Jews. Conversely, Protestant bystanders and their parents in significantly larger percentages belonged to political parties supporting autocracy and advocating exclusionary policies with respect to minorities and Jews. They were also far less likely to belong to resistance groups themselves or even to have family members who were involved in resistance activities (see Tables 3aI and 3aII).

As a consequence of religious sentiment and/or political bent, Protestant rescuers and bystanders differed strongly in their relationships with and perceptions of Jews, as well as of outgroups generally. Protestant rescuers were far more egalitarian: they were more likely to have Jewish friends and acquaintances and to be aware of Nazi intentions toward them earlier. Their feelings toward outsiders were more inclusive; they identified more with them, and felt more similar to Jews and Gypsies. And they were significantly more likely to reject any identification with Nazis (see Table 3aI).

Protestant bystanders, by contrast, were comparatively more ignorant of events affecting Jews, and ascribed the greatest merit to their particular ingroup while distancing themselves from or denigrating outsiders. They were significantly less likely to report having Jewish friends, and they alleged learning about Nazi intentions later. In significantly larger percentages, too, they acknowledged hearing negative stereotypes about Jews from their parents, and rejected outsiders. And this group, far more than any other, identified with Nazis (see Table 3aI).

The above findings suggest that a particularly strong work ethic, unless modified by other values, risks becoming linked to bigotry. Some current research supports just such a correlation in contemporary American society. In a study he published fifteen years ago, Adrian Furnham found that those who endorse the PWE tend to think stereotypically, and to reject values such as broadmindedness, equality, love, and harmony.[26] Findings of this nature come with an implied caution — excessive concern with industriousness, whether serving greed or the desire to achieve, can have disastrous results.

EMMA

Knud attributes many of his attitudes to economics. Bystanders who were more affluent and educated often chose to tell a different story. Eager to maintain their status under the Nazi regime, they were simultaneously less ready to acknowledge any loss of potency, preferring instead to define their passivity as neutrality rather than surrender; as free choice rather than capitulation. Emma, born in Hamburg in 1924, was among this group. Two years younger than Knud, and only a child when Hitler assumed power, she was also a bystander, along with her family.

> When the war started I was fifteen. At age fourteen, I joined the Hitler Youth and we were volunteered constantly for things. We collected for what was called "Winter Help"; we collected things for the needy. After about a year, I was drafted into the Labor Service. That was not the military exactly, but it was organized like the military. It was intended to relieve farmers who were shorthanded. We lived in a camp and wore uniforms. We worked on one farm for five or six weeks and then moved on to another farm. I milked cows and helped with the harvest, thrashing corn.
>
> When they asked for volunteers who wanted to work outside of Germany, I said "yes." I was sent to Poland, but obviously not to Polish farms. It turned out to be very political. I didn't realize that we were supposed to be model camps, showing the enemy how fantastic we were. They worked us twenty-four hours a day. We had political lectures every night, but they were never anti-Jewish, just anti-Polish. We were not allowed to associate with the Poles — that was made quite clear. They were "inferior" — that was also made quite clear.
>
> We were very isolated from the rest of the town. I thought I was back in the Stone Age; no water, no electricity, and they thrashed corn with two stones and a pony. The only time we had a connection with the town itself was when somebody had a baby. Then all of us had to march over there and sing some dumb songs.
>
> I was also a background for Rudolf Hoess in Poland. He came to Poland to make a speech and they selected guards from the Labor Service camp who were very Nordic looking to be the background for the weekly newsreel. I was

chosen. We were sent to Posen for three days, and there we had to sit under the hottest lights you can imagine for four hours. But I was glad to be there—away from chopping wood for three days. But there I really discovered just how much antagonism there was between Poles and Germans. The streetcars were segregated and people looked glum. This was a town where there was undoubtedly hunger and separation.

After Labor Service came War Service in an ammunition factory near Berlin where we worked on different projects. I was then eighteen years old. After that I went back to Hamburg and got a job. We were not allowed to go into nonpriority work, and I had my choice of three jobs. I chose a firm that made bouillon soup and I worked in the office.

With the exception of some occasional unpleasantness, Emma's description of her wartime years could well be that of any middle-class self-centered adolescent, resentful of external constraints and disdainful of the adults who imposed all kinds of obligations upon her. Yet she makes no moral judgments about them. She is amused at being chosen as an ideal Nordic blond, but says nothing in any way critical of Rudolf Hoess, a leading Nazi who later became the commandant of Auschwitz. Rather than criticizing her government for ruthless conquest and brutal treatment of Poles, she describes the relationship between Germans and Poles as "antagonistic," a term implying hostility between equally culpable parties. She studiously refrains from identifying the guilty actors who contributed to the "town where there was undoubtedly hunger and separation," preferring instead to describe it in the passive voice: an occurrence that just happened without initiation by any actors. And while she doesn't like the political lectures she receives about Poles, it is not because of any expressed sympathy for them or disapproval of the message bearers but rather because she simply didn't, and doesn't, "like politics."

Emma and her family studiously avoided politics: in fact they scorned it. "My father believed that anyone who dabbled in politics was automatically a crook." Neither parent belonged to any political party and claimed having no view on any political matter. What did "politics" mean to them? "Political" appeared to include any activity that might serve to identify them as anything but neutral on almost any matter of moral consequence. Thus, her parents "didn't mind it when she dated a young Jewish man," Emma said, and they did not object to her sister's Jewish friend in elementary school. But Emma was quick to warn the interviewer not to get the wrong idea. "I don't want you to think I was an anti-Nazi because I went out with a Jewish boy. In fact, I was very democratic. I went out with an SS man at the same time. Don't make me anti-Nazi. I don't want it to appear I was anything." Asked if she had admired any leaders during the war, she replied that she "didn't know any political leaders." Asked what she would tell today's young people if a party with goals similar to those of the Nazis came to power today, she said, "I would say emigrate to another country if you don't like the government." Political neutrality about their government apparently kept Emma and her family from the need to emigrate and apparently also protected Emma herself from the knowledge that emigration was often impossible. Political neutrality in their view apparently also protected them from being contaminated by "crooks."

Political neutrality and class insulation also kept Emma amply protected from needy people. "We didn't know anybody in trouble," said Emma. "Anybody" in this case might well have been "the rich" and "Protestants" only," the only two groups with whom Emma reported sharing a strong sense of similarity. It apparently did not include the Jews involved in two unpleasant incidents. When a neighbor who had observed the destruction of a Jewish clothing store during Kristallnacht told Emma's mother about it, the mother confessed to her family she didn't quite believe it. When both Emma and her mother saw an old man wearing the yellow star, her mother expressed outrage but didn't explain the reason for her anger to her adolescent daughter, who simply remained "very curious." Emma, like many other Protestants, apparently did not incline toward the soft sentiments associated with Sharing: her descriptions of the unfortunate people she met reflected little in the way of empathy and nothing in the way of the desire to relieve their distress.

Yet despite this very passive stand, Emma shared with many Protestants a sense of personal efficacy. She described herself as a high-risk taker, very adventurous, and very independent. But such inclinations were largely acted out within the safe boundaries of her family. Emma's father, a retired Navy captain, was an "arch Prussia," said Emma, and accustomed to being obeyed — they were at odds all the time. He tried hard to discipline his three girls, said Emma, but he was "amazed" to discover that unlike the men under his command who said "Yes, Sir" to every order he issued, his daughters rebelled at every turn. Emma claimed that many of the things she did would qualify her today as a "juvenile delinquent." She did not get along with her sisters at all, and she refused to be the "lady" that her mother very much wanted her to be. She also learned how to do exactly as she pleased even when apparently complying: "My mother was very fixed in her opinions. I finally avoided arguing with her by saying, 'Yes' to everything and then going my own way. With one of my sisters, it was just screaming back and forth." She also ran away from home on several occasions.

Yet Emma admired her father greatly and, despite herself, had actually internalized his values. He had taught her, she said, the Prussian code of honor: "total respect for other people's property and privacy. He would have considered stealing property or denouncing somebody as akin to murder." This code had influenced her a great deal, because she too finds it "awful when I hear of a child stealing something." Her mother taught her to have fun and laugh, and to appreciate the fact that "there is always a good side to life." From both her mother and father, she learned to be optimistic. And although the family argued with one another a great deal, they apparently enjoyed it as a competitive game, each one attempting to outwit the others: "Our family was like a courtroom; we would take another side just for the sake of argument. We were all amateur lawyers, and we all loved that sort of thing."

Singularly missing from any of the values her parents demonstrated or talked about was the importance of helping others or social responsibility of any kind. The family's apolitical stand reflected this, as did Emma's own activities even after the war. She reported never having done anything unusual to help others since the war, nor has she ever been involved in community helping activities. In her view, noninvolvement appears to be the most that might be expected of another. This leads her to "totally disagree" with "the collective guilt" imposed on Germans. "Most people," she said, "did not know any Jews or knew only very few Jews. Concentration camps were known — they were considered hard labor camps. I really don't know of anyone who knew what really went on in there unless they kept it a secret from me — but I doubt it."

Yet it was clear that the family knew something. Emma confessed that her mother felt some sympathy for Jews during the war, but "became antisemitic afterwards," even refusing to admit Jews into the house. Sympathy had to be predicated on some knowledge, but perhaps more important than any latent antisemitic sentiments the family may have harbored was their desire to appear independent of convention — as Emma herself expressed it, "to do something when it was no longer fashionable." Of course it did not take too much daring to feel some sympathy for Jews even during the Nazi regime, as long as it was not expressed in any way. Nor did it take much courage to express one's antisemitic feelings after the Nazi collapse. In this sense perhaps, Emma and her family were able to protect the self-image so valued among Protestants as people in control of their destiny. Ironically Protestant rescuers, who had in fact challenged their tyrannical masters overtly, thought significantly less well of themselves; apparently their self-expectations were different.

6

Catholics

ERNST

"Edelweiss Pirates" was a resistance group whose members were denounced as criminals and hanged if caught. The situation during the war didn't really make their activities crimes but members were executed anyway, without a chance to defend themselves.

A former member of a bombing squad who escaped from a concentration camp founded the group. Together with other deserters, forced laborers, and anybody who was persecuted by Nazis, our purpose was to sabotage the regime and help persecuted people. Our actions were pretty radical, and included shooting several Nazis, bombings, and looting in order to get supplies, including food for ourselves and others. Among the people we helped were five Jews: one mother with a daughter, two young brothers, and a young farmer.

I was not the initiator of any of the group's activities. I just helped supply them with food and weapons and lived with them. Rescue of Jews was not the main intent since any potential candidate for death was helped. The neighborhood knew about us but tolerated us.

It was easy to build a shelter of sorts in bombed-out cellars, and we probably would never have been noticed had we not been so active. The place eventually got raided and only one Jew and I survived. The others were hanged or disappeared. I got arrested but not hanged like the others: I never understood why. I was beaten with sticks, rubber clubs, and chains by anyone who thought they were "authorized" to do so. I also saw people in prison who had been tortured, beaten and covered with blood. But I didn't see that on the streets; they didn't allow themselves to do that at that time. I was rescued by the Americans after I had been in four different prisons.

There is little in the above to betray the fact that Ernst, the narrator, was no more than fourteen years old at the time of these events. Although he was German like Emma, the bystander we met in Chapter 5, and six years younger than she, the cultural milieu from which he emerged provided him with a radically different view of what was occurring. Unlike Emma, who retained so much of adolescence, Ernst was plunged into adulthood prematurely by the war.

Begun in April of 1944 in Koeln, a city of approximately 650,000 people, the Edelweiss Pirates' activities lasted only until September. The group, some fifteen to twenty adolescents ranging in age between ten and eighteen, were then living in a bombed out cellar and were largely ignored by their neighbors. Initially led by the older members, seventeen- and eighteen-year-olds, Ernst and two other boys, ages thirteen and fourteen, took over the leadership when the older boys were inducted into the Army. In the terror of Nazi Germany, their activities were extraordinary and rare but they were not unique. Some 2,000 boys and girls throughout Germany belonged to similar groups; all of them young people who engaged in some form of resistance. They were considered threatening enough so that in 1944 a concentration camp in Neuwied was designated primarily for boys under twenty years of age.[1] It may well be that Ernst spent some time there after his arrest.

All the Pirates members had known each other before the war. All of them were Catholics, living in "workers living quarters" (quarters reserved before Hitler for some members of the Communist Party), and all of them shared a similar political stance. "We were very opposed to the Nazi state and its crimes, and we just acted together as things came up," Ernst said. He could not remember when the first Jew joined them; as he explained, "Everything happened at the same time, and there really wasn't a 'first time.' They just took in whoever asked and they never turned anyone down; that was a self-understood policy shared by all the group." Their objective was to help all potential victims of the regime, and they paid heavily for their effort; as far as Ernst knew, only he and one other person, a Jewish male, survived.

By 1935, Ernst, then five years old, was essentially an orphan. Charged with being a Communist, his father was arrested that year and the family disbanded — his brothers and sisters went to live with relatives or friends, and he went to live with his Catholic grandparents. Yet he felt very much a part of a "good family community," for all of them lived in the same neighborhood. "Although we were very poor," he said, "we were a very close family." More than any other, his grandmother had a lasting influence on him, although he could not say exactly what he had learned from her. Like her, he described himself as "somewhat religious" during the war, becoming less so afterward. His grandmother overprotected him, he said, and as a consequence he became somewhat of a "fearful person." Nonetheless, he scored moderately high on personal potency, not entirely surprising since his activities required the ability to make independent decisions and the willingness to take risks.

Ernst began developing a particular sensitivity toward Jews at a very early age, not because of his equally young Jewish playmates, but largely due to his father's influence. "My father," he said, "warned me about teachers and posters that ridiculed and agitated against Jews." Although very young when his father was taken from him, he had a lasting sense of Jews as particular victims. While claiming only "a faint idea of what was going on — exact information about what happened in concentration camps did not generally leak out" — he was aware that Jewish neighbors "were taken away" sometime in 1938 or 1939, and he also knew about Kristallnacht. "I felt terrible," he said when first seeing a Jew wearing the yellow star; "I couldn't figure out what for; it was totally incomprehensible to me." His father may also have been responsible for his mature understanding of other ostensibly incomprehensible behavior. Rather than responding warmly to greetings, Jewish friends became aloof. "If you stood next to Jews and talked to them," he explained, "they felt uncomfortable because they didn't want to bring you or others into danger." He was able to feel sympathy for them despite the fact that he generally perceived Jews as belonging to "higher social levels." "They always make it," he said, "and get somewhere in many fields; they are ambitious." Acknowledging that their success "often led to envy among average Germans," he evidenced none himself despite the fact that he remained a kitchen worker throughout his life.

Ernst described himself as a "very helpful" person, and his concern for the afflicted and the needy, so evident during the war, persisted long thereafter. He directed a Citizen Center after the war, where he initiated activities to benefit orphans, including counseling them about jobs and personal problems, raising money on their behalf as well as contributing his own.

I began this chapter with Ernst's story for two reasons. One I've already alluded to: he presents a dramatic contrast with Emma, who, although sharing his nationality, represents a very different social world and culture. If his recollections are even somewhat accurate, Ernst had already begun to form his views by age five. While Emma and her mother had experienced some identical events as Ernst and his family — they had seen at least one Jew wearing the star, had heard about Kristallnacht, knew at least one Jewish neighbor who had simply disappeared—their interpretations and reactions were distinctly dissimilar. And reason two: he reflects several attributes that are significantly more characteristic of Catholics than of Protestants generally, and of Catholic rescuers as compared with Catholic bystanders.

Madeleine, a French rescuer, shares several of these same characteristics.

MADELEINE

Many Jews came to the Haute Savoie (a region in the Alps) from large cities or the capital, hoping to get to Switzerland. Because I had access to official cards and stamps at the courthouse where I worked, I was able to help many refugees, Alsaciens-Lorrains, Jews, and others. At the beginning people didn't know whether they could trust me. One day a woman came to see me. She said that she and her husband and three daughters had fled Montpellier, and asked if I could change her identification card. I talked about it to one of my directors whom I trusted. We changed her name and since she had no money, I helped her family get some clothing and also found a place for them to stay. The news spread quickly and many Jews came to me after that. During the next two or three years, hundreds came asking for help. Some wanted to get to Switzerland and sometimes they failed. Some were refused entry at the border or were even arrested and deported.

My boss approved my helping refugees since she was one herself from Alsace-Lorraine. But she was a bit anti-Jewish, so people preferred to talk to me. I would meet them outside the courthouse. I had troubles once. One of the courthouse directors had heard about the large quantity of identification cards I was issuing and threatened me, but then he left for another job. There were three successive directors at the courthouse and some of them were anti-Jewish but they never were able to discover our activities. They were too busy, especially the third one, fighting against the Resistance.

Two colleagues of mine were very helpful and lent me stamps that had to be locked up every night. With their help, I was able to find housing, jobs, and food rations for many people. I also succeeded once in getting out of jail an old Jewish lady and two Alsatians sentenced to death. My parents and I also took whole families in our home while they were looking for other places to live, but I tried my best to keep my family out of my activities. On the whole people were helpful or at least tolerant of us, but I was very careful with people working for the French militia—they worked for the Gestapo.

I helped the Resistance as much as I helped Jews. I worked as a messenger for them. I always tried to explain to the Resistance people, then and now, how hard the war was for the Jews. Many of them didn't, and still don't, know what happened to the Jewish people during the war. When I saw how

Jews were being persecuted, I had to rebel. I am only a poor French woman, but I did whatever I could to resist the Germans. I found it horrifying that more French people didn't react like me.

Madeleine, a nominal Catholic before the war, was twenty-one years old when she began her activities in 1942; she kept at them until liberation in August of 1944. By that time, she calculated that she had helped hundreds of people, all of them strangers and many, if not most of them, Jews.

The oldest of three children, Madeleine grew up in Challes-les-Eaux/Le Bourget du Lac, a small French town of some six hundred people. The family was a very close one, and affluent. Her New York–born father and her French mother owned a successful café in town, and she was the darling of a beloved aunt.

Even more than Ernst's account, Madeleine's is filled with language and emotions associated with altruism. Strong empathy for others began early in her life: "When I was eleven," she said, "I was very moved by a poem called '*La mort du colporteur*' and I think this had a lasting influence on me." Written in the nineteenth century by the well-known poet Alphonse de Lamartine, it describes the reluctance of a rural Catholic community to bury a poor Jewish peddler who died among them while on his travels. Madeleine's need to relieve others' distress was compelling, and she consistently evaluated herself as well as others in terms of their helpfulness and "openness."

A modest person, regarding herself as only somewhat self-confident, responsible, or assertive, she described herself as "very honest" and "very helpful." She had learned these values from many family members. From her aunt, who influenced her most, she learned "generosity, to be open, to help people." She was also strongly influenced by her mother's family, she said, "who are very generous and warm people." And at least one memorable religious leader espoused similar ideas: "He loved everybody," she said, "and taught the importance of helping others. He was open to everyone, no matter what their religion." She objected to friends whose religious beliefs made them "sometimes narrow-minded." Even her father, a member of and reasonably active in the right wing nationalist Croix de Feu, embraced tolerance as a most desirable value.[2] Ever ready to comfort those in pain wherever she could, she had managed to acquire a pass to visit prisoners, and it was there she saw just how badly some had been tortured—her grief was profound when Resistance friends were arrested or killed. Asked why she had helped, she replied, "Christian duty of helping others, compassion." After the war, she served as a volunteer for St. Vincent de Paul, an aid organization, and both she and her husband have been active in causes to combat racism and antisemitism.

Catholics and Protestants

How did Catholics compare with Protestants? Like Catholics generally as compared to Protestants generally, and even Catholic rescuers as compared with Protestant rescuers, Ernst and Madeleine did not regard themselves as particularly potent people (see Table 3bV). But like Catholics as compared with Protestants, Ernst and Madeleine did share many of the predispositions associated with Sharing.

Catholics generally as compared with Protestants generally, including Catholic rescuers as compared with Protestant rescuers, were significantly more marked by a Sharing predisposition. They scored significantly higher than Protestants on the Sharing factor, as well as many of its associated measures. More than Protestants, they expressed strong empathic feelings for those in distress and endorsed values relating to persistence at tasks once undertaken, as well as justice — that is, standards associated with equity or fairness. They were also far more likely to identify with the poor and to regard themselves as persons of personal integrity — very honest, helpful, and responsible. A pro-social action orientation, a strong sense of justice and personal integrity, as well as identification with the poor are all associated with altruistic behaviors, and they were more dominantly pronounced among Catholics (see Table 3bIV).

What can explain the more characteristic emphasis on Sharing among Catholics? Some believe it derives in part from what is alleged to be the more feminine aspects of Catholicism, one of which is the Catholic service itself. Catholic rituals, particularly before Vatican II, focused on alleged feminine characteristics such as imagery, emotionality, expressiveness and sentiment, observes historian Jay Dolan. Expressing a somewhat similar idea and expanding on concepts introduced by David Tracy, sociologist Andrew Greeley says Catholic rituals focus on the "analogic imagination," that is story, metaphor, art, and other forms of "poetry" to express religious ideas. By way of contrast, Protestant rituals have largely eliminated these modes of religious expression, depending instead on the "dialectical imagination" — that is, creed, catechism, rationality, and prose — to carry the message. While both are part of the Christian heritage and neither one is better than the other, says Greeley, they represent differences in styles that help explain many value differences between Protestants and Catholics.[3]

More often, feminine aspects associated with Catholicism are linked to what some call the Marian cult. Of all its symbols, the Virgin Mary is most often pointed to as the paramount feminine symbol in Catholicism. Inserting her into the spiritual hierarchy purportedly tempered the exclusive masculinity of the

Trinity. Merciful and approachable, the mother of God appeals particularly to women and the poor, offering them warmth and comfort, say Greeley and Kurtz. Greeley offers some empirical support for the proposition that a strong Mary image correlates positively with more feminine concerns such as good social relationships, pro-feminist orientations, and frequent prayer. That some feminine qualities may affect Catholic men as well as women is suggested in at least one study done recently in the United States. Of six cultural groups Antoine Vergote and his associates studied, he and Alvaro Tamayo found that Roman Catholic seminarians were most inclined to attribute maternal qualities to God. (The study also showed that these same subjects, as compared to laypersons, were significantly more attached to their mothers.)[4]

That Catholics are more inclined than Protestants toward Sharing would probably not surprise John Tropman, director of the Catholic Project. He asserts that Sharing is one of the core Catholic values constituting what he calls "the Catholic ethic." Tropman uses the term "ethic" in the same way that Max Weber does: as an "ideal" or "pure" type, a hypothetical construction to describe the essence of something rather than the actual phenomenon. As Tropman describes it, Sharing in the Catholic value system has several characteristics that distinguish it from the Protestant value system.[5]

Several characteristics make the Catholic Sharing ethic different, says Tropman. It occupies a dominant place in the Catholic value system, encompasses a broad range of people, and is marked by a special attitude that accompanies it. It means "not only the willingness to help others but the obligation to do so." Nor is it exclusively focused on helping only those at the bottom of the economic ladder; although having a "preferential option for the poor," it also includes all those in need. It also means giving in a manner that avoids a "one-down position," where the giver implies that the resource belongs to him or her alone and that the receiver needs to be appreciative. On the contrary, giving in the Catholic ethical sense "conveys a sense of equality between sharers" so that neither is aggrandized nor diminished by the act. Tropman is careful to point out, however, that the ethic is neither confined to Catholics nor necessarily descriptive of all Catholics, but that as compared with Protestantism, it is a dominant Catholic ideal.[6]

Tropman offers no empirical support for his assertions, leading some to question whether a Catholic ethic of Sharing is mere fantasy. *Christian Century* senior editor Martin Marty has his doubts. "What do I think of the Catholic ethic in American society?" he writes, "It would be a good idea." While he acknowledges Tropman's attempt at avoiding overgeneralization, he says that helping has also played a central role among Protestants and implies that the style is different. Who, after all, he asks, "invented the modern voluntary associations that set out to reform the world and engage in acts of mercy."[7] As Marty and others have pointed out, neither the Catholic ethic nor the Protestant ethic has precluded the concurrent existence of greed and cruel exploitation of others.

Our data suggest that Tropman nonetheless appeared to be right, at least in part, and that there is something to a particular Catholic style of Sharing, at least during the time and place of our study. What Tropman does not address is whether the Catholic Sharing predisposition extends to outgroups. Our data suggest that however real the Sharing orientation among Catholics appears to be, it may not be as widespread as he implies.

Catholics owe their Sharing dispositions to their religion, says Tropman. While a religious ethos may well contribute to this view, it may also be attributable in part to what some have called a *collectivist* culture. Collectivism can and is embraced by many different groups. Unlike Protestants, who are frequently described as being individualists, Catholics are more often described as belonging to a collectivist culture.

Group ties are tight in collectivist cultures: people tend to be strongly attached to their group, regard group norms and positive relationships with other group members as top priorities, and often subordinate their individual desires to group goals even if they suffer negative consequences as a result. Conversely, group ties are loose in individualistic cultures: people tend to see themselves and their obligations as different and separate from the group, and emphasize their personal goals even if they inconvenience the group.[8] The differences between these two cultures are summarized by social psychologist Harry Triandis as follows: (1) in collectivist cultures people largely define themselves as interdependent; in individualist cultures people largely define themselves as independent; (2) "personal and communal goals are closely aligned in collectivism and not at all aligned in individualism; (3) norms, obligations, and duties guide much of social behavior in collectivist cultures," whereas "attitudes, personal needs, rights, and contracts guide social behavior in individualistic cultures; and (4) an emphasis on relationships, even when they are disadvantageous, is common in collectivist cultures," whereas in individualist cultures "the emphasis is on rational analyses of the advantages and disadvantages of maintaining a relationship."[9] As Triandis rightly cautions, individualism and collectivism exist within every individual and in every society to different degrees, and within any culture there are people who act like collectivists or like individualists, but their distributions are different.

Interdependence, communal goals, strongly held shared norms and obligations, and an emphasis on relationships are characteristics of the Catholic ethic, writes John Tropman. These characteristics, which he calls "communal," are also basic elements defining collectivities. These communal elements, says Tropman, begin with the Catholic family and extend to the local parish community.[10]

The family "is a point of reference for an individual's decision making," reflected not only in family relationships but also in religious symbols, says Tropman.[11] The Holy Family of Jesus, Mary, and Joseph, for example, occupy a more central role in Catholic devotional practices than in Protestant practices. The forms of address for Catholic religious leaders are also familial: called fathers, brothers, mothers, and sisters, they parallel the family structure intended to embrace all Catholics, who are thus encouraged to see themselves as one big community united by kinship ties. And unlike Protestants, who have splintered into many sects, Catholics have remained a single religious entity or extended family despite their many differences.

If the above propositions are correct, we might anticipate that Catholics would score higher than Protestants on positive interpersonal relationships. But no significant differences emerge between Catholics and Protestants on overall family closeness or closeness to mother or father or even close friends. The only difference between them concerned relatives: Catholics more often lived among relatives. It may be that Catholics embraced a wider sense of family inclusion, preferring physical proximity to distance (see Table 3bIII).

If Catholics are more interdependent and bound together in a communal sense because of their Catholicism, we might expect that as compared with Protestants, Catholics might feel closer to their co-religionists. This, too, did not appear to be the case. To be sure, religious denominational identification provided a strong cultural identity for Catholics, but this association was no stronger than it was for Protestants. Regardless of their levels of religiosity — very religious, moderately religious, or not at all religious — Catholics and Protestants were likely to say they felt "most similar" to those who belonged to their own religious denomination (see Table 3aII).

Collectivist notions not only apply to family and community life but also have economic policy implications, according to some social commentators. One of the reasons Catholic ethics were antagonistic to capitalism, Max Weber postulated, is because of the impersonal human relations capitalism required.[12] That ordinary Catholics might more readily reject the very idea of capitalism is also suggested by what Tropman calls the Catholic preference for the poor, a proposition supported by our data. Compared with their Protestant counterparts, Catholics generally, as well as Catholic rescuers specifically, identified far more strongly with the poor. The very word "capitalism" continues to repel many Catholic intellectuals today, says Michael Novak, even when they in fact very much favor private property, investment, and private enterprise. Novak explains the reaction as stemming in part from capitalism's association with individualism rather than from concern with the common good.[13] Andrew Greeley's survey of 3,834 Catholics and 3,236 Protestants in seven countries appears to support the above claims. In all countries, says Greeley, Catholics as compared with Protestants more often emphasized equality and "communitarian" attitudes, and more often supported government programs to promote these goals, including government welfare programs, while Protestants were more likely to emphasize "freedom" and "individualism."[14]

In addition to their religious identification, what appeared to unite Catholics most was their sense of patriotism — stronger from youth on among all Catholic groups as compared with all Protestant groups. Among Catholics, however, religion and patriotism did not necessarily mean political involvement — far fewer Catholics than Protestants report affiliation with any political party (see Table 3aII). Unlike Protestants, who depended more on political clout to achieve their aims, Catholics appeared to rely more on their religious and national institutions to reach their goals.

Interdependent and more tightly bound by the governing norms of their own group, collectivist societies are allegedly less accepting of outsiders. But Catholics generally as compared with Protestants generally were significantly *more open* to groups other than their own. They did not differ with respect to their feelings of similarity to Jews or Turks, and their parents were neither more nor less likely to speak positively or disparagingly of Jews. But they claimed feeling more similar to Gypsies, and more like Protestants than Protestants felt toward them. If they were politically affiliated, the parties to which they belonged, as compared with those of politically affiliated Protestants, were significantly more likely to be inclusive — that is tolerant or advocates of rights for minorities and Jews. And more frequently they alleged having Jewish friends or knowing Jews, a claim perhaps related to the fact that Catholic respondents were also more likely to live among them (see Table 3aI).

The above suggests that Catholic culture generally may not be quite as collectivist as some have suggested, at least in the sense of excluding outgroups. *Yet it is Catholic rescuers, rather than bystanders, who appear to carry more of the Sharing propensities* that Tropman describes, as well as the inclination toward outgroup inclusion.

Catholic Rescuers and Catholic Bystanders

Catholic bystanders differed significantly from Catholic rescuers on many measures, several of them relevant to those suggested by Tropman.

Georges, a Belgian monk, reflects many of the characteristic attributes of Catholic bystanders.

GEORGES

Sickly as a young boy, studious and very religious, Georges joined the monastery at age twenty-seven. The reclusive life suited him, providing him with both a safe community and an opportunity to devote himself to study. He became a scholar of the Middle Ages, concentrating in his later years on a study of Flemish mysticism during the thirteenth century. When the war started, thirty-one-year-old Georges was then living in a Flemish-speaking monastery in the French section of Belgium, where he taught philosophy, theology, and Canon law. Here's how he described some of the important events in his life during the war.

> Beginning at the very first week of the war, people were all in trouble. They had nothing to eat. So we baked a lot of bread and distributed it to hundreds of people. I became the baker's assistant. We used the old system of baking and I baked nearly every day. We helped people survive.
>
> Next to the monastery we had a small house; people could stay there overnight. Some were transient refugees; some were underground people who had to be smuggled out of the monastery. It was not official but we did it. We supported them. One time we had a boarder, a member of the Resistance, and we had to ask him to leave. I told the committee that if the Germans came and caught him, he would be shot.

No different from most, Georges concentrated on surviving. "Survival made people do terrible things," he said, "a German soldier told me that on a train with Russian prisoners, one of them choked an officer to death so that he could steal his bread. If you want to survive, you have compassion for no one—neither your friend or enemy. You do everything just to survive." He was frightened that anything he might say or do could land him in a concentration camp. "A priest I knew," he said, "gave a sermon on Sunday and said something unfavorable to Hitler; he wound up in a concentration camp." He himself didn't do things publicly, but he would occasionally say unfavorable things to his trusted colleagues. "When Hitler was losing the war in Russia in '42, I said he had no experience with the Russian winter. Had the other side heard me, they would have sent me to a concentration camp." Georges acknowledged that living in a monastery provided him with an extra edge of protection.

But together with his fellow monks, he did take a few risks: not interfering with those who sought overnight shelter at the monastery was one, daring to suggest to some German soldiers that he was not entirely happy with the German occupation was another:

> All during the war, we had tours for visitors at the monastery: some days as many as twelve, even fifteen German soldiers. I would do the tour and we would share a glass of beer afterwards which we brewed ourselves. Some would come to shake hands afterwards and once I said: "Excuse me, I cannot shake hands with you. I have nothing against you personally, but you came uninvited and forced yourselves on my country. You shoot at my people. As long as this situation exists, I cannot shake hands with you." They all froze and I said to myself: "This could be the end of me." But one of them said "I understand" and we all relaxed. That was a very scary moment. If that had happened at the end of the war, they would have shot me. When they're winning, they're happy, but when they're losing they're angry.

Georges had learned to be prudent from his father. Like many more Catholic bystanders than rescuers, Georges had a poor relationship with his father. His father did not approve of his studious ambitions. "He wanted to use me to make money; I wanted to study and go to the university. To prepare, you had to spend six years studying Latin and Greek, but when I asked him if I could do that, he said no." Like many more Catholic bystanders, he endured physical abuse from his father. "He would teach me by kicking me," he said, "just because I didn't do whatever it was he wanted. Sometimes for coming home too late after school; most of the time unjustly. He would brag about me outside the house, saying to his friends, 'Oh, my boy is so intelligent.' But he was hideous at home."

Rather than confront his father, Georges usually obeyed him, another characteristic more common among bystanders. Early in life, he had learned to "use his head" rather than confront problems publicly. He credits his mother with having taught him this valuable lesson. A very religious Catholic, with whom he felt particularly close, she died of a very painful form of cancer, "in torment day and night." She taught him "how to take the troubles of life and integrate them," without fighting back. It was somewhat like gardening, he explained: "As using manure in a garden helps, so your sufferings will bring forth better fruit."

In keeping with this view, he advised other people to think before they acted, and did so when the Germans came into town. "People panicked and started to run away and I told them it's useless. When a flood comes, you can run perhaps five miles an hour but the flood runs ten miles an hour. But people stopped using their brains and depended on their feelings." As it happened, the army stayed for only a day but people didn't return until after several weeks. One of his major complaints about the underground was that they didn't always do things intelligently either. "It was not intelligent," he said, "to kill simple German soldiers, because then innocent people would have to pay for it. If they could kill the big shots, that would have been a different story."

Prudence also dictated his response to those in need. He admitted refusing help to some who had asked: "If they would ask for help and I could help them, I would do it. But if I couldn't, I couldn't." One of the people he refused to help was a known Resistance fighter. Willing to take some prudent risks, he was unwilling to take any that might be too costly.

Like many Catholics, Georges was an ardent patriot, but he was not a Belgian patriot. Born in Flanders, he expressed great loyalty to this region, rejecting what he called the "artificial state of Belgium." He claimed no political affiliation, but his political leanings were center to right. His fear of liberalism and Communism was far greater than his dread of Germans. He blamed the French Revolution for the destruction of "cultural treasures and much that was precious to religion," and for suppressing his monastic order. As for the Communists, he said, they are "worse than those Nazis. They kill all the intellectuals as soon as they occupy a country, as they did in Poland." In fact, he said, they were worse than the Nazis "because the Nazis used gas and that kills people fast," but the Communists killed an abbot he knew by "masturbating him to death." By way of comparison, German soldiers treated Georges and the monastery treasures relatively respectfully.

In fact, Georges went to considerable lengths to explain the differences among Germans and to justify their behaviors. "Germans are not Nazis," he said. "The SS was evil, not Germany." He insisted that the army didn't agree with the Nazis, and made careful distinctions between Germans who were Rhinelanders, "good and hospitable people," and the Prussians who were "militaristic and feel superior." He expressed great empathy for retreating German soldiers: "I saw it twice, and while I cannot say it broke my heart, it caused me great pain; not because they had not won but because there was no 'juice' in them. They were demoralized." As for the cause of the war, there was this crazy Hitler, but he cautioned, "Let's not forget the Treaty of Versailles in 1919 — England, Germany, and Italy and even America to some degree prepared the Second World War. The Treaty of Versailles was so bad that Germany had to go to war."

Largely insulated from the world around him, Georges had little contact with and paid little attention to people outside his faith circles. Answers concerning which groups he felt similar to fell into two polarized categories: he felt "very like" the poor and Catholics but could find nothing even remotely similar between himself and Jews, Turks, and Gypsies: "not at all like," he responded. He did in fact have a Jewish brother-in-law — actually a Catholic convert — but as Georges explained, even though his brother-in-law had converted before the war, "He was still Jewish in his heart — he never lost his Jewishness." Whatever Georges' relationship may have been to him, it did not apparently reduce his sense of estrangement from Jews generally. As for Protestants, he explained: "I didn't feel totally different from Protestants, because we are all Christians, but I didn't know any, so I didn't have to face the issue."

Like Georges, Catholic bystanders, more so than Catholic rescuers, sought survival through accommodation to external authorities. Their comparatively lower sense of self-esteem coupled with their conviction that power lay outside themselves led more bystanders to conclude that obedience is the most efficacious way to get on in the world (see Table V). Unlike Protestant bystanders, who also recognized the need for compliance with external demands but concurrently assumed a posture of internal strength, Catholic bystanders more characteristically complied out of an acknowledged sense of internal weakness. They scored significantly lower than Protestant bystanders on the Internal Mastery Factor, self-esteem, and an internal locus of control, as well as personal potency (see Table 3bV). Catholic bystanders, in short, emerge as a relatively fragile and anxious group, feeling they had little in the way of internal resources to master their environment.

Catholic rescuers, on the other hand, were more internally oriented. As compared with Catholic bystanders, they considered themselves more competent, and believing in their own abilities to make things happen rather than depending on others, they rejected obedience more often (see Table 3bV). This finding suggests that attributes associated with an internal sense of mastery may be essential for outgroup altruism. Yet, an inflated sense of mastery, as suggested by Protestant bystanders, particularly when it is externally oriented, can reflect an exaggerated self-centeredness that results in passivity to others' pain or even its infliction on others. Too weak a sense of internal mastery, as suggested by Catholic bystanders, can have the same results. Outgroup altruism, it appears, requires at least a moderate degree of internally oriented mastery attributes, sufficient to encourage the belief that objectives can be reached however difficult external circumstances might appear.

But Catholic bystanders differed from rescuers on many more matters than their different approaches to how to make it in the world.

As Tropman proposed, Catholics were significantly more inclined toward Sharing as compared with Protestants. It was an impressive difference; of the ten Sharing measures used to assess this inclination, five favored Catholics. This predisposition also favored Catholic rescuers even when compared with

Protestant rescuers. But these apparently more pronounced Catholic cultural values evaporate when Catholic rescuers are compared with Catholic bystanders. It is Catholic rescuers, significantly more than Catholic bystanders, who stand out by virtue of their Sharing dispositions. In larger percentages, they claimed learning values of care from their parents; they expressed a strong prosocial orientation, a heightened sense of social responsibility as well as personal integrity; and they continued their involvement in community helping even after the war. Catholic bystanders not only scored significantly lower on all these Sharing measures as compared with Catholic rescuers, but also evidenced no differences from Protestant bystanders on any Sharing measure (see Table 3bIV).

Catholic rescuers had at their disposal a set of Sharing values that distinguished them significantly from Catholic bystanders as well as Protestant rescuers. With respect to Sharing inclinations, Catholic rescuers scored particularly high and Catholic bystanders much lower.

The same contrast appears to be the case with family relationships: Catholic bystanders reflected poorer family relationships as compared with Catholic rescuers. In large measure, this appears to be the consequence of more negative family experiences with fathers particularly, who not only disciplined them more frequently but relied more often on physical discipline — strappings and beatings — sometimes administered in an alcoholic rage, and which recipients experienced as gratuitous. Whereas family relationships among Protestants generally tended to be similar, Catholics reflect both their most positive and negative aspects, with more positives accruing to Catholic rescuers (see Table 3bIII).

Yet despite their poorer family relationships, Catholic bystanders appeared to value their family connections. They expressed this primarily through helping relatives and neighbors, a matter that distinguished them from Protestant bystanders who invested significantly less energy in such personal activities. Some psychologists might say that given their frailties, they were simply more dependent on personal ties to sustain them. Others might incline to call this "interdependence" rather than "dependence," since bystanders not only report receiving help but also reciprocating.

The Catholic family ideal, as expressed by Tropman, appears to have found its most fertile field among Catholic rescuers. As compared with Catholic bystanders, rescuers were significantly more intimately connected with their families generally and their fathers particularly, and were rarely disciplined, the latter characteristic also distinguishing them from Protestant rescuers (see Table 3bIII).

Heavily influenced by their warm family ties, their war activities followed a course significantly different from that of bystanders. Like those of Ernst and Madeleine, family members of rescuers often belonged to resistance groups, as did they themselves, and some of their families also actively helped Jews (see Table 3aII). Although like Madeleine rescuers often preferred to keep their families ignorant of their activities out of concern for their safety, family members sometimes provided an interdependent helping network, providing information, food, false papers and the like.

ZENON

The strong Sharing disposition among Catholic rescuers clearly included outsiders. For Polish bystander Zenon, however, helpfulness rarely extended beyond parish boundaries.

> I was drafted into the army in 1939 and trained to be a horseman. The Polish Army used to have a cavalry and I was trained how to ride and fight on horseback. We were quickly defeated. We were to run and get rid of our uniforms and weapons and hide out. I hid in one of my uncle's farmhouses in a village about seventeen kilometers from Tarnow. When things quieted down, I came back home.
>
> Little by little, I managed to get a number of different jobs. I helped to make leather from cowhide that was used to make shoes — we killed the cows illegally. We would butcher them secretly, sell the meat, and exchange meat for clothing. We didn't have very good chemicals to process the leather, and the cowhide would sometimes stink too much. We were afraid that the neighbors might inform on us. I also used to make boots and shoes that we would sell illegally and trade for items such as kerosene for oil lamps, soap, and clothing.
>
> That was my primary involvement during the war — I needed to make a living. My wife, too, did many odd jobs, including bringing some sewing into the house. We needed money because we had a child. Sometimes we got sick and needed to pay a doctor — we often had colds.
>
> In 1943, I was hauling firewood to town by horse and wagon. A German stopped and beat me for slowing down the traffic.

Zenon was born in 1916 in Tarnow, Poland. His description of the war years largely mirrors his life. With an elementary education only, he earned his living as a shoemaker before and during the war, and remained one thereafter. He had never done anything unusual in any way before the war, nothing particularly adventurous, not even standing up for any belief. Neither he nor his parents belonged to any political party. He had never refused help to anyone during the war because he had never been asked. Although he considered himself very patriotic, he could think of nothing he had done to actively express that sentiment either. Besides the one beating he received, he was never mistreated by the Nazis.

His family relationships were not very good. From his influential mother, he had learned "to work hard, not to drink, to go to church regularly, to help and respect his elders, and not to lie because it is sinful and destructive and results in mistrust of people." As for his father, a carpenter:

> We did not communicate very well at all. He was often drunk and angry, and sometimes he beat me or punched me, for not obeying him or for not listening to what he told me to do, for talking back or for cursing him after he cursed me. Sometimes he even threw me out of the house, especially when he was very angry and partly drunk. I was very upset with the way he treated my mother, which sometimes bordered on violence. I sometimes saw her cry and I knew that something like that might have happened.

The only group of people he felt "very like" were fellow Catholics, and although very poor himself, he felt only "somewhat like" other poor people. As for all others, in no way did he think of them as similar to him. He had strong negative feeling toward Gypsies, because "they would steal things," and he didn't like the Germans "because they were arrogant." But his attitudes toward Jews were a bit more complex.

Except for some commercial transactions, Zenon knew little about the Jews among whom he lived. He had no Jewish friends and was unaware of any antisemitism in his country before the war. But his parents spoke about them often, and some of the comments were positive. His father, for example, spoke approvingly of his Jewish boss, whom he liked. And he himself had had some good experiences with Jewish merchants. "I remember some nice Jewish people who gave me candy as I walked by their shops because they saw I couldn't pay. Some Jews are very good—nice and good Poles," he added. But most of the comments Zenon heard were negative, and he tended to believe them. "Many were very mean, and rich too," his father told him. "They kept to themselves, they looked different, they spoke a funny language, and their Polish was not very good." "Jews are very smart and own all the businesses in town," his mother said; she warned him that sometimes they would take advantage of people. While not believing "everything that my mother told me," he could see lots of the same things himself. "They lived apart, in certain streets where mostly other Jews lived and there was not much mixing between the groups." He "didn't think much about it" when he saw Jews wearing the yellow star but felt sorry for them when he saw them beaten. After they were taken from the Tarnow Ghetto, he understood that "the poor devils were being killed off one by one."

Poor and abused as a child by his volatile father, Zenon had apparently learned that safety lay in passivity; it was the same lesson that Georges had learned. Zenon belonged to no political party or resistance group, concentrating his energies on survival for both himself and his family. Family, work, and church occupied all his time before, during, and after the war. Asked if he had done any helping activities recently, he said he contributed some four hours a month toward repairing the church. Although not a very religious man — he described himself as only "somewhat religious" — the church holds a very important place in his life as a source of security and community.

Like Zenon, many Catholics shared a strong sense of patriotism, stronger from youth on among all Catholic groups as compared with all Protestant groups. On this matter, there was no distinction between Catholic rescuers and bystanders (see Table 3aII).

But for Catholic rescuers, and their family members, patriotism included more direct political activity before the war, and resistance during the war. Significantly more rescuers and/or their relatives, as compared with bystanders and/or their relatives, participated in resistance activities and belonged to political parties before the war. For Catholic bystanders, political affiliation was far less common: identification with church and country appeared to suffice, without any apparent accompanying obligatory norms that required overt action against Nazism. On the whole, political participation mattered far less to Catholics generally as compared with Protestants generally, and even to Catholic rescuers as compared with Protestant rescuers: they were far less likely to be politically affiliated (see Table 3aII). Yet it was in the context of their left-leaning politics that some befriended Jews and learned about their needs.

In fact, Catholic rescuers, in significantly larger percentages than Catholic bystanders as well as Protestant rescuers (and Protestant bystanders), claimed having Jewish friends. Significantly more receptive to groups other than their own, as compared with Catholic bystanders as well as Protestant rescuers, they perceived themselves as more similar to several types of groups — Jews and Gypsies — and even more accepting of Protestants than Protestant rescuers were of Catholics. Given this type of receptivity, not surprisingly they reported having a greater diversity of friends, in terms not only of religion but also of social class (see Table 3aI). For more Catholic rescuers, Jews tended to be concrete persons they knew; for more Protestant rescuers, they often appeared to be abstractions.

Catholic bystanders, on the other hand, were significantly more likely to reject notions of similarity with others, and with respect to Jews, they were far more likely to have been raised in homes where parents voiced stereotypes. On the negative side, which they heard more often than did rescuers, they were likely to hear about Jewish untrustworthiness and undue influence; on the positive side they were likely to hear about the Jews' accomplishments, which more often than not engendered envy rather than affection (see Table 3aI).

CORINNE

Catholic rescue, it appears, as compared with Protestant rescue, often emerged from a culture that was more encompassing and broad, and included personal friendships with Jews. Without the benefit of a cultural context that explicitly endowed Jews with merit, proximity afforded little reason for bystanders to perceive them as worthy or even to notice them at all despite their physical presence. Corinne, a very religious French bystander, offers an example of this.

> During the war we lived in a village about forty kilometers from Limoges. Because we lived in the country, food was much easier to get, so we helped the rest of the family by sending them parcels of food. We sent packages to Paris, Bordeaux, Nice, or wherever they lived at the time.
>
> A Jewish student was hired to help me take care of the two children; she stayed with us one summer. We found work and lodging for some Alsaciens. And we listened constantly to the British radio in order to stay informed about Allied advances.

Born in Strasbourg, France, in 1917 to middle-class Catholic parents, Corinne, like her mother, was very devout throughout her life. Her moderately religious father was a government employee in the Department of Water and Forestry Management. The family relationships were "somewhat close" as she described them, and generally positive. The family unit was of critical importance to her. "We didn't care much about money," she said, "the unity of the family was important." In 1936, she received two university certificates: one in French and the other in Latin. Married in 1940, when she was twenty-three years old, she lived in Paris with her husband. She gave birth to two children during the war.

As with Georges, religion was the center of Corinne's life: "my principal preoccupation," she said. Shy and retiring, she found in the church a strong sense of belonging and security. She attended a Catholic elementary school, run by the Notre Dame de Sion, and a Catholic gymnasium. Catholic Action was her major activity before the war, and there she, along with a group of fellow students, studied religion. There she learned to value the "spiritual" dimension of life—"the importance of prayer, the responsibility one has toward others, honesty toward oneself and one's convictions."

Neither Corinne nor her husband was politically affiliated; the same was true of her parents. Her mother, however, did have strong political sentiments, progressive in some ways and rightist in others. A feminist of her time, she was an active member of the Feminine Action for the Emancipation of Women. Personal reasons may have contributed to her political sense: she taught her daughter not to trust or depend on men. But she was also a Royalist and associated with the Royalist movement.

Corinne herself was far more concerned about her country. A staunch patriot, she evaluated political leaders on the basis of whether they reflected national values or contributed to national survival. She very much admired Henri-Philippe Pétain, premier of Vichy France: in her view, he "embodied France." While she didn't quite approve of his government's anti-Jewish legislation, she excused it, saying, "It was the Germans who really ordered the Final Solution." She held de Gaulle in similar esteem: "He resisted and saved the country," she said. Hostile toward Germans "because of what happened in World War I," she felt "profound disgust and sadness" with the German occupation in World War II.

Three elements constituted the foundation of Corinne's world: her family, her religion, and her country. She registered little of what she may have seen outside these realms. Asked whether she had ever had a close friend of a different religion, she responded, "Yes, I had a friend who was a free thinker— no religion at all." Catholics were the only group with whom she felt "very like"—she rated Protestants "not very like," while rich and poor, Turks, Gypsies, and Nazis all received "not at all like."

Yet asked how similar she felt to other groups, Corinne ranked Jews higher than all other groups and only one level below that of Catholics: "somewhat like," she said. Her early background would not necessarily have predicted this. Her parents never spoke of them, and although Jews attended her elementary school, gymnasium, and university, she said she didn't know any. "In our social sphere," she said, "we did not associate with Jewish people. We did not care for them, we ignored them." But Jews were not as foreign to her as her circumstances might suggest. Her father did have one close Jewish friend, and her husband had one as well. She apparently did not object to the Jewish student hired by the family to help take care of the children for one summer. This relationship, as well as her husband's attitudes—"a very good (Jewish) friend visited him in the country often," she said—may have softened her disdain.

For some six years after the war, Corrine devoted herself to religious studies and helping children. She became active in the Association for Handicapped Children, where she undertook a variety of tasks, including editing a medical journal.

Corrine was devoted to her religion and her family, and although not immune from the prejudices she had learned in her early years, appeared to transcend them in some degree as a consequence of later experiences. A kind person, and not without some sympathy for Jews, Corrine had little reason to regard them as meriting particular attention. Given a religious context that regarded "inward spirituality" as sufficient, Corrine apparently did not doubt the virtue of her outward passivity.

Catholic rescuers presented a very different picture. As compared with Catholic bystanders and even Protestant rescuers, Catholic rescuers appeared most open to outsiders. Since as compared with Catholic bystanders and Protestants generally they were also most inclined toward a Sharing disposition, it can be argued that they most approximated what some have called the more "feminine" attributes of Catholicism. Since Catholic rescuers were also significantly less religious than Protestant rescuers, it may be that secular affiliations played a more important role among Catholics in contributing to rescue, whereas among Protestants, rescue more often emerged from tight religious collectivities at the center of which were normative agreements about the desirability of helping Jews. (Of course, "tight" religious collectivities, convents particularly, also played an important role among Catholics, as did secular affiliations among Protestants.) Clearly both groups, Catholics and Protestants, included rescuers who were able to transcend whatever narrow boundaries may have characterized their larger religious communities and embrace persecuted outsiders as insiders, although the values and dispositions through which they viewed these behaviors may not necessarily have been identical.

7

Patterns and Predictors

None of the groups here discussed qualifies as a dominantly "outgroup altruistic culture," yet all included a small percentage of individuals who acted heroically on behalf of an outgroup. The fact that such grandeur did exist under the most grotesque of circumstances suggests something extraordinarily hopeful about the human potential for good. Exploring the degree to which it may also exist in other cultures is an enterprise worthy of investigation.

In fact, if we bypass some of the components of conventional definitions of culture, including the one proposed here, something that might be called an outgroup altruistic culture may already exist. It would include a group of people from many diverse cultures who share more or less similar beliefs, attitudes, norms, and values regarding outgroup altruism but who do not necessarily share a sense of common identity that makes them distinct from others. Anthropologists Claudia Strauss and Naomi Quinn argue for just such investigations, that is, investigations that begin not necessarily with extant societies but rather with "public practices or a set of mental structures" and asking "who shares it?"[1] They agree that being part of a cultural group requires a set of shared values and attitudes but do not insist that it demands as a precondition a conscious identity, one that already ties people into an explicitly recognized relationship. A conscious identity may follow such inquiries, rather than precede them.

What attitudes and beliefs might constitute a core group of values reflective of an outgroup altruistic culture? And how homogeneous are participants likely to be? Rescuers suggest some preliminary answers. The five summary factors — Outgroup Relationships, Secondary Relationships (Religious/Secular), Primary Relationships, Sharing, and Mastery Orientation (Internal/External) — are a good place to begin.

Rescuers differed significantly from nonrescuers and bystanders on all five of the identified summary factors.

As compared with nonrescuers and bystanders, rescuers were significantly more open to outgroups generally (Outgroup Relationships factor), and better integrated into the major secular institutions of their society associated with rescue (Secular Secondary Relationships factor). Their family relationships were better (Primary Relationships) and they inclined more toward empathizing with and doing for others (Sharing factor). Rather than conforming with external authorities (External Mastery Orientation factor), as more nonrescuers did, they preferred to rely on their own internal resources, believing that they themselves could affect external events (Internal Mastery Orientation factor).

But are all these factors equally necessary to prompt a culture toward outgroup altruistic behaviors? The data suggest otherwise. Although all contributed significantly in predicting rescue, not all were equal; some predicted the outcome more than others did. And while rescuers from different cultural groups often resembled each other, the distribution of these factors also differed; a group weak on one factor would sometimes reflect some compensatory strength on another.

Which factors contributed most toward predicting rescue and how did groups compare with respect to their distribution? A discriminant function analysis suggested some answers.[2] I begin by noting how strongly each one of the five summary factors related to rescue, and I describe its distribution among all religiosity groups generally (very religious, somewhat religious, mildly religious, and irreligious) and between rescuers and nonrescuers in these same religiosity groups. The distribution of each of these same factors between Protestants and Catholics follows, accompanied by a comparison of Protestant and Catholics rescuers with their bystander counterparts. I begin with the factor contributing most, and in descending order I conclude with the factor contributing least. Some general implications follow.

Outgroup Relationships

The *Outgroup Relationships factor* — the types of relationships with outsider groups that the culture tolerated or encouraged — *was the strongest factor predicting rescue.* Of the five factors explored, it ranked as the most powerful predictor of rescue on the discriminant function (0.68). Loadings on the Outgroup Relationships factor included: Feelings of Similarity to Jews (0.68), Jewish Friends (0.57), Feelings of Similarity to Gypsies (0.56), Feelings of Similarity to Turks (0.51), Feelings of Similarity to Other Religious Denomination (0.49), Parental Negative Stereotyping of Jews (−0.41), Variety of Friendships (0.38), Jews in Neighborhood before the War (0.35), Jews in School (0.35), Empathy for Jews (0.33), Parental Values about Jews: Stereotypes (−0.28), Political Party Inclusiveness (0.28).

High scorers felt strongly similar to other groups, including Jews, Gypsies, Turks, and Christians of the other major denomination, and had Jewish friends as well as a variety of other vertical (social class) and horizontal (ethnic/religious) friends. More inclined toward egalitarian views and involvement with Jews, they claimed political affiliations that ranged from liberal to left. Conversely, low scorers more frequently rejected feelings of similarity to other groups, including Jews, Gypsies, Turks, and Christians of the other major denomination, and reported having fewer Jewish friends as well as fewer friends among diverse groups generally. Less inclined toward egalitarian views and involvement with Jews, they claimed political affiliations that ranged from center to right.

Which groups rated highest on Outgroup Relationships? Rescuers scored significantly higher than did nonrescuers and bystanders on the Outgroup Relationships factor (see Appendix B, Table 1aI). Among religiosity groups, the irreligious were the most liberal with respect to outgroups, and Catholics more so than Protestants.

The irreligious scored significantly higher than the somewhat religious on the Outgroup Relationship factor. They were more open to other groups overall as compared with the somewhat religious, and were more likely to be aware of Nazi intentions earlier as compared with the somewhat and very religious; as compared with all others, they were most likely to be affiliated with left-leaning political parties (see Table 2aI). But it is irreligious rescuers in particular who appear to be the most receptive to outsiders, and particularly toward Jews. As compared with all groups, irreligious rescuers were most likely to be affiliated with the political left, that is, groups advocating on behalf of minorities and Jews. As compared with somewhat and very religious rescuers, they claimed earlier knowledge of Nazi intentions regarding Jews, such salience probably deriving in part from the nature of their political affiliations as well as their school contexts, which as compared with the very religious in particular were far more likely to include Jews (see Table 2aI). They differed significantly from their nonrescuer counterparts on several items relating to Jews. Irreligious rescuers, as compared with their nonrescuer counterparts, claimed earlier awareness of Nazi intentions and greater empathy for Jews, heard more positive comments about Jews from their parents, and were also far more likely to affiliate with left-leaning political groups (see Table 2aI). Among irreligious rescuers, family and political values regarding Jews largely overlapped, resulting in an inclusive orientation that was particularly sensitive to their plight.

Conversely, of all groups, moderately religious nonrescuers — which include somewhat and mildly religious nonrescuers — were among the least liberal politically and the most exclusionary with respect to Jews. They scored significantly lower than their rescuer counterparts on the Outgroup Relationship factor generally, and tended largely to confine their relationships to others they deemed similar to themselves. They more often belonged to exclusionary political parties, identified more with Nazis, claimed fewer Jewish friends, heard more negative talk about Jews in their families of origin, and generally associated less with people outside their own particular religious group and social class (see Table 2aI). They even differed significantly from several other nonrescuer groups along some of these same measures, particularly regarding their relationships with Jews and their greater sense of similarity to Nazis (see Table 2aI). As compared with all other nonrescuer (and rescuer) groups, somewhat religious nonrescuers are noteworthy for more often claiming no Jewish friends, while mildly religious nonrescuers are distinguished by virtue of their strongest sense of identification with Nazis (see Table 2aI).

Catholics, as compared with Protestants, were also more open to outgroups; they scored significantly higher than Protestants on the Outgroup Relationships factor. In addition to other variables associated with this factor, they were more inclined to be affiliated with liberal/left political parties and also claimed more often to have Jewish friends (see Table 3aI). But it is Catholic rescuers in particular who evidence the greatest openness to outsiders. While they shared many similarities, Catholic rescuers nonetheless, as compared with Protestant rescuers, were more open to outgroups generally, particularly as manifested in their personal involvements with Jews, suggesting that general tolerance of and friendship with others may have played a more important role among members of this group (see Table 3aI).

What Catholic and Protestant rescuers also shared in common was the fact that as compared with their bystander counterparts, they scored significantly higher on the Outgroup Relationships factor and many of the single items included therein. In both groups, bystanders more often rejected outsiders and denied expressions of equality with others, particularly in relation to Jews (see Table 3aI). More than all other groups, Protestant bystanders identified with Nazis and belonged to rightist and fascist parties (see Table 3aI).

These findings point to the importance of openness to other groups as related to outgroup altruism. Yet, while openness ranked among the strongest correlates of rescue, it was not necessarily the most powerful condition for all groups. Despite the fact that very religious rescuers, for example, did not differ significantly from very religious nonrescuers on the Outgroup Relationships factor, the latter did not become rescuers. And although they were less open than Catholic rescuers and less involved with Jews, Protestant rescuers nonetheless risked their lives on behalf of Jews. For the very religious and Protestants, it appears that something else mattered more than openness. To a considerable degree, rescue depended on the nature of their secondary relationships.

Secondary Relationships

Secondary Relationships, the degree to which respondents felt integrated into the secondary institutions of their society, included both religious and secular ties. They were summarized in two ways.

The first summary factor was constructed from all the secondary relationship measures. The measures loading highly on this factor were Religiosity (0.79), Feelings of Similarity to Own Religious Denomination (0.71), and Patriotism Growing Up (0.54). Since this factor primarily reflected religious ties, it was labeled the Religious Secondary Relationships factor. The Religious Secondary Relationships factor was used to compare religious denomination groups, but in order to avoid circularity it was used neither to compare religiosity groups nor in the discriminant analysis.

The second summary factor was constructed from all the secondary relationship measures except for Religiosity. The measures loading highly on this factor were Resistance Groups: Self Belonged (0.62); Resistance Groups: Family Members Belonged (0.57); Defending Country Before the War (0.49); Patriotism Growing Up (0.49); and Political Party Membership (0.40). Since this factor primarily reflected secular ties, it was labeled the Secular Secondary Relationships factor. This factor was used to compare religious denomination groups and religiosity groups. It was also included as a predictor in the discriminant analysis and was the *second most powerful predictor of rescue* (0.58).

Rescuers, nonrescuers, and bystanders generally were similarly integrated into the religious institutions of their society; no significant differences emerged among them on the Religious Secondary Relationships factor (see Table 1aII). But rescuers, as compared with both nonrescuers and bystanders, emerged as more strongly integrated into those secular institutions supporting rescue. They were more engaged in anti-Nazi activities; they and their families more often belonged to resistance groups, in their view an expression of their patriotic sentiments; and they were more likely to be politically affiliated (see Table 1aII). But this pattern was not the same for all religiosity groups and denominations.

No overall significant differences occurred among religiosity groups with respect to their general integration into secular institutions, or between rescuers and their nonrescuer counterpart institutions (see Table 2aII). But the particular institutions that influenced each group varied. Irreligious rescuers, as compared with all other rescuer religiosity groups, appeared to be less influenced by patriotic sentiments. Very religious rescuers, as compared with irreligious rescuers, depended more on their religious associations as well as patriotic sentiments; a differentiating tendency that was also shared by moderately religious rescuers (see Table 2aI). As compared with their nonrescuer counterparts, moderately religious rescuers more often emerged from a social context that supported resistance to Nazis: more of their families and relatives were affiliated with resistance groups (see Table 2aII).

Protestants and Catholics reflected some of the same patterns and some important differences. While Protestants and Catholics generally did not differ in relation to their general integration into dominant secondary institutions, secular or religious, Protestant bystanders scored lower than Protestant rescuers on both, and particularly low on the Religious Secondary Relationships factor and Religiosity (see Table 3aII). Protestant rescuers, by contrast, scored higher on Religiosity than all other groups. Among Protestant rescuers, as compared with all other groups including Catholic rescuers, religiosity appeared to play a more important role in rescue. Like rescuers generally, Protestant rescuers and their family members, as compared with Protestant bystanders and their family members, were also more likely to join resistance groups (see Table 3aII).

Catholic rescuers, by contrast, did not differ from Catholic bystanders with respect to religious institutions but were more politically involved, and like rescuers generally, they and their families were also more likely to join resistance groups (see Table 3aII). While supportive religious institutions also played a role among Catholic rescuers, supportive secular affiliations — resistance groups and political networks — may have been equally or even more important. Overall, Catholic and Protestant rescuers, as compared with Catholic and Protestant bystanders, mirrored the pattern of rescuers and bystanders generally — they were far more likely to be affiliated with secular institutions associated with rescue — but religious affiliations appeared to play a much stronger role among Protestant rescuers.

Supportive secondary institutions are the "social capital" of outgroup altruism. They perform at least two functions: providing interpretations of the situation, and facilitating helping networks (e.g., recruiting others, offering emotional and material support). Networks can make the critical difference between success and failure. Cultures in which such supportive institutions do not exist are less likely to be oriented toward outgroup altruism in either attitudes or behavior. National and international affiliations are important, but local secondary institutions are probably more so.

Primary Relationships

Primary relationships, the degree to which respondents felt positively about relationships with their families of origin, *were the third most powerful predictor of rescue* (0.47). Highest loadings on this measure included Family Closeness (0.85), Closeness to Father (0.70), Closeness to Mother (0.68), Authoritarian Discipline (inverse relationship: −0.42), Ever Disciplined (inverse relationship: −0.40), and Close Friends Growing Up (0.32).

Rescuers scored significantly higher than nonrescuers and bystanders on the Primary Relationships factor; they felt closer to parents and families. Conversely, nonrescuer and bystander family experiences were far less positive (see Table 1bIII). While this was the general pattern, again it did not hold for all groups.

The general pattern did hold for the somewhat religious and the irreligious, among whom rescuers as compared with nonrescuers fared much better with their families. Somewhat religious nonrescuers were far more likely to suffer physical abuse at the hands of their fathers, which helps explain their poor relationships with them. Irreligious nonrescuers, who perceived their family relationships as generally more devoid of closeness, were more likely to see their parents as authoritarian. But no significant differences between rescuers and nonrescuers on Primary Relationships emerged among the very religious and the mildly religious (see Table 2bIII).

The irreligious once more stand out, this time not because of their strengths but because of an ostensible weakness: their relationships with their families of origin were relatively cool. As a general orientation, the irreligious scored significantly lower on the Primary Relationships factor than did the very and somewhat religious, despite the fact that their parents, more often than parents of the very religious, used reasoning as a disciplinary technique (see Table 2bIII). Among rescuers, irreligious rescuers scored significantly lower on the Primary Relationships factor than did somewhat religious rescuers; and among nonrescuers, irreligious nonrescuers scored lower than all other nonrescuer religiosity groups. Yet within the context of a culture that tended toward comparatively more aloof family relationships, irreligious rescuers developed closer relationships than did irreligious nonrescuers, in some measure perhaps due to their perception of parents as less authoritarian (see Table 2bIII).

Given the particularly strong liberalism of the irreligious with respect to outgroups, the above findings suggest that very good beginnings — that is, close family relationships — may not necessarily be critical in determining positive outgroup relationships. Of course, given the fact that all self-reports, particularly about past events, may not necessarily be true, it may be that the irreligious generally had closer family relationships than they reported, and that what they said was more related to a particular cultural image they had learned to value and wanted to project. The same may apply to those groups who reported more positive family relationships: the very religious and the somewhat religious. But this finding is nonetheless a provocative one, suggesting that the primacy of very strong early family relationships in influencing attitudes toward outgroups may not hold among all cultural groups, and that cultural definitions of appropriate relationships with outsiders may be just as important.

Yet the fact that irreligious rescuers, as compared with irreligious non-rescuers, had better relationships with their parents suggests the kinds of benefits that may exist in strong family beginnings. Even in a culture less inclined to give family relationships a high priority, those stronger in this regard may be more inclined toward outgroup altruism. The ability to commit to parents and politics was a distinguishing point for irreligious rescuers as compared with their irreligious counterparts, possibly indicating a stronger generalized readiness to accept obligations on behalf of others.

But relationships with parents do not help explain why Protestant rescuers and bystanders differed in their behaviors, although they do contribute toward understanding why Catholic rescuers and bystanders differed in theirs.

Protestants and Catholics scored similarly on the Primary Relationships factor, and in similar percentages reported family relationships as close and distant as well as shades in between. This occurred despite the fact that Protestants also report that they had been disciplined by parents more often. A somewhat similar pattern occurred among rescuers: Protestant rescuers and Catholic rescuers also scored similarly on the Primary Relationships factor despite the fact that Protestant rescuers also report having been disciplined more often and cooler relationships with their fathers (see Table 3bIII). No significant differences between Protestant rescuers and Protestant bystanders occur on any of the measures included in the Primary Relationships factor. Among Protestants, it appears, the quality of relationships with families of origin does not help clarify why rescuers and nonrescuers differed in their responses to Jews.

The situation is quite different for Catholic rescuers. Compared with Catholic bystanders, they scored significantly higher on the Primary Relationships factor, while Catholic bystanders scored particularly low on this same measure as compared with all other groups. Catholic rescuers had much stronger relationships with their fathers and families generally, while Catholic bystanders, disciplined more often and subjected to physical punishment, had the poorest relationships with their fathers and families generally as compared with all other groups (see Table 3bIII). In this respect they appear to be following a more conventionally accepted pattern; their early experiences apparently were sufficiently harsh so as to foment a lifelong rejection of outsiders. This pattern also helps to explain their views on sharing and mastery.

Sharing

The Sharing factor, the degree to which the culture supported distributing resources for others' welfare, *was the fourth contributor toward predicting rescue* (0.41). Loadings on this measure included: Prosocial Action Orientation (0.82), Social Responsibility Scale (0.80), Empathy Scale (0.73), Personal Integrity as a Child (0.46), Detachment (inverse relationship: −0.45), Community Helping Today (0.34), and Feelings of Similarity to Poor (0.26). High scorers reflected strong empathic feelings and persistence at tasks once begun, a sense of social responsibility, as well as a general valuing of involvement with others as an important way to live.

Rescuers generally were far more marked by a spirit of sharing than were nonrescuers and bystanders (see Table 1aIV). But there were some marked differences among religiosity and denominational groups on this measure.

The very religious generally, as compared with the somewhat religious and the irreligious generally, were more inclined toward sharing: they scored significantly higher than either of these groups on the Sharing factor. The relatively strong predisposition to share among the very religious was apparent even among very religious nonrescuers. They not only did not differ from very religious rescuers on this measure, but evidenced significantly stronger tendencies in this direction than did the somewhat religious and irreligious nonrescuers (see Table 2bIV). A stronger spirit of generosity appears to have been associated with very religious Christians as compared with those less religious.

But such differences evaporated among rescuers: very religious rescuers, moderately religious rescuers, somewhat religious rescuers, and irreligious rescuers reflected a similarly generous spirit. With the exception of the somewhat religious, among whom rescuers scored significantly higher than nonrescuers, all other rescuers did not differ significantly from their nonrescuer counterparts on the Sharing factor. Yet some differences on individual measures favored rescuers as compared with nonrescuers even when no overall Sharing factor difference emerged. As compared with their nonrescuer counterparts, very religious rescuers learned the value of care more often, while irreligious rescuers as well as somewhat religious rescuers placed higher value on personal integrity (see Table 2bIV).

Catholics and Protestants reflected a different pattern. Catholics, as compared with Protestants, expressed a far stronger sharing orientation, a distinction that also characterized Catholic rescuers as compared with Protestant rescuers. But it is Catholic rescuers, rather than Catholic bystanders, who account for this strong showing. Catholic rescuers scored higher than Protestant rescuers on five of the measures associated with Sharing, and as compared with Catholic bystanders, they scored higher on six of the associated measures. Catholic bystanders scored significantly lower than Catholic rescuers on the Sharing factor, including many of its associated measures, while also not differing from Protestant bystanders on the Sharing factor or any of its associated measures. Protestant rescuers, by contrast, did not differ significantly from Protestant bystanders on the Sharing factor or any of its associated measures, with one exception: more often, they report having learned caring values. Protestant bystanders, by contrast, scored lower than all other groups on caring values (see Table 3bIV).

The relatively weak emphasis on the Sharing factor among Protestant rescuers as compared with Catholic rescuers suggests that attitudes and values frequently associated with altruism — strong empathic feelings and persistence at tasks once begun, a sense of social responsibility as well as prizing involvement with others — contribute to outgroup altruistic behavior, but are not necessarily critical to its enactment. Some cultures may be more susceptible to such sentiments; others arrive at outgroup altruistic behaviors through other values and means, including institutional pressures.

Mastery

The Mastery measures formed *two* separate factors, reflecting an External and Internal Mastery Orientation. The *External Mastery Orientation* factor, reflecting the sense of mastery obtained through conformity with external criteria, ranked fifth and inversely with rescue (-0.35). High loadings included Obedience (0.84), Propriety (0.69), and Economic Competence (0.57). The *Internal Mastery Orientation*, reliance on internal sources for control of resources, *ranked sixth as a predictor of rescue* (0.30). Loadings on the Internal Mastery Orientation included Self-Esteem (0.72), Sense of Personal Potency as a Child (0.70), Internal Locus of Control (0.63), and Standing Up for Beliefs before the War (0.35).

Rescuers scored significantly lower than nonrescuers and bystanders on the External Mastery Orientation (Table 1bV). As a general orientation, the somewhat religious appeared to be most inclined in this direction, scoring higher than the very religious and mildly religious on the External Mastery factor. Rescuers at all levels of religiosity — very religious, somewhat religious, mildly religious, and irreligious — scored similarly on this measure, and with the exception of somewhat religious rescuers, they did not differ significantly from their nonrescuer counterparts. Somewhat religious nonrescuers not only scored higher than somewhat religious rescuers on the External Mastery Orientation, but scored highest of all other groups on this measure (Table 3bV).

Among Protestants and Catholics, rescuers and bystanders followed the pattern characteristic of rescuers and bystanders generally. Protestant and Catholic rescuers, as compared with Protestant and Catholic bystanders, scored significantly lower on the External Mastery Orientation. Conversely, Protestant and Catholic bystanders, as compared with their rescuer counterparts, were significantly more externally oriented. As compared with their rescuer counterparts, Protestant and Catholic bystanders were significantly more oriented toward obedience. But Protestant bystanders stand out above all by virtue of their strong external orientation; they scored highest of all groups on the External Mastery factor, focusing more than all other groups on economic competence and on matters of propriety (see Table 3bV).

Concomitant with their weaker inclination to depend on external authorities, rescuers generally as compared with nonrescuers and bystanders scored higher on the Internal Mastery Orientation factor (Table 1bV). But no differences on this factor occurred among any religiosity groups, including rescuers at all levels of religiosity as compared with their nonrescuer counterparts. Yet there is some suggestion of a stronger dependence on internal resources among the very religious and irreligious, both of whom distinguished themselves from the somewhat religious by their greater readiness to stand up for their beliefs, and among irreligious rescuers in particular, who as compared with mildly and very religious rescuers, as well as irreligious nonrescuers, had a stronger sense of self-esteem (Table 2bV).

While there was little difference among religiosity groups in relation to Internal Mastery, differences between Protestants and Catholics were sharper on that factor. Protestants generally, as compared with Catholics generally, had a stronger sense of reliance on their internal resources, an orientation that also distinguished Protestant bystanders as compared with Catholic bystanders. They had much greater confidence in their sense of personal potency: a distinction that characterized not only Protestants generally and Protestant bystanders as compared with their counterparts, but also Protestant rescuers as compared with Catholic rescuers. But Protestant bystanders also stand out by virtue of their self-esteem — higher than all other groups. Catholic bystanders stand out by virtue of a converse inclination. They scored lower than all other groups on the Internal Mastery factor, expressing the weakest sense of an internal locus of control and self-esteem (see Table 3bV). Catholic bystanders appeared to have the least amount of confidence in their internal capacities to find success in the world. It may well be that cultures marked by either too much dependence on external sources or too little confidence in their internal resources are not particularly good candidates for outgroup altruism.

A word of caution as well as several tentative implications follow from the above discussion. These comparisons were made in relation to a particular historical time and, given the limitations of the sample, are not necessarily reflective of these same groups generally either during the period under discussion or today. The purpose in describing them is less to suggest cultural characteristics of particular groups, and more to propose cultural characteristics generally conducive to or inhibitive of outgroup altruism. For graphic illustrations of the findings above as well as those that follow, see Appendix A, Figures 1–9.

The first proposition refers to the order of contributing factors, not unexpected in some ways and perhaps surprising in others. The fact that positive outgroup attitudes and relationships (Outgroup Relationships factor) contributed most to predicting outgroup altruism may not be unexpected; studies of bigotry and prejudice imply just such an association. The idea that openness can be expressed in diverse ways — politically, through personal involvements with outgroup members or simply egalitarian sentiments — but does not necessarily require all of them in order to result in outgroup altruism has perhaps not been emphasized enough.

But the fact that secondary relationships were a close second in order of importance might be unanticipated. The importance of secondary social institutions as interpreters of situations, particularly during crises, and as helping networking sources often tends to be overlooked or underrated. This relationship occupies a very high place here, in both its religious and secular character. While national secondary institutions are consequential, it seems likely that local institutions may be equally if not more important.

The second proposition emerges from consideration of the distribution of factor scores among rescuer groups. The fact that distribution patterns among rescuer groups varied suggests that outgroup altruistic behavior among groups does not necessarily depend on any single factor. For example, despite the fact that positive Outgroup Relationships contributed most to predicting rescue, not all rescuer groups scored similarly on this measure. Protestant rescuers, as compared with Catholic rescuers, scored significantly lower on the Outgroup Relationships factor; they also scored significantly lower than did Catholic rescuers on the Sharing factor. For this group, affiliation with religious and/or secular institutions that supported rescue may have played a more important role.

The third proposition derives from the finding that no single group reflected particular strengths on all factors identified as contributing to outgroup altruism. This suggests that outgroup altruistic behavior among groups does not necessarily depend on group superiority on all factors often associated with outgroup altruism. The irreligious, for example, who scored higher than many others with respect to relationships with outsiders, did not do very well on the Primary Relationships factor; the very religious were more inclined toward Sharing than were some other groups, but their Outgroup Relationships scores were relatively poorer. With no apparent particular cultural strengths inclining them toward outgroup altruism, the somewhat religious appeared to be least inclined in that direction — and indeed the distribution of rescuers in our sample is curvilinear, with the somewhat religious including a smaller proportion of rescuers than the irreligious and very religious. Yet rescuers also emerged from this group.

The fourth proposition is that not all cultures necessarily evolve toward more positive outgroup relationships in the same way. The classical pattern — one often proposed by personality scholars — suggests that acceptance of outsiders often begins in positive early family relationships; trusting and close relationships with parents tends to be associated with trust generally, including positive attitudes toward outsiders. Our data suggest some departure from this pattern in at least one cultural group. In comparison with all other religiosity groups, the irreligious generally claimed having the coolest relationships with their parents, while they also were the most receptive to outgroup relationships.

The final proposition is that outgroup altruistic patterns vary. Profiles of the groups' factor scores discussed here and graphed in Figures 6, 7, 8, and 9 illustrate their heterogeneous approaches. Among religiosity and denominational groups, no rescuer pattern is exactly the same as all others, and no rescuer/nonrescuer/bystander relationship is exactly the same as all others.

Yet something resembling a core shared pattern does occur among rescuers. As a single group, rescuers differ significantly from nonrescuers and bystanders on all summary factors. In almost all groups, as compared with their nonrescuer/bystander counterparts in the same group, rescuers distinguish themselves as significantly stronger on at least one of the summary factors noted above, and in several cases, on more. In all groups, as compared with their nonrescuer/bystander counterparts in the same group, rescuers distinguished themselves on several measures associated with the summary factors. And in all groups, a comparison of the overall Discriminant Function scores shows that among all religiosity and denominational groups, rescuers scored significantly higher than their nonrescuer and/or bystander counterparts in the same group. Apparently, a particular strength in one of the summary factors or their associated measures may be able to compensate for weaknesses in others, propelling a group toward an outgroup altruistic direction even when other relevant propensities appear to be fragile.

8

Culture and Outgroup Altruism

What type of culture is most predisposed toward outgroup altruism? Answers have frequently focused on cultures called "collectivist" and "individualistic."

Collectivist societies — that is, societies in which individuals are strongly bonded and personal identity derives largely from the group — are allegedly most likely to engage in ingroup altruism but are unlikely to behave altruistically toward outsiders, say several social scientists. Interdependent and pressured by cultural norms to help one another and the group, persons in collectivist societies behave altruistically toward each other reasonably often. But the very characteristics that lead to frequent acts of altruism on behalf of cultural cohorts can also lead to strong ethnocentric sentiments and exclusionary behaviors with respect to outgroups. In a world of limited resources, outsiders provoke much anxiety, threatening ingroup members' sense of identity, security, and favored position with bonded colleagues. In fact, say some scholars, the "tighter" the collective — that is, the stronger the bonds among group members — the more hostile its members tend to be toward outsiders.[1]

Individualistic societies — that is, cultures in which bonds among individuals are loose and personal identity is largely independent of others — are allegedly unlikely to engage in outgroup altruism and are much less likely as compared with collectivists even to engage in ingroup altruism. Since identity does not depend on the group, and personal and communal goals frequently diverge, people in individualistic societies are less likely to act on behalf of the public good. While it is true that individualists more often belong to numerous groups representing diverse interests and affiliations, in contrast to collectivist societies where individuals tend to identify with only a few groups largely representing similar interests, their relationships are shallow rather than intense.[2] As a consequence, conventional wisdom favors the view that individualistic cultures are less likely to engage in either form of altruism — ingroup or outgroup.

But is ingroup altruism "real" altruism? No, says Geert Hofstede. Helping cultural cohorts is self-serving, he argues; in fact it is little more than "group worship," leading to the worst types of outgroup excesses. Only outgroup helping merits the label "altruism," he says, and what determines that is neither collectivism nor individualism, but the degree of femininity in a culture.[3] In more feminine societies, social gender roles overlap and both men and women value being tender and concerned with the quality of life.[4]

And is it indeed the case that individualistic cultures are unlikely to engage in any form of altruism? No, says Shalom Schwartz: they just do it for different reasons than do collectivist cultures. Schwartz agrees that altruistic behavior in collectivist cultures is motivated by prescribed norms, the violation of which may result in the loss of group identification. "Autonomous cultures," the term Schwartz uses to describe what others essentially call individualistic cultures, do indeed value the individual as a unique entity, free to express ideas and thoughts as well as feelings. But autonomy is not synonymous with emotional detachment from others, he asserts, nor does it necessarily mean placing personal goals ahead of group goals. Participants in autonomous cultures place high value on egalitarianism, a concept that includes not only equality but also helpfulness, social justice, tolerance of outgroups, and world peace. Contrary to popular thought, they do act prosocially on behalf of the public good and do so voluntarily, out of the learned belief that helping others serves egalitarian values. Schwartz thus proposes that both outgroup and ingroup altruism occur in individualistic societies, and further implies that in either case such behaviors are of a higher moral order since they are freely chosen rather than the results of external pressure.[5]

This study addresses some of these issues, albeit indirectly. One of them concerns outgroup altruism in collectivist and individualistic societies; the other the relationship of egalitarianism to ingroup and outgroup altruism.

Tight collectives, even tight religious collectives, do not inevitably exclude outgroup helping. Many very religious rescuers belonged to tight collectives: the Reformed Church in the Netherlands,[6] women's religious orders,[7] the

Huguenots of Le Chambon,[8] and the priests of Assisi,[9] among others.[10] One reason for their success was the very nature of their "tightness." Tight collectivities had the benefit of "thick" or "dense" social networks; especially trustworthy relatives, friends, and colleagues known to share similar values and attitudes. "Social capital" of this type is particularly advantageous in carrying out subversive or underground activities.[11] Like their counterparts who did not rescue, very religious collectivities who did were highly insulated from the larger society and many knew Jews only in the abstract. But attitudes among very religious rescuer collectivities often favored Jews even while they may have also included common prejudices.[12] Clearly, then, tight collectivities do not necessarily exclude outgroup altruism, but in fact may be forcefully and powerfully oriented toward it. It all depends on the ideology of the group.

But is this altruism in its best? That is, do such efforts, prompted as they are by group pressures — neighbors, friends and authority figures — really qualify as "altruism?" Echoing Hofstede and Schwartz, political scientist Michael Gross argues it does not. He agrees that what he calls "infrastructural variables and micromobilization contexts" — that is, "organization, material support, and supporting social networks" — were absolutely necessary to sustain collective action among rescuers; indeed, he believes that rescues of this sort accounted for more successes than did individual rescues. But external sources, in the form of legitimate and "astute political leadership," mobilized these groups by manipulating information and providing necessary material support. Real altruism, Gross says, is self-motivated and an individual action, not a collective one.[13]

Is Schwartz correct in implying that individualistically oriented societies are inclined toward not only ingroup but also outgroup altruism? And do individualists approach altruism from a higher moral plane than collectivists, as Gross proposes? Our data suggest some tentative responses.

The irreligious most approximate what might be called an individualistically oriented culture. As compared with all other groups, for example, they were most inclined toward loose ties with family and country as well as with religious institutions. Consistent with Schwartz's notion of the value of egalitarianism among individualists, they ranked highest on their receptivity to outsiders. And they, along with the very religious, included a significantly higher percentage of rescuers as compared with the moderately religious. But it is irreligious rescuers, rather than irreligious nonrescuers, who appear most egalitarian in their views. While not significantly different in their overall receptivity to outsiders, irreligious rescuers as compared with irreligious nonrescuers were far more interested in Jews and empathic toward them, and also far more likely to be affiliated with politically inclusive political parties. This suggests that a general sense of egalitarianism does not necessarily extend to all outsider groups but in fact may be particularistic, including some groups and excluding others. Additionally, while the irreligious generally had looser ties with families than did other groups, irreligious rescuers as compared with irreligious nonrescuers claimed stronger family attachments. While egalitarian attitudes are important, acting altruistically on behalf of outgroups may require a particularly inclusive form of egalitarianism, as well as a readiness to commit to others.

Yet to the extent that egalitarianism may be based on the internalized principle of a universally shared humanity, outgroup altruism undertaken in its name may have the higher moral ground than outgroup altruism undertaken because of loyalty to a collective's norm.

But it is not clear just how independent alleged individualists really are. Individual values and personality are never completely autonomous: they are always linked to the culture of which they are a part. Family and political culture, whose values largely converged in relation to the merits of outsiders, strongly influenced irreligious rescuers. They also provided a context for friendships with Jews and such friendships prompted many irreligious rescuers. In that context, it can even be argued that altruism based on personal preference — such as that suggested by friendship — is no more noble than altruism based on notions of religious duty as interpreted by a religious collective.[14]

Moral questions aside, in place of collectivism and individualism, neither of which may adequately assess a cultural predisposition toward outgroup altruism, the concepts *extensive* and *constricted* cultures may be more applicable. In our 1988 study of rescuers, Sam Oliner and I used these terms to describe two types of personalities with different implications for ingroup and outgroup altruism.[15]

Extensive personalities, we said, have a powerful sense of attachment to others and a strong feeling of responsibility for the welfare of others, including those outside their immediate familial or communal circles. A prototypical extensive personality orientation, we proposed, is nurtured in close attachments to family, from whom children learn values of care and generosity, and positive attitudes toward others including outsider groups. Such children in turn develop similar attitudes, judging and forming attachment to others on the basis of affection rather than ethnicity, nationality, or other such bounded parameters. Extensive personalities are thus more likely to engage in both ingroup and outgroup altruism.

Conversely, constricted personalities attach to others weakly and, rather than accepting responsibility for others' welfare, relate to them instrumentally — that is, as potentially useful objects. A prototypical constricted personality orientation, we proposed, is developed in experiences of deprivation, beginning with families of origin. Family relationships are not particularly good and are often characterized by aloof or abusive fathers who, together with mothers, frequently express distrust of others and hostility toward outsiders. Children raised in such environments become more centered on themselves and their own needs, paying scant attention to others. Having learned to "experience the external world as largely peripheral except insofar as it may be instrumentally useful," they reserve their sense of obligation to a small circle from whom they hope to benefit. Anxious to protect their fragile status, they exclude outsiders, not only refusing to accept any sense of responsibility for their welfare but also often prepared to ostracize them so as to ensure their own safety. Constricted personalities are thus unlikely to engage in either ingroup or outgroup altruism.

We proposed the above as prototypical developments, a composite portrait from the significant personality differences distinguishing rescuers from bystanders. We cautioned that in real life, both were rarely found in their pure forms. These same concepts can also be applied to cultures and with the same caveat.[16]

What would an extensive culture look like? Extensive cultures have positive views of outsiders and are characterized by families and secondary institutions — religious and/or secular — that promote egalitarian ideas and broad social responsibility norms. Parental relationships are rooted in affection and intimacy: discipline is reasonable, sometimes experienced as almost imperceptible, and perceived as such by children. Parents teach sharing values — particularly in relation to caring for others — and express their appropriateness not only in relation to family and ingroups, but also in relation to outsiders. Children emerge from such social contexts with a strong sense of internal mastery — that is, ready to take action in the world based on their sense of self-worth and internalized beliefs. They also emerge with a sharing predisposition, ready to accept responsibility for and care for others. Extensive cultures empathize with the distressed and the less privileged, and aspire to be helpful and socially responsible. They reject stereotyping, particularly negative stereotyping, inclining more to understand and credit those disparaged by such views. Besides family, their institutional commitments may vary — they may focus on politics or religion, nation or local community. Whatever these may be, they bring to them a sense of the world as a community and of humanity writ large. Rooted in personal attachments and global ties, they are not only aware of the immediate context of their lives but also sensitive to world events. Such cultures are likely to be responsive to ingroup and outgroup concerns, and act altruistically on behalf of both — even heroically should the need arise.

Constricted cultures, on the other hand, regard outsiders with distrust and are characterized by family and secondary institutions — religious and/or secular — that promote exclusionary ideas and narrow views of social responsibility. Parents incline toward aloof and sometimes abusive discipline — often rationalizing such means as the proper ways of socializing children to their duties. Fathers in particular are prone to such relationships, modeling for their children the arrogant exercise of power in constraining the weak, and thus teaching them to do likewise. Parents thus promote the idea that acquiescence to external powers is the key to success. Parents discourage sharing with others generally and with outsiders particularly, and children learn to view sharing as a means of currying favor and enhancing one's status in the world. Affiliations with secondary institutions — religious and/or secular — are reserved for those that promise status and security by rejecting outsiders. Children in such cultural contexts develop a very different idea of how to garner social resources. More internally fragile, participants socialized in such cultures may develop a very low sense of self-worth or, as a compensatory device, project themselves as overconfident — far more worthy than others.

The same caveat that applies to personalities also applies to these descriptions of cultures. Each of these can be considered an "ideal type" rather than a real world prototype. Cultures that evidence all the attributes and behaviors of extensivity would be as difficult to find as those that evidence all the attributes of constrictedness. No society could exist on altruism alone, even less so on outgroup altruism alone; without some solid measure of individual and group self-interest, survival itself would be jeopardized. But neither could any society exist without some foundation of altruism; without some solid measure of readiness for self-sacrifice on behalf of the group, no social group could last.

But can societies exist without outgroup concern? In this shrunken world, perhaps not even in the short term. The issue is how to find a balance between legitimate self-interest and altruism, including outgroup altruism. Such a balance might be termed what Mariano Grondona calls an "intermediate morality": neither the highest nor the lowest, but seeking one's own well-being while also accepting responsibility for others.[17] Societies that are concerned predominantly with success and achievement risk being out of balance unless they also cultivate a sense of sharing and look with favor toward outgroups. Strong sharing cultures are likely to be more positively oriented toward outsiders, but unless they also have a modicum of mastery in the sense of potency, they may fail to act on behalf of others despite their generally benevolent attitudes. Cultures that do not nurture their young with care are not strong candidates for outgroup altruism; neither are cultures whose dominant social institutions do not support outgroups. Rather than a bipolar distribution, with cultures dominantly belonging to one category or another, extensivity and constricted-ness are better conceptualized as a continuum, with cultures inclining more in one direction or another.

Like the cultural groups studied here, heroic outgroup altruists are likely to constitute only a small percentage of many if not most extant cultural groups. Assessing a culture's propensity for outgroup altruism may require not only comparing one culture with another — that is, intercultural similarities and differences — but also understanding intracultural similarities and differences. Predicting rescue in this study often depended on the significant differences not only among cultures, but between rescuers and others in the same group. Such intragroup differences suggest some capacity to be "different." A weak family attachment may signify little in a culture that is dominantly oriented toward weak family attachments, but a strong family attachment in some group within that same culture may signify a readiness to abandon other cultural norms that do not favor a sense of attachment and connectedness with others. Similarly, a weak sense of personal potency may signify little in a culture that is dominantly oriented toward low personal potency, but a stronger sense of potency in some group within that same culture may signify a particularly strong readiness to act. Deviance from what is cultural-normative can have negative consequences, such as the codes of criminals or terrorists, but it may also have positive consequences.

Can cultures change? They not only can but do. Some beliefs are very resis-tant to change, remaining much the same over generations. Routine ways of thinking and behaving are learned through frequent repetition: since they are also often rewarded, the motivation to modify them is very weak. Old patterns may become so customary and accepted that alternative scenarios can scarcely be envisaged. Habitual behaviors, say Strauss and Quinn, "will always be the behaviors of choice because they are the only familiar and perhaps the only imaginable possibility." But encouragingly they add that cultures are "not bounded, timeless systems of meanings" and they do change.[18] Change can be shallow or cosmetic, in which case regression to old patterns remains a constant possibility. But sometimes cultural change is deep and discontinuous with the old. In most cases, it is also likely to be very slow.

How do cultures change? The core of such an effort is likely to require the development of appropriate norms. Émile Durkheim recognized years ago that the collective, common, and widespread ideas about right and wrong that exist outside of individuals have a controlling effect on their lives; he called them "social facts."[19] Just how consequential cultural norms are in regulating human behavior is a matter of dispute, but no social scientist believes they are without importance. Some ascribe greater importance to the human capacity for autonomous decision making, while others believe that norms regulate most of human behavior.

Elliot Sober and David Wilson belong to the "norms as strong regulators" group. Their survey of cultures around the world persuaded them that "human behavior is very tightly regulated by social norms in most cultures around the world." Culture, they say, "regulates not only the smallest of patterns of behavior and all conceivable activity," but also the most dangerous and life-threatening, including situations in which sacrificing one's life is appropriate. In fact, they say, the regulation "is strong enough to induce participants in that culture to act without hesitation or thought."[20]

As norms can lead to the most ignoble behaviors, so they also inspire the most noble actions. "Most people calibrate their conscience against a level of minimum decency expected of people in their peer group or culture," says Jonathan Glover, and "when the level drifts downward, people can commit horrible crimes with the confidence that comes from knowing that 'everyone does it.'"[21] Nazi Germany is an apt example of this observation. But the converse also holds. When the level of what is considered human decency ascends, people can do marvelous deeds with the same confidence, knowing that "everyone does it." This appears to describe what happened in some of the rescue communities noted here and, as depicted by Philip Hallie, is exactly what happened in Le Chambon, where members of this French Huguenot community opened their doors to Jews as a self-understood matter.[22] This does not mean, however, that individual personality does not matter. On some level, individuals retain their autonomy and personal choices — even when violation of accepted norms invites strong punishment — provided of course that they can even envision alternative behaviors. Culture, after all, does not determine personality, but it does strongly influence it.

How can norms change? Cultural leaders — religious, political, and institutional leaders of all types — need to authorize change by articulating norms clearly. Norms tend to be stated as abstractions; translating them into specific rules is problematic. "Love your neighbor," for example, is a maxim many religious groups espouse. This laudable precept poses two immediate problems. One relates to the word "love." Just exactly what does love require? Love for some means unconditional acceptance of others, without regard for their behavior; for others it can include very harsh measures ostensibly intended for the other's welfare. The concept "neighbor" is equally troublesome. Confined to family alone for some, it may also include "clan" or ethnic, religious, or national community for others. On rare occasions, it may also include certain outgroups but not others; more rarely, it may extend to the whole of the human and nonhuman world.

But more than clearly articulated and specific norms are needed to change culture. As the anthropologist Clifford Geertz emphasizes, culture is all about "meaning," and "meaning is socially constructed."[23] Meaning — an interpretation of life and a worldview — does not arise from within the mind of a single person, says Geertz. Rather, meaning develops from the social context — that is, through regularly interacting networks in which people learn to understand one another's language, gestures, myths, scripts, feelings, rituals, visual objects, music, and historical memories, among other signs and symbols, and arrive at some shared interpretation of what the world is about. According to Geertz, "meaning, in the form of interpretable signs — sounds, images, feelings, artifacts, gestures — comes to exist only within language games, communities of discourse, intersubjective systems of reference, ways of worldmaking; that it arises within the frame of concrete social interaction in which something is a something for you and a me, and not in some secret grotto in the head; and it is through and through historical, hammered out in the flow of events."[24]

Norms have to be incorporated into the cultural life of the group, and that requires interacting networks — sometimes referred to as communities of discourse or communities of memory — who adapt and exchange appropriate language, gestures, standards of evaluations and artifacts among other symbols and signs.[25] If changing culture requires changing the meaning of interpretable signs as networks interact routinely, it is most likely to be successful if based on consciously retrieving and elaborating on relevant historical events and life experiences.

If cultural change is directed to embrace outsiders, it is also likely to require attention to particular social processes. A case in point is Hitler's Germany, which within a decade of his ascent to power witnessed a remarkably swift and radical cultural change. An illustrative example of how this occurred in one agency is described by George Browder in his study of Nazi Germany's security forces — the Gestapo (Geheime Staatspolizei — political police or secret police), the SS (Schutzstaffel — auxiliary police), Sipo (Sicherheitspolizei — security police), Kripo (Kriminalpolizei — regular detectives), and SD (Sicherheitsdienst — SS security office). A police force of ordinary men in pre-Nazi Germany, they quickly evolved into what Browder calls "Hitler's enforcers," becoming involved in mass murder and "the worst horrors of the Third Reich." Browder offers a detailed portrait of how this occurred.[26]

Most participants in the security offices of pre-Nazi Germany, says Browder, began as "ordinary men of varied dispositions"; professionals whose personalities were not significantly different from the population at large. Only a minority could be described as brutally inclined or viciously antisemitic, and some were even "idealistic," persuaded that they were serving their country in some transcendent way. In fact, he believes that "most of these men would probably have served similar agencies among the western allied powers just as well as their counterparts actually did, and without any infamy."[27] Rather than villains, he claims, they would have become our heroes.

Just how did they become transformed from a professional police force to masters of brutality? Applying and extending Herbert Kelman's theoretical model,[28] Browder demonstrates how four processes worked to effect the unthinkable:

1. *Authorization:* Sanctions by legitimately recognized officials encouraging participants to feel that ordinary moral considerations do not apply
2. *Routinization:* The incorporation of behaviors as normative and habitual routines, largely eliminating the need to think about decisions or consider any moral crises that might be involved
3. *Dehumanization:* A process that denies the humanity of victims in preparation for their brutalization
4. *Bolstering:* A supporting group system to help participants "cope with any moral or ethical dissonance" by reinforcing conformity to the new standards and assuring them of the virtue of the new behaviors

These processes, incorporated into the habitual routines of daily work, coupled with a bureaucratic structure that fragmented tasks so that means and ends were rarely considered, and largely removed from actual contact with the victims, rendered personal feelings irrelevant.

While not absolving participants of personal culpability and responsibility, Browder sees this as largely a matter of blind "entrapment" into social roles. With rare exceptions, most of these same men, along with most Germans, returned to their pre-war roles after the war ended, becoming once again law-abiding and civil citizens. The rapidity with which the change toward normality occurred was also quite astonishing. Was Nazi culture then a shallow phenomenon, an "aberration" as some have suggested, or is it the case that the current cultural milieu is merely harboring the next wave of violence? Unlike their parents, many second- and third-generation Germans are confronting their past, offering hope for the future.

The story of these Nazi security officers raises a provocative question. If people in given cultural contexts can be entrapped into evil roles, can they also be entrapped into altruistic ones? It seems plausible that the very same social processes identified by Kelman and described by Browder, but serving different objectives, can help facilitate it. Whereas *authorization* in Nazi Germany required participants to discard their moral principles with respect to Jews, Gypsies, and other outsiders, authorization in the service of outgroup altruism would explicitly affirm norms accepting outsiders' moral rights and entitlements. Under the Nazi regime, *routinization* invited habitual procedures that became progressively more brutal, while routinization in the service of outgroup altruism would facilitate humane treatment of outsiders as a habitual response in relation to small as well as more consequential decisions. Whereas under the Nazi regime the objective was dehumanization of the other, *humanization* would be the objective in a culture designed to service outgroup altruism. *Bolstering,* the group support system that helped co-brutalizers dispense with moral problems, in the service of outgroup altruism would mean encouraging groups to support and reinforce altruistic behaviors in the face of doubt or skepticism.

These four processes largely converge with notions of cultural change implied by Geertz, among others. Although authorization may come from leaders, change focuses on the social context. Kelman's processes require interacting networks who meet regularly, and among whom new meanings begin to arise by modifying language, rituals, art, and music, as well as other signs and symbols. As participants learn new interpretations and expectations, new feelings and motivations can direct new kinds of behavior.

A similar spirit characterizes the social processes that I and Sam Oliner called "caring," and which we proposed should infuse social institutions generally. In times of peace but particularly in times of crises, people tend to depend on the values, beliefs, and relationships they already have. In uncertain circumstances, reliance on the familiar and the trusted appear to be the best way to restore some semblance of order, predictability, and meaning in their lives. Traditional cultural leaders play a vital role,[29] but so do the learned routines governing social institutions — family, as well as religious, political, and business institutions — under more normal circumstances. Should such institutions incorporate some elements of care in their habitual behaviors, this may well abort tyranny before it becomes a political reality.

"Care" needs to encompass attachment to people who exist in the immediate context, we suggested, as well as to diverse others. We proposed eight social processes that can serve varied institutions interested in infusing care into their social relationships. The first four focus on attaching processes with people in immediate settings. They include opportunities for:

1. *Bonding:* Forming a sense of community with others
2. *Empathizing:* Understanding others' feelings
3. *Learning caring norms:* Finding out what caring norms might be
4. *Practicing care and assuming personal responsibility:* Actually participating in caring activities

The second set of four processes is intended to include diverse others. They include opportunities for:

5. *Diversifying:* Making an intentional effort to interact with different types of people in a collegial way
6. *Networking:* Learning how to develop shared objectives with different groups of people
7. *Resolving conflicts:* Learning and implementing conflict resolution strategies
8. *Establishing global connections:* Linking the here and now with people and places far and near in the service of care

Such behaviors, we proposed, can help modify the culture of the institutions in which we live our normal lives, and can be instituted by ordinary people from inside or outside the institution, and from the top as well as the bottom.[30]

"Care" and "altruism," as we have used these terms, are similar but not identical. Care, like altruism, requires "assuming personal responsibility for others' welfare," but with respect to cost, a minimalist position is sufficient. Altruism implies high risks or great personal sacrifices; care does not require either. Nor does care require outgroup helping, although the social processes we proposed were directed toward both ingroups and outgroups. Altruism as generally conceptualized may also be directed toward ingroups or outgroups, although some argue that it be reserved for outgroup helping only.

The object of the caring processes we proposed is to create a caring culture within social institutions. The importance of culture cannot be overestimated, for as Geertz points out, people do not make their decisions entirely out of their own thinking and impulses — they are strongly influenced by the social context, although not determined by it. Individuals whose personality predispositions may not necessarily be inclined toward outgroup benevolence may nonetheless make considerable sacrifices on behalf of outsiders under the right cultural conditions.

A culture likely to predispose individuals toward outgroup altruism is inclined to view that outgroup positively, includes primary and secondary social institutions that support similar values, is inclined toward sharing resources with others, and is more oriented toward internal principles rather than compliance with external authorities. The fact that positive outgroup attitudes and relationships contributed most to predicting outgroup altruism in this study is not unexpected; many scholars of outgroup altruism emphasize this point. The idea that openness can be expressed in diverse ways — politically, through personal involvements or simply egalitarian sentiments — but does not necessarily require all of them to result in outgroup altruism has perhaps not been emphasized enough. But the fact that secondary relationships were a close second in order of importance might be unanticipated. The importance of secondary social institutions as interpreters of situations and networking opportunities, particularly during crises, often tends to be overlooked or underrated. It occupies a very high place here, both in its religious and secular character. While positive views toward outsiders contributed most to rescue and supportive secondary institutions ranked second, the paths toward outgroup altruism varied. None of the rescuer groups studied here — very religious, moderately religious, or irreligious, Protestants or Catholics — reflected all the above strengths.

Can such inclinations alter the course of potential destruction as we have come to know it? It may not do much to alter the behavior of potential perpetrators, but it may help avoid the bystander syndrome.[31] The lesson of the Holocaust, says Zygmunt Bauman, is that given a situation that makes good choices very costly, too many people choose what looks rational rather than moral. Evil then proceeds on its dirty path: "Hoping that most people most of the time will refrain from doing rash, reckless things. . . . Evil needs neither enthusiastic followers nor an applauding audience — the instinct of self-preservation will do, encouraged by the comforting thought that it is not my turn yet, thank God: by lying low, I can still escape."[32] Institutions that incorporate care routinely and inclusively — families, religious groups, workplaces, and other associations — and cultures that focus on outgroup altruism values may help people recognize and abort the evil before it spreads.

Highly self-motivated individuals acting with minimal attention to the culture of which they are a part and out of largely independent judgments do exist, but they are few in number. People responding to others in the spirit of love, as the philosopher Emmanuel Levinas would have it — "the incessant watching over the other," where "not only am I more responsible than the other but I am even responsible for everyone else's responsibility" — are probably rarer still.[33] Yet apparent altruistic responses to others, including outsiders, do occur, and probably more often than most acknowledge but not necessarily out of such dispositions.

Some conceptions of altruism insist that motives are the primary distinguishing element of true altruism, and that only motivations directed toward another's welfare as the ultimate concern meet this criterion. This disqualifies an apparent altruistic behavior — even a high-risk behavior — motivated by conformity to cultural norms or routines, even if the consequences for the victims are indistinguishable from the nobler variety. Rather than dismissing such behavior as little more than compliance based on pressure from others or fear of group disapproval — in other words, little more than another form of self-centeredness — some may prefer to call this "consequential altruism."

The events of September 11, 2001, when more than three thousand persons were murdered in New York's Twin Towers, Washington D.C.'s Pentagon, and in the four airplanes that carried the responsible terrorists, offer a glimpse of the ambiguity of motives as well as what might have been the results of consequential altruism. The heroes of that day were many: the firefighters, police, and medical personnel who went far beyond their duty in doing their best to rescue people, many at the cost of their lives, as well as the untold numbers of ordinary people who also died in similar attempts. Editorializing on these individuals a year later, the *New York Times* wrote:

> Whatever they did they almost certainly did with powerful feelings, caught as they were in a cataclysm. They acted with emotions that can't really be named, emotions that clarified their actions and made their heroism seem inevitable to us in the aftermath — although heroism, by definition, is never inevitable. . . . But we'll never know how many selfless acts were committed in the interval between the first death and the last — in the stairwells of the World Trade Center, the halls of the Pentagon, the aisles of the four airliners — any more than we'll know whose nerve gave out or whose emotions paralyzed them that morning, who might have acted but couldn't.[34]

Were these behaviors entirely dependent on emotions of the moment? And were they entirely selfless? To what degree can they be attributed to habits emerging out of learned cultural values and norms routinely governing the social institutions of which they were a part — their professional occupational cultures, religious or political cultures, or simply the political culture of American society? While we will never know the answers to these questions, one thing is certain: many were rescued, whatever the motives of the rescuers.

Consequential altruism is altruistic inasmuch as it benefits the other, but it may be the result of unknown or diverse motives. While cultures may strive to cultivate more exalted motives, consequential altruism may be the highest normative level most cultures can reach, and in terms of its effect, it may reach the broadest numbers of people. Although it is unlikely to make the need for higher-level altruism obsolete, a world in which altruistic behavioral norms have a prominent place seems not at all a bad place to live, provided of course that such norms include outsiders as well as insiders.

Appendix A
Methodology

My purpose here was to explore the relationship between religious culture and outgroup altruism and, more specifically, the relationship between altruistically associated values and attitudes of Christian participants in Western and Eastern Europe and the rescue of Jews during the period of the Holocaust. Two broad questions guided the study: (1) How did levels of religiosity — very religious, moderately religious, and irreligious — relate to rescue? More specifically, (a) what altruistically associated values and attitudes distinguished religious rescuers from less religious rescuers, and (b) how did very religious, moderately religious, and irreligious rescuers differ from each other and from their nonrescuer/bystander counterparts? (2) How did Catholics and Protestants approach rescue? More specifically, what altruistically associated values and attitudes distinguished Catholic and Protestant rescuers from each other and from their similarly religiously affiliated nonrescuer/bystander counterparts?

The Sample

The sample includes 510 persons living in several countries in Nazi-occupied Europe: 346 rescuers and 164 nonrescuers. Nonrescuers included 97 bystanders and 67

Note: For more details on the sample, questionnaire, and collection of data, see Samuel P. Oliner and Pearl M. Oliner, *The Altruistic Personality: Rescuers of Jews in Nazi Europe* (Free Press, 1988).

actives. Most of the respondents are from Poland, Germany, France, and Holland, but respondents from Italy, Denmark, Belgium, and Norway are also included. Most still lived in their native countries at the time we interviewed them; some had immigrated to Canada and the United States.

Approximately 95 percent of rescuers were authenticated as such by Yad Vashem. Based on interviews with rescued survivors, and using criteria similar to those established by Yad Vashem, the Altruistic Personality and Prosocial Behavior Institute at Humboldt State University identified an additional 5 percent.

Yad Vashem is Israel's memorial to the victims of the Holocaust. Part of its charge is to honor those who risked their lives to rescue Jews. To qualify as an honoree, the rescued survivor (or friends or relatives) needs to submit evidence of the deed to a Yad Vashem–appointed commission of eighteen members. In addition to examining submitted documents, the commission conducts interviews. Selections are made very carefully and take considerable time. In 1988, the time of our original study, Yad Vashem had identified approximately 6,000 rescuers. As of 2002, that number had increased to more than 19,000.[1] Three overriding criteria determine selection: the rescuer had to be motivated by humanitarian considerations only, risked his or her own life, and received no remuneration of any kind for his or her act.

Yad Vashem's criteria for identifying rescuers thus largely converged with those used by the Altruistic Behavior and Prosocial Behavior Institute to define altruism. "An altruistic act of rescue," as Sam Oliner and I wrote in 1988, "(1) involved a high risk to the actors, (2) was accompanied by no external rewards, (3) was voluntary, and (4) had to be directed toward helping a Jewish person."[2]

We cannot claim that our sample is representative of the total population of rescuers. The exact number of rescuers is not yet known and may well never be known. Not all rescued survivors have submitted the names of their rescuers to Yad Vashem; some because they do not know of Yad Vashem or its work, others because of other reasons including the fact that they may be unaware of the process or how to obtain the necessary papers. Since simply learning to live with some semblance of normality after the war sapped their energies, many lacked the motivation; still others died. Yad Vashem itself has been unable to keep up with all its work because the staff is small, the list of applicants long, and the process of authentication cumbersome.

The purpose of our 1988 research was to study rescuers, but in order to examine how specific factors might distinguish rescuers from others we included a comparison group of nonrescuers. Nonrescuers include people not identified as rescuers but who lived in the same countries during the same period as rescuers. During the course of the interviews, an important difference emerged among respondents in this group in response to the question of whether they had done anything out of the ordinary during the war to help others or to resist the Nazis. Of the 164 nonrescuers, 67 responded affirmatively, claiming they had participated in resistance activities or helped Jews. While we had no reason to doubt these claims but since we had no independent verification of these activities, we called this group "actives." We called the 97 respondents who said they had done nothing to help anyone during the war "bystanders." Depending on sizes of samples, statistical comparisons included here sometimes include rescuers and all nonrescuers (that is, "actives" and "bystanders") as well as rescuers and bystanders only. As with rescuers, we cannot claim that the nonrescuer sample constitutes a representative group.

The measure we used to assess level of religiosity was based on respondents' self-categorization as "very religious," "somewhat religious," "not very religious," or "not at all religious." For most of our respondents, we had three such measures relating to different time periods: during childhood, before the war, and at the time of the interview. Ultimately, however, we chose the childhood measure; a decision based on pragmatic considerations. While the majority of our interviewees had responded to all three of these questions, the interviews we used with earlier respondents included only the childhood measure. Rather than excluding these respondents, we decided to use the same measure for the entire sample. While the degree of religiosity varied over the years — some individuals who were very religious in their youth became less so with advancing years, while the reverse was true for others — overall there was a strong significant multiple correlation between the degree of youthful religiosity and that of later years.[3]

Using the above criteria, our religiosity sample included 504 respondents: 341 rescuers and 163 nonrescuers. Since bystander sample sizes were small, we used the larger sample sizes of nonrescuers for statistical comparisons. The 504 religiosity sample included 150 very religious, 190 somewhat religious, 106 mildly religious, and 58 irreligious respondents. The respondents who rated themselves as "very," "somewhat," "not very," and "not at all" religious are herein referred to as "very," "somewhat," "mildly," and "irreligious" rescuers. The 341 rescuers included 111 very religious, 117 somewhat religious, 71 mildly religious, and 42 irreligious respondents. The 163 nonrescuers included 39 very religious, 73 somewhat religious, 35 mildly religious, and 16 irreligious respondents. Rescuers and nonrescuers did not differ significantly in their average level of religiosity.

With respect to religious denomination, respondents who claimed an affiliation with a Protestant or Catholic group while growing up were included in the analyses involving religious denomination; those who claimed another affiliation or no affiliation during this period were omitted from these analyses. Only a very few later changed or dropped their affiliation; several maintained it even when they claimed to have become irreligious. Of the total of 510 respondents, 183 were Protestants, 292 were Catholics, 7 reported having another affiliation, and 28 reported having no religious affiliation in their youth. The 183 Protestant respondents included 137 rescuers, 14 actives, and 32 bystanders. The 292 Catholic respondents included 181 rescuers, 50 actives, and 61 bystanders. Since bystander groups were sufficiently proportionally equivalent to allow for statistical comparisons, we included bystanders in comparing Protestants and Catholics but omitted the active nonrescuers. The final religious denominational sample thus included 411 respondents: 137 Protestant rescuers and 32 Protestant bystanders, and 181 Catholic rescuers and 61 Catholic bystanders.

The Questionnaire

The questionnaire consisted of approximately 450 items; 75 percent of which were forced choice, the remainder open-ended. In addition, each respondent was asked to describe his or her wartime activities in detail. The questionnaire administered to nonrescuers was much the same as that given to rescuers, except that instead of being asked to describe their rescue activity and its setting, the nonrescuers were asked to describe their particular activities and lives during the war.

Respected academicians in the corresponding countries trained and supervised interviewers. Interviews, conducted in the native language of the respondents, were taped. They commonly lasted several hours. They were subsequently translated into English, transcribed, coded, and analyzed; analyses were both qualitative and quantitative in character.

Coding and Analysis

The 1988 study included all items from the questionnaire. For the purpose of this study, only those variables that appeared to relate to core conceptual categories were selected. The five selected core conceptual categories were derived largely from social scientists whose work appeared to have the most direct connection to our own, and also appeared to be most relevant in predicting outgroup altruism. These core categories constituted five summary factors, as described below. A more exact description of each of the summary factors and their associated variables is given in Table 8.

The first summary factor, Outgroup Relationships and its sixteen associated measures, was intended to assess the respondents' types of relationships with outsider groups. It includes attitudes toward and relationships with outgroup members, where outgroups include others having a different religious or ethnic status, and particularly focused on Jews. Positive values toward outgroups are commonly associated with outgroup altruism.

The second summary factor, the Secondary Relationships summary factor and its eight associated measures, assesses the respondents' types of secondary relationships. It includes respondents' religious and secular ties, the latter including affiliations with political parties and resistance groups, as well as identification with the national community. The influence of supportive secondary institutions on altruistic behavior, including outgroup altruism, has not been investigated by social scientists as often as other variables.

The third summary factor, the Primary Relationships summary factor and its eleven associated measures, concentrates primarily on assessing respondents' feelings about their families of origin but also includes other personal relationships. Positive relationships with families of origin are also often associated with altruism.

The fourth summary factor, the Sharing summary factor and its ten associated measures, assesses the degree to which respondents in each group supported values encouraging the distribution of resources—social and material—for others' welfare. Feelings of empathy, particularly toward others' pain, as well as a sense of care, social responsibility, and personal integrity, are commonly associated with altruism.

I am indebted to John Tropman, director of the Catholic Ethic Project, who developed the concept "sharing" in describing core Catholic values. While the spirit in which it is used here is essentially similar to his, it is not necessarily defined in exactly the same way.[4] The concept "prosocial," often used by psychologists and others to describe positive social behaviors, most approximates "sharing"; it includes many of the same individual variables identified above. But prosocial behaviors may also include many positive social behaviors that, although worthy, are not necessarily focused on sharing—for example, appropriate attire, courtesy, honesty.

The fifth summary factor, Mastery Orientation, and its seven associated measures, was intended to assess the means the culture encouraged to achieve power and control. It includes an External Mastery Orientation (with three associated measures) and an Internal Mastery Orientation (with four associated measures). An External Mastery Orientation reflects a tendency to achieve mastery through compliance with external criteria. An Internal Mastery Orientation reflects a tendency to achieve mastery through dependence on one's internal resources. Altruism is often associated with a rejection of an external orientation in favor of an internal one.

The Mastery construct appears largely similar to Schwartz's "mastery" conception,[5] and Bakan's[6] and Wiggins's "agency" construct,[7] but is not entirely congruent with any of the foregoing. Mastery values, says Schwartz, "emphasize active mastery of the social environment through self-assertion";[8] values he found associated with it include being successful, ambitious, independent, daring, capable, and choosing one's own goals. It also appeared to be similar to the concept "agency" as originally proposed by Bakan and later further developed by Wiggins. Mastery, says Wiggins, "is manifest in strivings for mastery and power," and includes assertion and extroversion.[9] Individualism appears to be a critical component of such conceptions of mastery, a point that Wiggins in particular emphasizes: "the condition of being a differentiated individual" is its core.

As conceptualized here, the "condition of being a differentiated individual" is not essential for Mastery; influence and control rather than self-differentiation are more central to our view of Mastery. In that sense, Mastery may be achieved through self-differentiation—an individualistic approach—or through conformity and compliance with powerful others.[10] The critical distinction between these two conceptions rests on whether Mastery is sought through an internal power source or through an external power source.

Data Collection

An international team of selected social scientists helped choose interviewees, and helped train as well as supervise interviewers. They included Samuel P. Oliner (professor of sociology at Humboldt State University in the United States, executive director of the Altruistic Personality Research Project, and author of several books and articles on the subject of altruism), Professor Janusz Reykowski (internationally known social psychologist at the Polish Academy of Science who has written broadly on the subject of altruism), Dr. Zuzanna Smolenski (a child development specialist also at the Polish Academy of Science), Professor Jürgen Falter (political scientist at the Freie Universität in Berlin and a specialist in the rise of Nazism), Professor André Kaspi (a historian and international relations expert at the Sorbonne), Professor Richard Van Dyck (a psychiatrist at the University of Ledien), Dr. Michele Sarfatti and Professor Luisella Mortara Ottolenghi (both historians at the Centro di Documentazione Ebraica Contemporanea in Milan), and Susan Schwartz (a clinical psychologist and marriage, family, and child counselor in Oslo).

Almost all the interviews took place between 1980 and 1988; a few occurred thereafter. Most interviews occurred in the countries where interviewees lived during the war, and most were conducted in their native languages. All questionnaires had been appropriately translated so as to make this possible. A few interviews took place in the United States and Canada, where some interviewees had immigrated after the war. Completed taped interviews were sent to the headquarters of the Altruistic Personality Project at Humboldt State University, where Sam Oliner coordinated and monitored their translation and transcription. Most translators shared the native language of the interviewee but had lived in the United States for several years and thus had considerable proficiency in English as well.

Coding and Analysis

We included both quantitative and qualitative methods in our analyses. Responses to forced-choice questions were coded numerically. Verbal responses to open-ended questions were coded into response categories. The direction of coding for ordinally scaled items gave higher number codes for responses indicating more of the variable.

First-order factor analyses, using principal-components factor analysis with varimax orthogonal rotation, were conducted on selected groups of items that related to similar topics, in order to group related items into factor scales. Standardized factor scores were created for each respondent on each of the resulting factors.

The variables and factors were then arranged into five categories of measures reflecting Outgroup Relationships, Secondary Relationships, Primary Relationships, Sharing, and Mastery. Second-order factor analyses were then conducted on the measures within each category to obtain summary factors for each category. The primary principal-component factor was used to summarize the measures within each of the categories, with the exception of the Mastery category. The measures in the Mastery category split into two separate orthogonal factors, which reflected Internal and External Mastery orientations.

A discriminant analysis was then conducted to investigate the six summary factors as predictors of rescuer versus bystander status. The discriminant analysis also combined the summary factors to obtain a discriminant function that best distinguished rescuers from bystanders. Standardized discriminant function scores were created for each respondent.

Groups were compared on each of the measures and factors using two-way analysis of covariance while statistically controlling for gender and age. For the religiosity groups, rescuers and nonrescuers in the four religiosity levels were compared on each of the measures using Duncan post hoc pairwise comparisons following two-way 2 × 4 analysis of covariance. The 2 × 4 analysis of covariance analyzed variation in scores among the two rescuer status groups (rescuers and nonrescuers) and the four religiosity levels (very, somewhat, mildly, and irreligious) while statistically controlling for gender and age. For the religious affiliation groups, Catholic and Protestant rescuers and bystanders were compared on each of the measures using Duncan post hoc pairwise comparisons following two-way 2 × 3 analysis of covariance. The 2 × 3 analysis of covariance analyzed variation in scores among the two religious affiliations (Catholic and Protestant) and three rescuer status groups (rescuers, actives, and bystanders) while statistically controlling for gender and age.

Limitations

We subjected our statistical procedures to rigorous requirements and careful scrutiny, allowing us to speak with considerable confidence about our findings. Yet despite the care we gave to our methodology and analytical procedures, we need to acknowledge limitations.

1. Our sample is not random, and we cannot determine to what extent it may be representative of the populations under consideration. As a consequence, the findings are not fully generalizable. Yet since many of our results are consistent with those of other studies, primarily those done in recent years in the United States, it seems safe to suggest that our findings appear to go beyond a limited historical time and space.

2. Retrospective research — that is, research done after the fact — is usually suspect on the grounds that respondents are not necessarily the same people they were at the time of their decisions. Since in this case respondents were interviewed more than thirty years after the end of World War II, a strong basis for questioning interview responses exists. Research suggests, however, that people tend to recall early events in their lives more accurately than they do later ones, particularly those related to traumas. Additionally, many core personality items tend to remain fairly stable over time.

3. The fact that rescuer interviewees knew they were chosen because they were rescuers might have resulted in a "halo effect." "Putting on a good face" for interviewers is a constant peril in survey research; it is a particular temptation for those who have already been identified as possessing some strong virtue. Nonrescuers, too, might have recognized at some point during the interview that an uncommon number of questions focused on Jews and may also have wanted to present the best image of themselves. Further compounding such possible distortions is the fact that

both rescuers and nonrescuers received a considerable amount of public attention during the years preceding the interviews. Nonetheless, because interviews were commonly extended over several hours, and some critical questions were asked more than once during that time, it was difficult for most to sustain an inauthentic posture for too long. In addition, while interviews do not necessarily tell us what people really believe or the values they hold, as Claudia Strauss and Naomi Quinn remind us, they can tell us what they take for granted and what they see as contestable.[11]

4. Objection might be made regarding the use of personality measures to assess intercultural differences. Hofstede, for example, argues that personality items are appropriate for making intracultural comparisons only and are not valid for making cross-cultural comparisons. Triandis and Wiggins, on the other hand, imply that personality dimensions appropriate for making intracultural comparisons are also appropriate for making intercultural comparisons.[12]

Although these limitations suggest reasons for caution, all research of this nature has its weaknesses. Statistical correlations at best can only suggest relationships and probabilities. Laboratory experiments would overcome several of the above problems and more directly address causation, but clearly they would be impossible to conduct in this context. And laboratory experiments have their own limitations, among which removal from "real-life" situations is primary. To its credit, a study such as this one captures the authenticity, intensity, and complexity associated with real life-and-death situations and behaviors.

Appendix B

Table 1a. Rescuer, Nonrescuer, and Bystander Group Comparisons
Results of Duncan post hoc comparisons following analysis of variance comparing groups on each variable, indicating significant group differences at the 0.05 level

Variable	A Rescuer vs. Nonrescuer	B Rescuer vs. Bystander
DISCRIMINANT FUNCTION	R > N	R > B
I. OUTGROUP RELATIONSHIPS		
Outgroup Relationships Factor	R > N	R > B
A. Feelings of Similarity to Outsiders		
1. Feelings of Similarity to Gypsies	R > N	R > B
2. Feelings of Similarity to Jews	R > N	R > B
3. Feelings of Similarity to Nazis	n	R < B
4. Feelings of Similarity to Other Religious Denomination	n	n
5. Feelings of Similarity to Turks	n	n

Table 1a. Continued

Variable	A Rescuer vs. Nonrescuer	B Rescuer vs. Bystander
B. Jews		
1. Early Awareness of Nazi Intentions	R > N	R > B
2. Empathy for Jews	R > N	R > B
3. Jewish Friends	R > N	R > B
4. Jewish Presence		
a. Jews in Neighborhood	n	n
b. Jews at School	n	n
5. Parental Values about Jews		
a. Negative Stereotypes	R < N	R < B
b. Positive Stereotypes	R > N	n
c. Stereotypes	n	R < B
d. Talked about Jews	R > N	n
C. Political Party Inclusiveness	R > N	R > B
D. Variety of Friends	R > N	R > B
II. SECONDARY RELATIONSHIPS		
Religious Secondary Relationships Factor	n	n
Secular Secondary Relationships Factor	R > N	R > B
A. Religious Ties		
1. Feelings of Similarity to Own Religious Denomination	n	n
2. Religiosity	n	n
B. Secular Ties		
1. Friendliness of Neighbors	n	n
2. Patriotism		
a. Defending Country before War	n	n
b. Patriotism Growing Up	n	n
3. Political Party Membership	R > N	R > B
4. Resistance Groups	n	n
a. Family Members Belonged	R > N	R > B
b. Self Belonged	R > N	R > B

R = rescuer; N = nonrescuer; B = bystander; n = not significant.
See Table 8 for the definition and construction of variables listed in the same order.

Table 1b. Rescuer, Nonrescuer, and Bystander Group Comparisons
Results of Duncan post hoc comparisons following analysis of variance comparing
groups on each variable, indicating significant group differences at the 0.05 level

Variable	A Rescuer vs. Nonrescuer	B Rescuer vs. Bystander
III. PRIMARY RELATIONSHIPS		
Primary Relationships Factor	R > N	R > B
A. Close Friends Growing Up	n	n
B. Families of Origin		
1. Closeness to Father	R > N	R > B
2. Closeness to Mother	R > N	n
3. Family Closeness	R > N	R > B
C. Parental Discipline		
1. Ever Disciplined	n	n
2. Type of Discipline		
a. Authoritarian	n	n
b. Chores	n	n
c. Physical	n	R < B
d. Reasoning	n	n
D. Personal Helping Today	n	n
E. Relatives in Community	n	n
IV. SHARING		
Sharing Factor	R > N	R > B
A. Care	R > N	R > B
B. Community Helping Today	R > N	R > B
C. Detachment	n	n
D. Empathy	n	n
E. Equity		
1. Church Valuing of Equity	n	n
2. Parental Valuing of Equity	n	n
F. Feelings of Similarity to Poor	n	R > B
G. Personal Integrity	R > N	R > B
H. Prosocial Action Orientation	n	R > B
I. Social Responsibility	R > N	R > B

Table 1b. Continued

Variable	A Rescuer vs. Nonrescuer	B Rescuer vs. Bystander
V. MASTERY		
External Mastery Factor	R < N	R < B
A. External Mastery		
1. Economic Competence	n	n
2. Obedience	R < N	R < B
3. Propriety	n	n
Internal Mastery Factor	R > N	R > B
B. Internal Mastery		
1. Internal Locus of Control	n	R > B
2. Personal Potency	R > N	n
3. Self-Esteem Scale	n	n
4. Stand Up for Beliefs	R > N	R > B

R = rescuer; N = nonrescuer; B = bystander; n = not significant.
See Table 8 for the definition and construction of variables listed in the same order.

Table 2a. Religiosity Cell and Group Comparisons
Results of Duncan post hoc comparisons following analysis of variance comparing groups on each variable, indicating significant group differences at the 0.05 level

Variable	A: 1 vs. 2 vs. 3 vs. 4	B: R1 vs. R2 vs. R3 vs. R4	C: N1 vs. N2 vs. N3 vs. N4	D: R1 vs. N1	E: R2 vs. N2	F: R3 vs. N3	G: R4 vs. N4	I: Interaction
DISCRIMINANT FUNCTION	n	n	n	R1 > N1	R2 > N2	R3 > N3	R4 > N4	n
I. OUTGROUP RELATIONSHIPS								
Outgroup Relationships Factor	1 > 3	n	n	n	R2 > N2	R3 > N3	n	n
A. Feelings of Similarity to Outsiders								
1. Feelings of Similarity to Gypsies	n	R2 < R1,R4	n	n	n	R3 > N3	R4 > N4	n
2. Feelings of Similarity to Jews	n	n	n	n	R2 > N2	R3 > N3	R4 > N4	n
3. Feelings of Similarity to Nazis	1 < 3	n	N2,N3 > N4	n	R2 < N2	n	n	N2 high
4. Feelings of Similarity to Other Religious Denomination	2 < 4	R1 < R4	n	R1 < N1	n	n	n	n
5. Feelings of Similarity to Turks	n	R1 < R4	n	n	n	n	n	n
B. Jews								
1. Early Awareness of Nazi Intentions	1 > 3,4	R1 > R3,R4	n	R1 > N1	n	R3 > N3	n	n
2. Empathy for Jews	2 > 3	R2 > R3	n	R1 > N1	R2 > N2	n	n	n
3. Jewish Friends	n	R2 > R4	N1 > N3	R1 > N1	R2 > N2	R3 > N3	n	N3 low

Table 2a. Continued

Variable	A 1 vs. 2 vs. 3 vs. 4	B R1 vs. R2 vs. R3 vs. R4	C N1 vs. N2 vs. N3 vs. N4	D R1 vs. N1	E R2 vs. N2	F R3 vs. N3	G R4 vs. N4	I Interaction
4. Jewish Presence								
a. Jews in Neighborhood	n	n	n	n	n	n	n	n
b. Jews at School	1,2,3 > 4	R1,R2,R3 > R4	n	n	n	n	n	n
5. Parental Values about Jews								
a. Negative Stereotypes	n	n	N3 > N4	R1 > N1	n	R3 < N3	n	n
b. Positive Stereotypes	n	n	N1 < N3	n	n	n	n	n
c. Stereotypes	n	n	N3 > N4	n	n	R3 < N3	n	n
d. Talked about Jews	n	n	N2 < N3	n	R2 > N2	n	R4 > N4	R4 high
C. Political Party Inclusiveness	1 > 2,3,4	R1 > R2,R3,R4	n	R1 > N1	R2 > N2	n	n	n
D. Variety of Friends	n	n	n	n	n	R3 > N3	n	n
II. SECONDARY RELATIONSHIPS								
Religious Secondary Relationships Factor	1 < 2 < 3 < 4	R1 < R2 < R3 < R4	N1 < N2 < N3 < N4	n	n	n	n	n
Secular Secondary Relationships Factor	n	n	n	n	n	n	n	n

Variable	A 1 vs. 2 vs. 3 vs. 4	B R1 vs. R2 vs. R3 vs. R4	C N1 vs. N2 vs. N3 vs. N4	D R1 vs. N1	E R2 vs. N2	F R3 vs. N3	G R4 vs. N4	I Interaction
A. Religious Ties								
1. Feelings of Similarity to Own Religious Denomination	1 < 2 < 3,4	R1 < R2 < R3, R4	N1, N2 < N3, N4	R1 < N1	n	n	n	n
2. Religiosity	1 < 2 < 3 < 4	R1 < R2 < R3 < R4	N1 < N2 < N3 < N4	n	n	n	n	n
B. Secular Ties								
1. Friendliness of Neighbors	n	n	n	n	n	n	n	n
2. Patriotism								
a. Defending Country before War	n	n	n	n	n	n	n	n
b. Patriotism Growing Up	1 < 2 < 3,4	R1 < R2,R3,R4	N1 < N3,N4	n	n	n	n	n
3. Political Party Membership	1,4 > 3	n	n	n	n	n	R4 > N4	n
4. Resistance Groups								
a. Family Members Belonged	n	n	n	n	R2 > N2	R3 > N3	n	n
b. Self Belonged	n	n	n	n	n	n	n	n

1 = irreligious; 2 = mildly religious; 3 = somewhat religious; 4 = very religious

R = rescuer; N = nonrescuer; n = not significant.

Interaction column shows group means that are highest or lowest for variables with significant overall interaction. See Table 8 for the definition and construction of variables listed in the same order.

Table 2b. *Religiosity Cell and Group Comparisons*

Results of Duncan post hoc comparisons following analysis of variance comparing groups on each variable, indicating significant group differences at the 0.05 level

Variable	A 1 vs. 2 vs. 3 vs. 4	B R1 vs. R2 vs. R3 vs. R4	C N1 vs. N2 vs. N3 vs. N4	D R1 vs. N1	E R2 vs. N2	F R3 vs. N3	G R4 vs. N4	I Interaction
III. PRIMARY RELATIONSHIPS								
Primary Relationships Factor	1 < 3,4	R1 < R3	N1 < N2,N3,N4	R1 > N1	n	R3 > N3	n	n
A. Close Friends Growing Up	3 < 4	n	n	n	n	n	n	n
B. Families of Origin								
1. Closeness to Father	1 < 2,3,4	R1 < R3	N1 < N2,N3,N4	n	n	R3 > N3	n	n
2. Closeness to Mother	1,2 < 3,4	R2 < R3	n	n	n	n	n	n
3. Family Closeness	1 < 3,4; 2 < 4	R1 < R3,R4	N1 < N2,N3,N4	R1 > N1	n	R3 > N3	n	n
C. Parental Discipline								
1. Ever Disciplined	n	n	n	n	n	n	n	n
2. Type of Discipline								
a. Authoritarian	n	n	n	R1 < N1	n	n	n	n

Variable	A 1 vs. 2 vs. 3 vs. 4	B R1 vs. R2 vs. R3 vs. R4	C N1 vs. N2 vs. N3 vs. N4	D R1 vs. N1	E R2 vs. N2	F R3 vs. N3	G R4 vs. N4	I Interaction
b. Chores	1 > 2,3,4	n	N1 > N2,N3,N4	n	n	n	n	n
c. Physical	1 < 2	n	N1 < N3	n	n	R3 < N3	n	n
d. Reasoning	1 > 4	n	n	n	n	n	n	n
D. Personal Helping Today	n	n	n	n	n	n	n	n
E. Relatives in Community	n	R3 > R4	n	n	n	n	R4 < N4	n
IV. SHARING								
Sharing Factor	1,3 < 4	n	N1,N3 < N4	n	n	R3 > N3	n	n
A. Care	n	n	n	n	n	n	R4 > N4	n
B. Community Helping Today	3 > 4	R3 > R4	n	n	n	n	n	n
C. Detachment	n	n	N3 < N4	n	n	n	n	n
D. Empathy	n	n	n	n	n	n	n	n
E. Equity								
1. Church Valuing of Equity	n	n	n	n	n	n	R4 < N4	n
2. Parental Valuing of Equity	n	n	n	n	n	n	n	n
F. Feelings of Similarity to Poor	n	n	n	n	n	n	n	n
G. Personal Integrity	1 < 3,4	n	N1 < N2,N3,N4	R1 > N1	n	R3 > N3	n	n
H. Prosocial Action Orientation	1 < 2,3,4	n	N1 < N4	n	n	n	n	n
I. Social Responsibility	1,3 < 4	n	n	n	n	n	n	n

Table 2b. Continued

Variable	A 1 vs. 2 vs. 3 vs. 4	B R1 vs. R2 vs. R3 vs. R4	C N1 vs. N2 vs. N3 vs. N4	D R1 vs. N1	E R2 vs. N2	F R3 vs. N3	G R4 vs. N4	I Interaction
V. MASTERY								
External Mastery Factor	2,4 < 3	n	N1 < N3	n	n	R3 < N3	n	N3 high
A. External Mastery								
1. Economic Competence	3 > 4	R3 > R4	n	n	n	n	n	N3 high
2. Obedience	n	n	N1 < N3,N4	n	n	R3 < N3	n	N3 high
3. Propriety	n	n	n	n	n	n	n	N3 high
Internal Mastery Factor	n	n	n	n	n	n	n	n
B. Internal Mastery								
1. Internal Locus of Control	n	n	n	n	n	n	n	n
2. Personal Potency	n	n	n	R1 > N1	n	n	n	n
3. Self-Esteem Scale	n	R1 > R2,R4	n	n	n	n	n	n
4. Stand Up for Beliefs	1,4 > 3	n	n	n	n	n	n	n

1 = irreligious; 2 = mildly religious; 3 = somewhat religious; 4 = very religious

R = rescuer; N = nonrescuer; n = not significant.

Interaction column shows group means that are highest or lowest for variables with significant overall interaction. See Table 8 for the definition and construction of variables listed in the same order.

Table 3a. Religious Affiliation Cell and Group Comparisons
Results of Duncan post hoc comparisons following analysis of variance comparing groups on
each variable, indicating significant group differences at the 0.05 level

Variable	A P vs. C	B PR vs. CR	C PB vs. CB	D PR vs. PB	E CR vs. CB	F Interaction
DISCRIMINANT FUNCTION	n	PR < CR	n	PR > PB	CR > CB	n
I. OUTGROUP RELATIONSHIPS						
Outgroup Relationships Factor	P < C	PR < CR	n	PR > PB	CR > CB	n
A. Feelings of Similarity to Outsiders						
1. Feelings of Similarity to Gypsies	P < C	n	n	PR > PB	CR > CB	n
2. Feelings of Similarity to Jews	n	n	n	PR > PB	CR > CB	n
3. Feelings of Similarity to Nazis	n	PR < CR	PB > CB	PR < PB	n	PB high
4. Feelings of Similarity to Other Religious Denomination	P < C	PR < CR	n	n	n	n
5. Feelings of Similarity to Turks	n	n	n	n	n	n
B. Jews						
1. Early Awareness of Nazi Intentions	P > C	PR > CR	n	PR > PB	n	n
2. Empathy for Jews	P > C	n	PB > CB	n	CR > CB	n
3. Jewish Friends	P < C	PR < CR	n	PR > PB	CR > CB	n
4. Jewish Presence						
a. Jews in Neighborhood	P < C	n	n	n	n	n
b. Jews at School	n	n	n	n	n	n
5. Parental Values about Jews						
a. Negative Stereotypes	n	n	n	PR < PB	CR < CB	n
b. Positive Stereotypes	n	n	n	n	n	n
c. Stereotypes	n	n	n	n	CR < CB	n
d. Talked about Jews	n	n	n	n	n	n
C. Political Party Inclusiveness	P < C	n	PB < CB	PR > PB	n	PB low
D. Variety of Friends	n	n	n	n	CR > CB	n
II. SECONDARY RELATIONSHIPS						
Religious Secondary Relationships Factor	n	n	PB < CB	PR > PB	n	PB low
Secular Secondary Relationships Factor	n	n	n	PR > PB	CR > CB	n
A. Religious Ties						
1. Feelings of Similarity to Own Religious Denomination	n	n	n	n	n	n
2. Religiosity	n	PR > CR	PB < CB	PR > PB	n	PR high, PB low
B. Secular Ties						
1. Friendliness of Neighbors	P > C	PR > CR	n	n	n	PR high
2. Patriotism						
a. Defending Country before War	n	n	n	PR < PB	n	n
b. Patriotism Growing Up	P < C	PR < CR	PB < CB	n	n	n

Table 3a. Continued

Variable	A P vs. C	B PR vs. CR	C PB vs. CB	D PR vs. PB	E CR vs. CB	F Interaction
3. Political Party Membership	P > C	PR > CR	PB > CB	n	CR > CB	n
4. Resistance Groups						
a. Family Members Belonged	n	n	n	PR > PB	CR > CB	n
b. Self Belonged	P < C	n	n	PR > PB	CR > CB	n

P = Protestant; C = Catholic; R = rescuer; B = bystander; n = not significant.

Interaction column shows group means that are highest or lowest for variables with significant overall interaction. See Table 8 for the definition and construction of variables listed in the same order.

Table 3b. Religious Affiliation Cell and Group Comparisons

Results of Duncan post hoc comparisons following analysis of variance comparing groups on each variable, indicating significant group differences at the 0.05 level

	A	B	C	D	E	F
Variable	P vs. C	PR vs. CR	PB vs. CB	PR vs. PB	CR vs. CB	Interaction
III. PRIMARY RELATIONSHIPS						
Primary Relationships Factor	n	n	n	n	CR > CB	CB low
A. Close Friends Growing Up	n	n	n	n	n	n
B. Families of Origin						
1. Closeness to Father	n	PR < CR	n	n	CR > CB	CB low
2. Closeness to Mother	n	n	n	n	n	n
3. Family Closeness	n	n	PB > CB	n	CR > CB	CB low
C. Parental Discipline						
1. Ever Disciplined	P > C	PR > CR	n	n	CR < CB	n
2. Type of Discipline						
a. Authoritarian	n	n	n	n	n	n
b. Chores	n	n	n	n	n	n
c. Physical	n	n	n	n	CR < CB	n
d. Reasoning	n	n	n	n	n	n
D. Personal Helping Today	n	n	PB < CB	n	n	PB low
E. Relatives in Community	P < C	PR < CR	n	n	n	n
IV. SHARING						
Sharing Factor	P < C	PR < CR	n	n	CR > CB	n
A. Care	n	n	n	PR > PB	CR > CB	PB low
B. Community Helping Today	n	n	n	n	CR > CB	n
C. Detachment	n	n	n	n	n	n
D. Empathy	n	n	n	n	n	n
E. Equity						
1. Church Valuing of Equity	P < C	PR < CR	n	n	n	n
2. Parental Valuing of Equity	P < C	PR < CR	n	n	n	CR high
F. Feelings of Similarity to Poor	P < C	PR < CR	n	n	CR > CB	n
G. Personal Integrity	P < C	PR < CR	n	n	CR > CB	n
H. Prosocial Action Orientation	P < C	PR < CR	n	n	CR > CB	n
I. Social Responsibility	n	n	n	n	CR > CB	n
V. MASTERY						
External Mastery Factor	n	n	n	PR < PB	CR < CB	PB high
A. External Mastery						
1. Economic Competence	n	n	PB > CB	PR < PB	n	PB high
2. Obedience	n	n	n	PR < PB	CR < CB	n
3. Propriety	n	n	n	n	n	PB high
Internal Mastery Factor	P > C	n	PB > CB	n	CR > CB	CB low

Table 3b. Continued

Variable	A P vs. C	B PR vs. CR	C PB vs. CB	D PR vs. PB	E CR vs. CB	F Interaction
B. Internal Mastery						
1. Internal Locus of Control	n	n	PB > CB	n	CR > CB	CB low
2. Personal Potency	P > C	PR > CR	PB > CB	n	n	n
3. Self-Esteem	n	n	PB > CB	PR < PB	CR > CB	PB high, CB low
4. Stand Up for Beliefs	n	n	n	n	n	n

P = Protestant; C = Catholic; R = rescuer; B = bystander; n = not significant.

Interaction column shows group means that are highest or lowest for variables with significant overall interaction.

Table 4a. Rescuer, Nonrescuer, and Bystander Group Means and N's

Variable	A Rescuer Mean	(N)	B Nonrescuer Mean	(N)	C Bystander Mean	(N)
DISCRIMINANT FUNCTION	0.27	(346)	−0.46	(164)	−0.95	(97)
I. OUTGROUP RELATIONSHIPS						
Outgroup Relationships Factor	0.16	(346)	−0.34	(164)	−0.63	(97)
A. Feelings of Similarity to Outsiders						
1. Feelings of Similarity to Gypsies	1.94	(157)	1.51	(115)	1.38	(69)
2. Feelings of Similarity to Jews	3.13	(184)	2.55	(125)	2.39	(76)
3. Feelings of Similarity to Nazis	1.18	(192)	1.35	(116)	1.50	(74)
4. Feelings of Similarity to Other Religious Denomination	2.70	(165)	2.68	(112)	2.57	(69)
5. Feelings of Similarity to Turks	1.85	(67)	2.02	(58)	1.82	(34)
B. Jews						
1. Early Awareness of Nazi Intentions	2.32	(324)	2.12	(154)	2.08	(90)
2. Empathy for Jews	0.06	(322)	−0.13	(155)	−0.17	(92)
3. Jewish Friends	0.07	(340)	−0.14	(161)	−0.28	(97)
4. Jewish Presence						
a. Jews in Neighborhood	1.69	(328)	1.66	(143)	1.63	(84)
b. Jews at School	0.00	(308)	0.00	(151)	0.02	(86)
5. Parental Values about Jews						
a. Negative Stereotypes	−0.07	(291)	0.15	(139)	0.29	(78)
b. Positive Stereotypes	0.03	(291)	−0.06	(139)	−0.08	(78)
c. Stereotypes	−0.04	(291)	0.09	(139)	0.25	(78)
d. Talked about Jews	0.04	(339)	−0.09	(161)	−0.10	(95)
C. Political Party Inclusiveness	0.10	(346)	−0.21	(164)	−0.28	(97)
D. Variety of Friends	0.07	(224)	−0.11	(150)	−0.22	(92)
II. SECONDARY RELATIONSHIPS						
Religious Secondary Relationships Factor	0.00	(346)	0.00	(164)	−0.08	(97)
Secular Secondary Relationships Factor	0.10	(346)	−0.21	(164)	−0.60	(97)
A. Religious Ties						
1. Feelings of Similarity to Own Religious Denomination	3.39	(191)	3.53	(137)	3.52	(84)
2. Religiosity	0.03	(342)	−0.05	(163)	−0.01	(97)
B. Secular Ties						
1. Friendliness of Neighbors	3.43	(304)	3.29	(147)	3.32	(85)
2. Patriotism						
a. Defending Country before War	1.22	(232)	1.27	(158)	1.31	(97)
b. Patriotism Growing Up	3.32	(236)	3.44	(156)	3.28	(94)

Table 4a. Continued

Variable	A Rescuer		B Nonrescuer		C Bystander	
	Mean	(N)	Mean	(N)	Mean	(N)
3. Political Party Membership	1.24	(341)	1.13	(159)	1.13	(95)
4. Resistance Groups						
a. Family Members Belonged	1.60	(290)	1.37	(147)	1.22	(85)
b. Self Belonged	1.41	(340)	1.26	(160)	1.00	(97)

See Table 8 for the definition and construction of variables listed in the same order.

Table 4b. Rescuer, Nonrescuer, and Bystander Group Means and N's

Variable	A Rescuer Mean	(N)	B Nonrescuer Mean	(N)	C Bystander Mean	(N)
III. PRIMARY RELATIONSHIPS						
Primary Relationships Factor	0.13	(346)	−0.27	(164)	−0.41	(97)
A. Close Friends Growing Up	3.01	(343)	2.90	(162)	2.89	(97)
B. Families of Origin						
1. Closeness to Father	3.38	(219)	3.18	(144)	3.01	(87)
2. Closeness to Mother	3.60	(232)	3.44	(149)	3.43	(90)
3. Family Closeness	0.10	(343)	−0.22	(163)	−0.33	(96)
C. Parental Discipline						
1. Ever Disciplined	1.83	(242)	1.87	(160)	1.89	(96)
2. Type of Discipline						
a. Authoritarian	−0.04	(240)	0.07	(150)	0.08	(88)
b. Chores	−0.01	(240)	0.02	(150)	−0.03	(88)
c. Physical	−0.06	(240)	0.09	(150)	0.14	(88)
d. Reasoning	0.00	(240)	0.00	(150)	−0.08	(88)
D. Personal Helping Today	0.04	(234)	0.03	(155)	−0.02	(94)
E. Relatives in Community	1.44	(321)	1.51	(148)	1.42	(84)
IV. SHARING						
Sharing Factor	0.09	(346)	−0.18	(164)	−0.39	(97)
A. Care	0.11	(307)	−0.23	(146)	−0.33	(83)
B. Community Helping Today	0.07	(234)	−0.12	(155)	−0.25	(94)
C. Detachment	−0.04	(346)	0.09	(164)	0.15	(97)
D. Empathy	57.40	(346)	57.07	(164)	56.68	(97)
E. Equity						
1. Church Valuing of Equity	−0.03	(151)	0.09	(58)	−0.28	(20)
2. Parental Valuing of Equity	0.02	(307)	−0.04	(146)	0.04	(83)
F. Feelings of Similarity to Poor	2.99	(207)	2.86	(146)	2.73	(89)
G. Personal Integrity	0.07	(243)	−0.11	(159)	−0.19	(96)
H. Prosocial Action Orientation	0.04	(346)	−0.09	(164)	−0.21	(97)
I. Social Responsibility	26.32	(346)	25.72	(164)	25.18	(97)
V. MASTERY						
External Mastery Factor	−0.09	(346)	0.19	(164)	0.33	(97)
A. External Mastery						
1. Economic Competence	−0.02	(307)	0.03	(146)	0.06	(83)
2. Obedience	−0.06	(307)	0.12	(146)	0.21	(83)
3. Propriety	1.20	(307)	1.26	(146)	1.29	(83)

Table 4b. Continued

Variable	A Rescuer		B Nonrescuer		C Bystander	
	Mean	(N)	Mean	(N)	Mean	(N)
Internal Mastery Factor	0.08	(346)	−0.16	(164)	−0.28	(97)
B. Internal Mastery						
1. Internal Locus of Control	13.38	(346)	13.00	(164)	12.67	(97)
2. Personal Potency	0.06	(243)	−0.09	(159)	−0.12	(96)
3. Self-Esteem	29.92	(346)	29.47	(164)	29.31	(97)
4. Stand Up for Beliefs	1.35	(224)	1.24	(152)	1.20	(91)

See Table 8 for the definition and construction of variables listed in the same order.

Table 5a. Religiosity Group Means and N's

Variable	A Irreligious Mean	(N)	B Mildly Rel. Mean	(N)	C Somewhat Rel. Mean	(N)	D Very Rel. Mean	(N)
DISCRIMINANT FUNCTION	0.02	(58)	−0.03	(106)	−0.04	(190)	0.16	(150)
I. OUTGROUP RELATIONSHIPS								
Outgroup Relationships Factor	0.25	(58)	−0.01	(106)	−0.10	(190)	0.03	(150)
A. Feelings of Similarity to Outsiders								
1. Feelings of Similarity to Gypsies	1.97	(31)	1.63	(62)	1.66	(116)	1.95	(62)
2. Feelings of Similarity to Jews	3.11	(35)	2.82	(71)	2.84	(129)	2.97	(73)
3. Feelings of Similarity to Nazis	1.08	(39)	1.20	(71)	1.36	(122)	1.20	(74)
4. Feelings of Similarity to Other Religious Denomination	2.47	(15)	2.52	(64)	2.71	(124)	2.90	(72)
5. Feelings of Similarity to Turks	1.62	(13)	1.74	(31)	1.98	(49)	2.16	(31)
B. Jews								
1. Early Awareness of Nazi Intentions	2.42	(57)	2.28	(102)	2.21	(177)	2.21	(138)
2. Empathy for Jews	−0.05	(54)	0.09	(97)	−0.05	(184)	0.02	(139)
3. Jewish Friends	0.14	(57)	0.08	(104)	−0.06	(187)	−0.05	(148)
4. Jewish Presence								
a. Jews in Neighborhood	1.72	(53)	1.73	(98)	1.66	(174)	1.65	(141)
b. Jews at School	0.15	(51)	0.07	(94)	0.01	(175)	−0.13	(135)
5. Parental Values about Jews								
a. Negative Stereotypes	−0.11	(49)	0.07	(86)	0.06	(165)	−0.08	(125)
b. Positive Stereotypes	−0.12	(49)	0.04	(86)	0.01	(165)	0.00	(125)
c. Stereotypes	−0.17	(49)	0.04	(86)	0.06	(165)	−0.03	(125)
d. Talked about Jews	−0.05	(58)	−0.05	(104)	0.01	(187)	0.03	(146)
C. Political Party Inclusiveness	0.67	(58)	−0.06	(106)	−0.04	(190)	−0.17	(150)
D. Variety of Friends	−0.10	(39)	0.07	(89)	−0.01	(151)	−0.01	(94)

Table 5a. Continued

Variable	A Irreligious Mean	(N)	B Mildly Rel. Mean	(N)	C Somewhat Rel. Mean	(N)	D Very Rel. Mean	(N)
II. SECONDARY RELATIONSHIPS								
Religious Secondary Relationships Factor	−1.24	(58)	−0.67	(106)	0.26	(190)	0.63	(150)
Secular Secondary Relationships Factor	−0.08	(58)	−0.06	(106)	0.00	(190)	0.06	(150)
A. Religious Ties								
1. Feelings of Similarity to Own Religious Denomination	2.50	(20)	3.05	(75)	3.65	(147)	3.67	(84)
2. Religiosity	−1.19	(55)	−0.57	(106)	0.13	(190)	0.70	(150)
B. Secular Ties								
1. Friendliness of Neighbors	3.31	(52)	3.29	(92)	3.40	(168)	3.46	(134)
2. Patriotism								
a. Defending Country before War	1.28	(43)	1.23	(91)	1.25	(159)	1.21	(96)
b. Patriotism Growing Up	2.72	(43)	3.21	(91)	3.53	(161)	3.53	(96)
3. Political Party Membership	1.29	(58)	1.19	(105)	1.15	(187)	1.25	(146)
4. Resistance Groups								
a. Family Members Belonged	1.58	(50)	1.52	(90)	1.50	(167)	1.55	(126)
b. Self Belonged	1.40	(58)	1.42	(102)	1.34	(188)	1.34	(147)

See Table 8 for the definition and construction of variables listed in the same order.

Table 5b. Religiosity Group Means and N's

Variable	A Irreligious Mean	(N)	B Mildly Rel. Mean	(N)	C Somewhat Rel. Mean	(N)	D Very Rel. Mean	(N)
III. PRIMARY RELATIONSHIPS								
Primary Relationships Factor	−0.36	(58)	−0.10	(106)	0.06	(190)	0.12	(150)
A. Close Friends Growing Up	2.82	(56)	2.96	(106)	2.91	(188)	3.11	(150)
B. Families of Origin								
1. Closeness to Father	2.87	(39)	3.35	(83)	3.41	(148)	3.29	(91)
2. Closeness to Mother	3.28	(40)	3.39	(90)	3.64	(155)	3.61	(95)
3. Family Closeness	−0.30	(58)	−0.08	(106)	0.04	(189)	0.11	(148)
C. Parental Discipline								
1. Ever Disciplined	1.84	(44)	1.82	(94)	1.88	(164)	1.81	(98)
2. Type of Discipline								
a. Authoritarian	−0.05	(45)	−0.01	(91)	0.01	(158)	0.01	(94)
b. Chores	0.34	(45)	−0.08	(91)	0.01	(158)	−0.11	(94)
c. Physical	−0.17	(45)	0.10	(91)	0.01	(158)	−0.02	(94)
d. Reasoning	0.14	(45)	0.03	(91)	0.02	(158)	−0.12	(94)
D. Personal Helping Today	0.03	(44)	0.00	(90)	0.00	(158)	0.13	(95)
E. Relatives in Community	1.48	(56)	1.50	(98)	1.50	(175)	1.39	(135)
IV. SHARING								
Sharing Factor	−0.32	(58)	0.01	(106)	−0.06	(190)	0.18	(150)
A. Care	−0.01	(47)	0.09	(91)	−0.12	(170)	0.06	(140)
B. Community Helping Today	−0.11	(44)	−0.03	(90)	−0.01	(158)	0.07	(95)
C. Detachment	−0.05	(58)	0.02	(106)	0.14	(190)	−0.16	(150)
D. Empathy	55.87	(58)	57.17	(106)	57.54	(190)	57.69	(150)
E. Equity								
1. Church Valuing of Equity	0.15	(11)	−0.05	(42)	0.02	(92)	−0.01	(63)
2. Parental Valuing of Equity	0.06	(47)	−0.02	(91)	−0.01	(170)	−0.02	(140)
F. Feelings of Similarity to Poor	2.83	(36)	3.00	(81)	2.91	(149)	2.99	(86)
G. Personal Integrity	−0.29	(45)	−0.05	(92)	0.04	(165)	0.10	(98)
H. Prosocial Action Orientation	−0.29	(58)	0.04	(106)	0.01	(190)	0.08	(150)
I. Social Responsibility	25.55	(58)	26.25	(106)	25.77	(190)	26.71	(150)
V. MASTERY								
External Mastery Factor	−0.10	(58)	−0.10	(106)	0.19	(190)	−0.11	(150)
A. External Mastery								
1. Economic Competence	−0.04	(47)	−0.02	(91)	0.10	(170)	−0.11	(140)
2. Obedience	−0.10	(47)	−0.07	(91)	0.07	(170)	0.01	(140)

Table 5b. Continued

Variable	A Irreligious		B Mildly Rel.		C Somewhat Rel.		D Very Rel.	
	Mean	(N)	Mean	(N)	Mean	(N)	Mean	(N)
3. Propriety	1.26	(47)	1.19	(91)	1.26	(170)	1.19	(140)
Internal Mastery Factor	0.23	(58)	−0.03	(106)	−0.05	(190)	−0.02	(150)
B. Internal Mastery								
1. Internal Locus of Control	13.79	(58)	13.14	(106)	13.15	(190)	13.25	(150)
2. Personal Potency	0.02	(45)	0.05	(92)	−0.06	(165)	0.03	(98)
3. Self-Esteem Scale	30.57	(58)	29.48	(106)	30.07	(190)	29.29	(150)
4. Stand Up for Beliefs	1.43	(40)	1.29	(90)	1.25	(155)	1.38	(90)

See Table 8 for the definition and construction of variables listed in the same order.

Table 6a. Religiosity Cell Means and N's

Variable	A Irreligious Rescuer Mean (N)	B Mildly Rel. Rescuer Mean (N)	C Somewhat Rel. Rescuer Mean (N)	D Very Rel. Rescuer Mean (N)	E Irreligious Nonrescuer Mean (N)	F Mildly Rel. Nonrescuer Mean (N)	G Somewhat Rel. Nonrescuer Mean (N)	H Very Rel. Nonrescuer Mean (N)
DISCRIMINANT FUNCTION	0.27 (42)	0.22 (71)	0.28 (117)	0.27 (111)	−0.63 (16)	−0.54 (35)	−0.57 (73)	−0.16 (39)
I. OUTGROUP RELATIONSHIPS								
Outgroup Relationships Factor	0.36 (42)	0.22 (71)	0.13 (117)	0.08 (111)	−0.05 (16)	−0.47 (35)	−0.47 (73)	−0.12 (39)
A. Feelings of Similarity to Outsiders								
1. Feelings of Similarity to Gypsies	2.29 (17)	1.63 (38)	1.86 (64)	2.21 (38)	1.57 (14)	1.63 (24)	1.42 (52)	1.54 (24)
2. Feelings of Similarity to Jews	3.26 (23)	3.12 (43)	3.05 (75)	3.21 (43)	2.83 (12)	2.36 (28)	2.56 (54)	2.63 (30)
3. Feelings of Similarity to Nazis	1.00 (26)	1.04 (47)	1.27 (70)	1.29 (48)	1.23 (13)	1.50 (24)	1.48 (52)	1.04 (26)
4. Feelings of Similarity to Other Religious Denomination	2.00 (10)	2.65 (40)	2.73 (71)	2.91 (43)	3.40 (5)	2.29 (24)	2.68 (53)	2.90 (29)
5. Feelings of Similarity to Turks	1.00 (7)	1.61 (18)	2.00 (25)	2.24 (17)	2.33 (6)	1.92 (13)	1.96 (24)	2.07 (14)
B. Jews								
1. Early Awareness of Nazi Intentions	2.52 (42)	2.35 (69)	2.29 (108)	2.24 (101)	2.13 (15)	2.15 (33)	2.09 (69)	2.14 (37)
2. Empathy for Jews	0.06 (39)	0.18 (65)	−0.01 (115)	0.07 (100)	−0.33 (15)	−0.08 (32)	−0.11 (69)	−0.11 (39)
3. Jewish Friends	0.11 (41)	0.22 (70)	0.07 (116)	−0.06 (109)	0.23 (16)	−0.21 (34)	−0.27 (71)	0.00 (39)

Table 6a. Continued

Variable	A Irreligious Rescuer Mean (N)	B Mildly Rel. Rescuer Mean (N)	C Somewhat Rel. Rescuer Mean (N)	D Very Rel. Rescuer Mean (N)	E Irreligious Nonrescuer Mean (N)	F Mildly Rel. Nonrescuer Mean (N)	G Somewhat Rel. Non-rescuer Mean (N)	H Very Rel. Nonrescuer Mean (N)
4. Jewish Presence								
a. Jews in Neighborhood	1.75 (40)	1.75 (68)	1.65 (110)	1.65 (106)	1.62 (13)	1.70 (30)	1.67 (64)	1.66 (35)
b. Jews at School	0.24 (37)	0.10 (62)	0.02 (107)	-0.19 (99)	-0.09 (14)	0.00 (32)	0.00 (68)	0.03 (36)
5. Parental Values about Jews								
a. Negative Stereotypes	-0.13 (34)	0.01 (59)	-0.08 (100)	-0.09 (94)	-0.07 (15)	0.19 (27)	0.27 (65)	-0.03 (31)
b. Positive Stereotypes	-0.02 (34)	0.10 (59)	0.00 (100)	0.02 (94)	-0.33 (15)	-0.10 (27)	0.03 (65)	-0.09 (31)
c. Stereotypes	-0.17 (34)	0.01 (59)	-0.07 (100)	0.00 (94)	-0.19 (15)	0.11 (27)	0.26 (65)	-0.12 (31)
d. Talked about Jews	0.03 (42)	0.05 (70)	-0.01 (116)	0.11 (107)	-0.26 (16)	-0.26 (34)	0.06 (71)	-0.17 (39)
C. Political Party Inclusiveness	0.89 (42)	0.14 (71)	0.05 (117)	-0.16 (111)	0.11 (16)	-0.46 (35)	-0.17 (73)	-0.21 (39)
D. Variety of Friends	-0.03 (25)	0.12 (56)	0.09 (83)	0.03 (59)	-0.23 (14)	-0.03 (33)	-0.14 (68)	-0.07 (35)
II. SECONDARY RELATIONSHIPS								
Religious Secondary Relationships Factor	-1.23 (42)	-0.62 (71)	0.26 (117)	0.59 (111)	-1.30 (16)	-0.79 (35)	0.26 (73)	0.74 (39)
Secular Secondary Relationships Factor	0.08 (42)	0.03 (71)	0.11 (117)	0.13 (111)	-0.52 (16)	-0.25 (35)	-0.17 (73)	-0.11 (39)

Variable	A Irreligious Rescuer Mean (N)	B Mildly Rel. Rescuer Mean (N)	C Somewhat Rel. Rescuer Mean (N)	D Very Rel. Rescuer Mean (N)	E Irreligious Nonrescuer Mean (N)	F Mildly Rel. Nonrescuer Mean (N)	G Somewhat Rel. Non-rescuer Mean (N)	H Very Rel. Nonrescuer Mean (N)
A. Religious Ties								
1. Feelings of Similarity to Own Religious Denomination	2.17 (12)	2.98 (46)	3.63 (81)	3.67 (51)	3.00 (8)	3.17 (29)	3.68 (66)	3.67 (33)
2. Religiosity	−1.18 (40)	−0.51 (71)	0.15 (117)	0.70 (111)	−1.21 (15)	−0.70 (35)	0.09 (73)	0.70 (39)
B. Secular Ties								
1. Friendliness of Neighbors	3.37 (38)	3.33 (61)	3.45 (103)	3.48 (98)	3.14 (14)	3.23 (31)	3.34 (65)	3.39 (36)
2. Patriotism								
a. Defending Country before War	1.30 (27)	1.18 (56)	1.23 (88)	1.20 (60)	1.25 (16)	1.31 (35)	1.27 (71)	1.22 (36)
b. Patriotism Growing Up	2.70 (27)	3.20 (59)	3.51 (89)	3.44 (61)	2.75 (16)	3.22 (32)	3.56 (72)	3.69 (35)
3. Political Party Membership	1.31 (42)	1.20 (71)	1.18 (115)	1.29 (109)	1.25 (16)	1.18 (34)	1.10 (72)	1.11 (37)
4. Resistance Groups								
a. Family Members Belonged	1.66 (35)	1.64 (59)	1.58 (102)	1.58 (91)	1.40 (15)	1.29 (31)	1.37 (65)	1.46 (35)
b. Self Belonged	1.48 (42)	1.46 (69)	1.40 (116)	1.38 (109)	1.19 (16)	1.33 (33)	1.25 (72)	1.24 (38)

See Table 8 for the definition and construction of variables listed in the same order.

Table 6b. Religiosity Cell Means and N's

Variable	A Irreligious Rescuer Mean	(N)	B Mildly Rel. Rescuer Mean	(N)	C Somewhat Rel. Rescuer Mean	(N)	D Very Rel. Rescuer Mean	(N)	E Irreligious Nonrescuer Mean	(N)	F Mildly Rel. Nonrescuer Mean	(N)	G Somewhat Rel. Non-rescuer Mean	(N)	H Very Rel. Nonrescuer Mean	(N)
III. PRIMARY RELATIONSHIPS																
Primary Relationships Factor	-0.14	(42)	-0.01	(71)	0.26	(117)	0.19	(111)	-0.95	(16)	-0.27	(35)	-0.25	(73)	-0.08	(39)
A. Close Friends Growing Up	2.90	(41)	2.96	(71)	2.94	(116)	3.15	(111)	2.60	(15)	2.97	(35)	2.86	(72)	3.00	(39)
B. Families of Origin																
1. Closeness to Father	3.04	(26)	3.40	(53)	3.55	(83)	3.30	(56)	2.54	(13)	3.27	(30)	3.22	(65)	3.26	(35)
2. Closeness to Mother	3.36	(25)	3.43	(56)	3.71	(91)	3.68	(60)	3.13	(15)	3.32	(34)	3.53	(64)	3.49	(35)
3. Family Closeness	-0.14	(42)	0.01	(71)	0.18	(117)	0.18	(109)	-0.71	(16)	-0.27	(35)	-0.17	(72)	-0.08	(39)
C. Parental Discipline																
1. Ever Disciplined	1.82	(28)	1.83	(59)	1.86	(93)	1.79	(61)	1.88	(16)	1.80	(35)	1.92	(71)	1.84	(37)
2. Type of Discipline																
a. Authoritarian	-0.22	(29)	-0.02	(58)	-0.02	(91)	0.02	(61)	0.26	(16)	0.01	(33)	0.06	(67)	0.01	(33)
b. Chores	0.24	(29)	-0.07	(58)	0.01	(91)	-0.09	(61)	0.52	(16)	-0.09	(33)	0.02	(67)	-0.14	(33)
c. Physical	-0.14	(29)	0.07	(58)	-0.15	(91)	0.01	(61)	-0.23	(16)	0.14	(33)	0.22	(67)	-0.06	(33)
d. Reasoning	0.19	(29)	0.01	(58)	0.05	(91)	-0.15	(61)	0.05	(16)	0.07	(33)	-0.03	(67)	-0.07	(33)

Variable	A Irreligious Rescuer Mean	(N)	B Mildly Rel. Rescuer Mean	(N)	C Somewhat Rel. Rescuer Mean	(N)	D Very Rel. Rescuer Mean	(N)	E Irreligious Nonrescuer Mean	(N)	F Mildly Rel. Nonrescuer Mean	(N)	G Somewhat Rel. Non-rescuer Mean	(N)	H Very Rel. Nonrescuer Mean	(N)
D. Personal Helping Today	-0.01	(29)	0.06	(56)	-0.03	(89)	0.14	(59)	0.11	(15)	-0.11	(34)	0.03	(69)	0.11	(36)
E. Relatives in Community	1.50	(42)	1.48	(66)	1.50	(109)	1.33	(100)	1.43	(14)	1.53	(32)	1.48	(66)	1.57	(35)
IV. SHARING																
Sharing Factor	-0.20	(42)	0.13	(71)	0.09	(117)	0.15	(111)	-0.64	(16)	-0.22	(35)	-0.30	(73)	0.27	(39)
A. Care	0.09	(33)	0.16	(62)	-0.05	(105)	0.20	(103)	-0.25	(14)	-0.06	(29)	-0.24	(65)	-0.32	(37)
B. Community Helping Today	-0.06	(29)	0.07	(56)	0.07	(89)	0.14	(59)	-0.22	(15)	-0.18	(34)	-0.11	(69)	-0.04	(36)
C. Detachment	-0.06	(42)	-0.07	(71)	0.10	(117)	-0.17	(111)	-0.01	(16)	0.18	(35)	0.20	(73)	-0.14	(39)
D. Empathy	56.07	(42)	57.46	(71)	58.08	(117)	57.16	(111)	55.36	(16)	56.59	(35)	56.66	(73)	59.18	(39)
E. Equity																
1. Church Valuing of Equity	0.27	(7)	0.03	(29)	0.01	(65)	-0.17	(49)	-0.07	(4)	-0.22	(13)	0.03	(27)	0.54	(14)
2. Parental Valuing of Equity	0.19	(33)	0.08	(62)	0.00	(105)	-0.07	(103)	-0.24	(14)	-0.22	(29)	-0.01	(65)	0.12	(37)
F. Feelings of Similarity to Poor	3.00	(23)	3.06	(50)	2.98	(82)	2.94	(52)	2.54	(13)	2.90	(31)	2.82	(67)	3.06	(34)
G. Personal Integrity	-0.10	(29)	-0.02	(59)	0.16	(93)	0.10	(61)	-0.64	(16)	-0.10	(33)	-0.11	(72)	0.10	(37)
H. Prosocial Action Orientation	-0.23	(42)	0.09	(71)	0.11	(117)	0.04	(111)	-0.45	(16)	-0.07	(35)	-0.15	(73)	0.20	(39)
I. Social Responsibility	25.65	(42)	26.53	(71)	26.01	(117)	26.75	(111)	25.30	(16)	25.68	(35)	25.37	(73)	26.58	(39)
V. MASTERY																
External Mastery Factor	0.05	(42)	-0.24	(71)	0.04	(117)	-0.16	(111)	-0.47	(16)	0.17	(35)	0.42	(73)	0.04	(39)
A. External Mastery																
1. Economic Competence	0.05	(33)	-0.06	(62)	0.11	(105)	-0.14	(103)	-0.25	(14)	0.05	(29)	0.09	(65)	-0.01	(37)
2. Obedience	-0.03	(33)	-0.12	(62)	-0.04	(105)	-0.03	(103)	-0.25	(14)	0.04	(29)	0.24	(65)	0.13	(37)

Table 6b. Continued

Variable	A Irreligious Rescuer Mean	(N)	B Mildly Rel. Rescuer Mean	(N)	C Somewhat Rel. Rescuer Mean	(N)	D Very Rel. Rescuer Mean	(N)	E Irreligious Nonrescuer Mean	(N)	F Mildly Rel. Nonrescuer Mean	(N)	G Somewhat Rel. Non-rescuer Mean	(N)	H Very Rel. Nonrescuer Mean	(N)
3. Propriety	1.30	(33)	1.15	(62)	1.21	(105)	1.20	(103)	1.14	(14)	1.28	(29)	1.34	(65)	1.16	(37)
Internal Mastery Factor	0.38	(42)	-0.02	(71)	0.06	(117)	0.04	(111)	-0.16	(16)	-0.06	(35)	-0.23	(73)	-0.18	(39)
B. Internal Mastery																
1. Internal Locus of Control	13.96	(42)	13.23	(71)	13.23	(117)	13.43	(111)	13.36	(16)	12.98	(35)	13.03	(73)	12.75	(39)
2. Personal Potency	0.06	(29)	0.01	(59)	0.04	(93)	0.12	(61)	-0.06	(16)	0.12	(33)	-0.20	(72)	-0.10	(37)
3. Self-Esteem Scale	31.44	(42)	29.36	(71)	30.40	(117)	29.27	(111)	28.30	(16)	29.73	(35)	29.55	(73)	29.37	(39)
4. Stand Up for Beliefs	1.48	(25)	1.36	(55)	1.27	(86)	1.40	(57)	1.33	(15)	1.17	(35)	1.22	(69)	1.33	(33)

See Table 8 for the definition and construction of variables listed in the same order.

Table 7a. Religious Affiliation Group and Cell Means and N's

Variable	A Protestant Mean	(N)	B Catholic Mean	(N)	C Protestant Rescuer Mean	(N)	D Catholic Rescuer Mean	(N)	E Protestant Bystander Mean	(N)	F Catholic Bystander Mean	(N)
DISCRIMINANT FUNCTION	-0.12	(183)	0.08	(292)	0.07	(137)	0.36	(181)	-0.91	(32)	-0.98	(61)
I. OUTGROUP RELATIONSHIPS												
Outgroup Relationships Factor	-0.20	(183)	0.06	(292)	-0.03	(137)	0.25	(181)	-0.86	(32)	-0.57	(61)
A. Feelings of Similarity to Outsiders												
1. Feelings of Similarity to Gypsies	1.52	(89)	1.81	(165)	1.73	(52)	1.99	(91)	1.11	(27)	1.49	(41)
2. Feelings of Similarity to Jews	2.81	(100)	2.89	(186)	3.01	(68)	3.15	(100)	2.18	(22)	2.46	(50)
3. Feelings of Similarity to Nazis	1.32	(125)	1.22	(157)	1.06	(84)	1.33	(87)	2.14	(29)	1.09	(43)
4. Feelings of Similarity to Other Religious Denomination	2.40	(125)	2.93	(152)	2.41	(82)	2.99	(83)	2.33	(30)	2.74	(39)
5. Feelings of Similarity to Turks	1.72	(36)	2.00	(82)	1.77	(22)	1.98	(41)	2.00	(7)	1.60	(25)
B. Jews												
1. Early Awareness of Nazi Intentions	2.39	(170)	2.14	(276)	2.46	(127)	2.18	(172)	2.21	(29)	2.04	(57)
2. Empathy for Jews	0.07	(171)	-0.05	(274)	0.09	(127)	0.02	(169)	0.04	(31)	-0.23	(58)

Table 7a. Continued

Variable	A Protestant		B Catholic		C Protestant Rescuer		D Catholic Rescuer		E Protestant Bystander		F Catholic Bystander	
	Mean	(N)	Mean	(N)	Mean	(N)	Mean	(N)	Mean	(N)	Mean	(N)
3. Jewish Friends	−0.15	(182)	0.06	(285)	−0.10	(137)	0.17	(176)	−0.43	(32)	−0.24	(61)
4. Jewish Presence												
a. Jews in Neighborhood	1.60	(168)	1.71	(271)	1.62	(129)	1.71	(174)	1.55	(29)	1.67	(51)
b. Jews at School	−0.03	(162)	−0.01	(266)	−0.08	(121)	0.00	(162)	0.19	(28)	−0.06	(55)
5. Parental Values about Jews												
a. Negative Stereotypes	0.05	(144)	−0.02	(259)	−0.01	(108)	−0.10	(162)	0.35	(24)	0.29	(51)
b. Positive Stereotypes	−0.04	(144)	0.02	(259)	−0.01	(108)	0.05	(162)	−0.10	(24)	−0.04	(51)
c. Stereotypes	−0.02	(144)	0.03	(259)	−0.02	(108)	−0.04	(162)	0.04	(24)	0.38	(51)
d. Talked about Jews	0.06	(179)	−0.02	(288)	0.09	(133)	0.02	(179)	0.04	(32)	−0.14	(60)
C. Political Party Inclusiveness	−0.22	(183)	0.06	(292)	0.00	(137)	0.06	(181)	−1.14	(32)	0.15	(61)
D. Variety of Friends	−0.04	(133)	0.03	(215)	0.01	(87)	0.13	(117)	−0.21	(32)	−0.23	(57)

Variable	A Protestant		B Catholic		C Protestant Rescuer		D Catholic Rescuer		E Protestant Bystander		F Catholic Bystander	
	Mean	(N)	Mean	(N)	Mean	(N)	Mean	(N)	Mean	(N)	Mean	(N)
II. SECONDARY RELATIONSHIPS												
Religious Secondary Relationships Factor	−0.03	(183)	0.11	(292)	0.08	(137)	0.05	(181)	−0.52	(32)	0.22	(61)
Secular Secondary Relationships Factor	−0.08	(183)	0.05	(292)	0.01	(137)	0.14	(181)	−0.58	(32)	−0.57	(61)
A. Religious Ties												
1. Feelings of Similarity to Own Religious Denomination	3.38	(128)	3.49	(200)	3.42	(84)	3.36	(107)	3.33	(30)	3.63	(54)
2. Religiosity	0.11	(182)	0.04	(292)	0.20	(136)	0.03	(181)	−0.23	(32)	0.18	(61)
B. Secular Ties												
1. Friendliness of Neighbors	3.58	(163)	3.28	(258)	3.58	(118)	3.32	(161)	3.39	(31)	3.27	(52)
2. Patriotism												
a. Defending Country before War	1.25	(139)	1.23	(221)	1.22	(93)	1.21	(116)	1.41	(32)	1.28	(61)
b. Patriotism Growing Up	3.12	(137)	3.59	(225)	3.15	(94)	3.57	(119)	2.90	(29)	3.49	(61)
3. Political Party Membership	1.29	(180)	1.13	(286)	1.30	(136)	1.17	(178)	1.29	(31)	1.03	(60)
4. Resistance Groups												
a. Family Members Belonged	1.51	(162)	1.52	(244)	1.57	(120)	1.61	(145)	1.21	(29)	1.28	(53)
b. Self Belonged	1.31	(180)	1.40	(286)	1.36	(136)	1.45	(177)	1.00	(32)	1.00	(61)

See Table 8 for the definition and construction of variables listed in the same order.

Table 7b. Religious Affiliation Group and Cell Means and N's

Variable	A Protestant Mean	(N)	B Catholic Mean	(N)	C Protestant Rescuer Mean	(N)	D Catholic Rescuer Mean	(N)	E Protestant Bystander Mean	(N)	F Catholic Bystander Mean	(N)
III. PRIMARY RELATIONSHIPS												
Primary Relationships Factor	−0.01	(183)	0.02	(292)	0.04	(137)	0.21	(181)	−0.12	(32)	−0.51	(61)
A. Close Friends Growing Up	3.02	(183)	2.98	(289)	3.07	(137)	2.99	(180)	2.75	(32)	3.02	(61)
B. Families of Origin												
1. Closeness to Father	3.27	(133)	3.35	(202)	3.25	(91)	3.52	(107)	3.20	(30)	2.92	(53)
2. Closeness to Mother	3.59	(138)	3.52	(215)	3.61	(93)	3.59	(117)	3.65	(31)	3.36	(56)
3. Family Closeness	0.06	(182)	−0.01	(290)	0.09	(136)	0.14	(180)	−0.05	(32)	−0.42	(60)
C. Parental Discipline												
1. Ever Disciplined	1.92	(142)	1.81	(229)	1.92	(96)	1.77	(122)	1.88	(32)	1.90	(60)
2. Type of Discipline												
a. Authoritarian	0.10	(140)	−0.04	(219)	0.06	(96)	−0.09	(120)	0.20	(30)	0.02	(54)
b. Chores	−0.07	(140)	−0.03	(219)	−0.10	(96)	−0.01	(120)	−0.01	(30)	−0.04	(54)
c. Physical	0.07	(140)	−0.01	(219)	0.06	(96)	−0.11	(120)	0.13	(30)	0.08	(54)
d. Reasoning	0.05	(140)	−0.05	(219)	0.04	(96)	−0.06	(120)	0.01	(30)	−0.11	(54)

	A Protestant		B Catholic		C Protestant Rescuer		D Catholic Rescuer		E Protestant Bystander		F Catholic Bystander	
Variable	Mean	(N)	Mean	(N)	Mean	(N)	Mean	(N)	Mean	(N)	Mean	(N)
D. Personal Helping Today	-0.02	(132)	0.07	(226)	-0.01	(90)	0.06	(120)	-0.31	(29)	0.13	(61)
E. Relatives in Community	1.39	(171)	1.52	(267)	1.36	(131)	1.50	(164)	1.41	(27)	1.42	(55)
IV. SHARING												
Sharing Factor	-0.11	(183)	0.10	(292)	-0.03	(137)	0.20	(181)	-0.41	(32)	-0.34	(61)
A. Care	0.05	(160)	-0.05	(266)	0.11	(121)	0.08	(165)	-0.45	(25)	-0.27	(55)
B. Community Helping Today	0.08	(132)	-0.06	(226)	0.16	(90)	-0.01	(120)	-0.09	(29)	-0.31	(61)
C. Detachment	-0.04	(183)	0.05	(292)	-0.06	(137)	0.00	(181)	-0.00	(32)	0.21	(61)
D. Empathy	57.01	(183)	57.70	(292)	57.16	(137)	57.79	(181)	56.19	(32)	57.11	(61)
E. Equity												
1. Church Valuing of Equity	-0.21	(83)	0.14	(121)	-0.23	(65)	0.10	(83)	-0.46	(9)	-0.12	(10)
2. Parental Valuing of Equity	-0.13	(160)	0.07	(266)	-0.19	(121)	0.16	(165)	0.09	(25)	0.01	(55)
F. Feelings of Similarity to Poor	2.60	(123)	3.12	(209)	2.68	(80)	3.21	(111)	2.43	(30)	2.86	(57)
G. Personal Integrity	-0.14	(141)	0.10	(230)	-0.07	(96)	0.20	(123)	-0.30	(31)	-0.10	(61)
H. Prosocial Action Orientation	-0.11	(183)	0.11	(292)	-0.07	(137)	0.17	(181)	-0.21	(32)	-0.19	(61)
I. Social Responsibility	25.94	(183)	26.32	(292)	26.13	(137)	26.52	(181)	25.39	(32)	25.21	(61)

Table 7b. Continued

Variable	A Protestant Mean	(N)	B Catholic Mean	(N)	C Protestant Rescuer Mean	(N)	D Catholic Rescuer Mean	(N)	E Protestant Bystander Mean	(N)	F Catholic Bystander Mean	(N)
V. MASTERY												
External Mastery Factor	0.03	(183)	0.00	(292)	−0.05	(137)	−0.11	(181)	0.62	(32)	0.24	(61)
A. External Mastery												
1. Economic Competence	0.01	(160)	−0.01	(266)	−0.03	(121)	−0.02	(165)	0.35	(25)	−0.07	(55)
2. Obedience	0.03	(160)	0.00	(266)	0.00	(121)	−0.09	(165)	0.26	(25)	0.23	(55)
3. Propriety	1.23	(160)	1.22	(266)	1.21	(121)	1.19	(165)	1.40	(25)	1.25	(55)
Internal Mastery Factor	0.14	(183)	−0.13	(292)	0.12	(137)	−0.01	(181)	0.30	(32)	−0.57	(61)
B. Internal Mastery												
1. Internal Locus of Control	13.36	(183)	13.15	(292)	13.35	(137)	13.35	(181)	13.59	(32)	12.17	(61)
2. Personal Potency	0.20	(141)	−0.13	(230)	0.22	(96)	−0.08	(123)	0.16	(31)	−0.25	(61)
3. Self-Esteem Scale	30.01	(183)	29.48	(292)	29.61	(137)	29.89	(181)	31.80	(32)	28.27	(61)
4. Stand Up for Beliefs	1.33	(131)	1.27	(217)	1.38	(89)	1.30	(114)	1.17	(29)	1.19	(58)

See Table 8 for the definition and construction of variables listed in the same order.

Table 8. Construction of the Summary Variables and Their Associated Measures

Constructed Variable	Items

Discriminant Function

This discriminant function emerged from discriminant analysis using the summary factors as predictors of rescuer versus bystander status. The predictors were the summary factors reflecting External Mastery, Internal Mastery, Sharing, Primary Relationships, Secular Secondary Relationships, and Outgroup Relationships. The discriminant function that best predicted rescuer versus bystander status had the following loadings:

Loading	Predictor
0.68	Outgroup Relationships factor
0.58	Secular Secondary Relationships factor
0.47	Primary Relationships factor
0.41	Sharing factor
−0.35	External Mastery factor
0.30	Internal Mastery factor

I. Outgroup Relationships

The *Outgroup Relationships factor* summarized the outgroup relationship measures and assessed the respondents' orientation to outgroups. It ranked as the most powerful predictor of rescue (0.68). Measures loading highly on this factor included Feelings of Similarity to Jews (0.68), Jewish Friends (0.57), Feelings of Similarity to Gypsies (0.56), Feelings of Similarity to Turks (0.51), Feelings of Similarity to Other Religious Denomination (0.49), Parental Values about Jews-Negative Stereotypes (inversely related, −0.41), Variety of Friends (0.38), Jews in Neighborhood (0.35), Jews in School (0.35), Empathy for Jews (0.33), Parental Values about Jews-Stereotypes (inversely related, −0.28), and Political Party Inclusiveness (0.28).

A. Feelings of Similarity to Outsiders

1. Feelings of Similarity to Gypsies	A single item (D21b) on which respondents rated on a 1–4 scale how similar they felt to Gypsies.
2. Feelings of Similarity to Jews	A single item (D21f) on which respondents rated on a 1–4 scale how similar they felt to Jews.
3. Feelings of Similarity to Nazis	A single item (D21h) on which respondents rated on a 1–4 scale how similar they felt to Nazis.
4. Feelings of Similarity to Other Religious Denomination	This variable has a 1–4 scale and is derived from Catholic respondents' feelings of similarity to Protestants (D21d) and Protestant respondents' feelings of similarity to Catholics (D21c).

Note: Measures within categories are listed in alphabetical order. All variables with loadings stronger than 0.25 on each factor are listed. Item numbers in parentheses refer to the questions in the questionnaire, which is printed in Appendix C of Oliner and Oliner (1988).

Table 8. Continued

Constructed Variable	Items
5. Feelings of Similarity to Turks	A single item (D21e) on which respondents rated on a 1–4 scale how similar they felt to Turks.

B. Jews

1. Early Awareness of Nazi Intentions	A single item based on respondents' answers (to E7) asking on what occasion they became aware of what the Nazis intended to do to the Jews. Responses were coded on a 1–3 scale: 1 = after the liberation; 2 = during the occupation; and 3 = before the occupation. Higher scores represent earlier awareness.
2. Empathy for Jews	This factor emerged from questions on feelings about Jews in distress.

Loading	Item
0.44	(D23) Feeling of distress about Kristallnacht (if in Germany) or (D23a) Feeling of distress about anti-Semitism (if in another country)
0.44	(E8) Feeling of distress at seeing Jews wearing the yellow star

3. Jewish Friends — One of two factors that emerged from the respondents' answers to seven items regarding Jewish friends and acquaintances.

Loading	Item
0.68	(D12) Had Jewish friends before the war
0.65	(C16) Had close Jewish friends growing up
0.39	(D4) Spouse had Jewish friends before war

4. Jewish Presence

a. Jews in Neighborhood — A single item (E4) indicating whether any Jews lived in the respondent's neighborhood before the war.

b. Jews at School — This factor emerged from responses to three items about Jews attending school with the respondent.

Loading	Item
0.73	(C3b) Jews at gymnasium
0.54	(C2a) Jews at elementary school
0.25	(C5b) Jews at university

Constructed Variable	Items
5. Parental Values about Jews	
a. Negative Stereotypes	One of four factors that emerged from nine categories of responses regarding what parents said about Jews while the respondent was growing up (B14a,B24a,B34a).

Loading	*Item*
0.50	Negative stereotyping of Jews
0.49	Neutral differentiation of Jews
0.33	Other negative comments about Jews

b. Positive Stereotypes	One of four factors that emerged from nine categories of responses regarding what parents said about Jews while the respondent was growing up (B14a,B24a,B34a).

Loading	*Item*
0.35	Other positive comments about Jews
0.26	Positive stereotyping of Jews

c. Stereotypes	One of four factors that emerged from nine categories of responses regarding what parents said about Jews while the respondent was growing up (B14a,B24a,B34a).

Loading	*Item*
0.54	Neutral stereotyping of Jews
0.54	Positive stereotyping of Jews
0.31	Negative stereotyping of Jews

d. Talked about Jews	This factor emerged in response to items indicating whether mother, father, or a significant other person ever talked about Jews while the respondent was growing up.

Loading	*Item*
0.62	(B24) Mother talked about Jews
0.60	(B34) Father talked about Jews
0.47	(B14) Significant other talked about Jews

Table 8. Continued

Constructed Variable	Items
C. Political Party Inclusiveness	A factor that emerged from the respondent's political party (D15a) and family members' political parties (B10a, B20a, B30a, D10a). Political parties with documented histories were rated on four characteristics: democratic position (1 = autocratic, 2 = democratic), economic position (1 = right, 2 = center, 3 = left), position toward minorities (1 = exclusionary, 2 = tolerant, 3 = inclusive), and position toward Jews (1 = exclusionary, 2 = tolerant, 3 = inclusive).

Loading   *Item*

Loading	Item
0.79	Family's party Jewish inclusiveness position
0.78	Respondent's party Jewish inclusiveness position
0.75	Family's party minorities inclusiveness position
0.75	Respondent's party minorities inclusiveness position
0.73	Family's party leftist economic position
0.73	Respondent's party leftist economic position
0.53	Family's party democratic position
0.42	Respondent's party democratic position

D. Variety of Friends — This factor emerged from two questions about friendships while growing up.

Loading	Item
0.50	(C14) Had friends of different religion
0.50	(C15) Had friends of different social class

II. Secondary Relationships

The secondary relationship measures included both religious and secular ties, and they were summarized in two ways.

The first summary factor was constructed from all the secondary relationship measures. The measures loading highly on this factor were Religiosity (0.79), Feelings of Similarity to Own Religious Denomination (0.71), and Patriotism Growing Up (0.54). This factor primarily reflected religious ties and was thus named the

Constructed Variable	Items

Religious Secondary Relationships factor. This factor was used in comparing religious denomination groups, but in order to avoid circularity it was not used in comparing religiosity groups or in the discriminant analysis.

The second summary factor was constructed from all the secondary relationship measures except for Religiosity. The measures loading highly on this factor were Resistance Groups—Self Belonged (0.62), Resistance Groups—Family Members Belonged (0.57), Defending Country before War (0.49), Patriotism Growing Up (0.49), and Political Party Membership (0.40). This factor primarily reflected secular ties and was thus named the *Secular Secondary Relationships factor.* It was used to compare religious denomination groups and religiosity groups. Included as a predictor in the discriminant analysis, it was the second most powerful predictor of rescue (0.58).

A. Religious Ties

1. Feelings of Similarity to Own Religious Denomination	This variable has a 1–4 scale and is derived from Catholic respondents' feelings of similarity to Catholics in general (D21c), and Protestant respondents' feelings of similarity to Protestants in general (D21d).
2. Religiosity	A factor relating to religiosity of self, parents, and spouse.

Loading	Item
0.86	(D14) Religiosity before the war
0.74	(D12a) Religiosity today
0.74	(C9) Religiosity while growing up
0.63	(B29) Father's religiosity
0.62	(B19) Mother's religiosity
0.47	(D9) Spouse's religiosity before the war

B. Secular Ties

1. Friendliness of Neighbors	A single item (A16) indicating respondents' rating on a 1–4 scale of how friendly and helpful the neighbors were when they were growing up.
2. Patriotism	
a. Defending Country before War	A single item (D19) that asked if the respondent had ever done anything unusual to defend or support the country before the war.
b. Patriotism Growing Up	A single item (C18j) reflecting on a 1–4 scale how patriotic the respondent felt growing up.

Table 8. Continued

Constructed Variable	Items
3. Political Party Member-ship	A single item (D15) that asked if the respondent had belonged to a political party before the war.
4. Resistance Groups	
a. Family Members Be-longed	A single item (E59) that asked if the respondent's family members engaged in any kind of resistance activities during the war.
b. Self Belonged	A single item (E15) that asked if the respondent was ever a member of a resistance group.

III. Primary Relationships

The *Primary Relationships factor* assessed the degree to which respondents felt positively about families of origin and other personal relationships in childhood. It was the third most powerful predictor of rescue (0.47). Measures loading highly on this factor included Family Closeness (0.85), Closeness to Father (0.70), Closeness to Mother (0.68), Authoritarian Discipline (inverse relationship, −0.42), Ever Disciplined (inverse relationship, −0.40), and Close Friends Growing Up (0.32).

A. Close Friends Growing Up	A single item (C11) with a 1–4 scale relating to the extent to which the respondent had close friends growing up.
B. Closeness to Father	A single item (B31) with a 1–4 scale reflecting how close respondents felt to their father growing up.
C. Closeness to Mother	A single item (B21) with a 1–4 scale reflecting how close respondents felt to their mother growing up.
D. Family Closeness	This factor emerged from four items measuring the respondent's attachments to family or another significant person while growing up.

Loading	*Item*
0.72	(A14) Closeness of family members
0.53	(B21) Closeness to mother
0.52	(B31) Closeness to father
0.30	(B11) Closeness to significant other person

E. Parental Discipline	
1. Ever Disciplined	A variable with a 0–3 scale reflecting the number of individuals respondents reported disciplining them growing up (on questions B13, B23, B33).

Constructed Variable	Items

2. Type of Discipline

a. Authoritarian

One of four factors that emerged in relation to types of parental discipline and behaviors for which respondents were disciplined (from questions B23a–b and B33a–b).

Loading	Item
0.40	Father scolding
0.40	Father physical punishment
0.39	Father punishing disobedience
0.38	Mother scolding
0.28	Father cathartic punishment
0.27	Mother punishing disobedience

b. Chores

One of four factors that emerged in relation to types of parental discipline and behaviors for which respondents were disciplined (B23a–b and B33a–b).

Loading	Item
0.80	Father chores
0.67	Mother chores
0.40	Father deprivation
0.28	Mother deprivation

c. Physical

One of four factors that emerged in relation to types of parental discipline and behaviors for which respondents were disciplined (B23a–b and B33a–b).

Loading	Item
0.42	Mother punishing cheating
0.38	Mother punishing aggression
0.38	Father physical punishment
0.37	Father punishing cheating
0.28	Mother physical punishment

d. Reasoning

One of four factors that emerged in relation to types of parental discipline and behaviors for which respondents were disciplined (23a–b and 33a–b).

Loading	Item
0.45	Father punishing failure
0.44	Mother punishing failure
0.38	Mother reasoning
0.36	Father reasoning
0.30	Mother punishing disruption
0.21	Father punishing disruption

Table 8. Continued

Constructed Variable	Items
F. Personal Helping Today	One of two factors that emerged in relation to post-war helping behavior, based upon responses to thirteen questions (F7–F10g).

	Loading	*Item*
	0.69	(F9b) Helped friend during past year
	0.55	(F9a) Helped relative during past year
	0.55	(F9c) Helped neighbor during past year
	0.44	(F9d) Helped stranger during past year

Constructed Variable	Items
G. Relatives in the Community	A single item (E71) reflecting whether there were relatives other than family living in the community during the war.

IV. Sharing

The *Sharing factor* assessed the degree of support for distributing resources for others' welfare. It ranked fourth as a predictor of rescue (0.41). Measures loading on this factor included Prosocial Action Orientation (0.82), Social Responsibility Scale (0.80), Empathy Scale (0.73), Personal Integrity as a Child (0.46), Detachment (inverse relationship, -0.45), Community Helping Today (0.34), and Feelings of Similarity to Poor (0.26).

Constructed Variable	Items
A. Care	One of four factors that emerged from eleven categories of responses reflecting values learned from father, mother, and significant other (from B12, B22, B32).

	Loading	*Item*
	0.87	Parental valuing of universal care
	0.76	Parental valuing of care

Constructed Variable	Items
B. Community Helping Today	One of two factors that emerged in relation to post-war helping behavior in response to thirteen questions (F7–F10g).

	Loading	*Item*
	0.78	(F10e) During past year, how often have you given speeches or lectures or written letters on behalf of an issue or cause?
	0.77	(F10f) During past year, how often have you investigated, collected, or prepared information on behalf of an issue or cause?

Constructed Variable	Items

Loading	Item
0.71	(F10d) During past year, how often have you made telephone calls or helped raise money on behalf of a group or cause?
0.52	(F10c) During past year, how often have you taught children or adults or counseled anyone about jobs or personal problems?
0.50	(F8) Are you or have you recently been involved in helping activities in your community, such as volunteer work with charities, schools, churches, etc?
0.49	(F10a) During past year, how often have you led recreational activities for children or adults?
0.37	(F7) After the war, did you ever do anything unusual to help someone?
0.37	(F10b) During past year, how often have you helped feed the sick or the aged or visited the ill?
0.32	(F10g) During past year, how often have you contributed money or goods to some cause?
0.27	(F9d) During past year, have you given help to a stranger?

C. Detachment

One of three factors that emerged from a factor analysis of forty-two personality items (in F14) relating to feelings at the present time. High scores reflect greater detachment from events and persons.

Loading	Item
0.50	(F14.14) It's no use worrying about current events or public affairs; I can't do anything about them anyway.
0.38	(F14.22) Letting people down is not so bad, because you can't do good all the time for everybody.

Table 8. Continued

Constructed Variable	Items

	Loading	*Item*
	0.37	(F14.15) When I work on a committee, I usually let other people do most of the planning.
	0.36	(F14.36) I wish I could have more respect for myself.
	0.35	(F14.16) I feel I have little influence over what happens to me.
	0.34	(F14.5) I often find that what is going to happen will happen.
	0.33	(F14.30) People would be a lot better off if they would live far away from other people and never have anything to do with them.
	0.31	(F14.31) I get nervous if others are nervous.

D. Empathy — A scale consisting of nineteen items from the Empathy Scale, developed by Mehrabian and Epstein (1972) and modified by Midlarsky (1981). Respondents rated their agreement with each item on a 1–4 scale. Responses were coded and summated so that higher scores reflect higher emotional empathy.

E. Equity

a. Church Valuing of Equity — One of four factors that emerged from thirteen categories reflecting values learned from religious leaders (in response to question C10).

Loading	*Item*
0.86	Church valuing of equity
0.77	Church valuing of universal equity

b. Parental Valuing of Equity — One of four factors that emerged from eleven categories reflecting values learned from father, mother, and significant other (B12, B22, B32).

Loading	*Item*
0.70	Parental valuing of universal equity
0.62	Parental valuing of equity

F. Feelings of Similarity to Poor — A single item (D21B) on which respondents rated on a 1–4 scale how similar they felt to poor people.

Constructed Variable	Items
G. Personal Integrity	One of two factors that emerged from ten self-attributed personal qualities when respondents grew up (C18a–j).

Loading	Item
0.52	(C18d) Able to take responsibility
0.52	(C18a) Honest
0.45	(C18h) Helpful
0.34	(C18i) Willing to stand up for beliefs

Constructed Variable	Items
H. Prosocial Action	One of three factors that emerged from a factor analysis of forty-two personality items relating to present time. High scores reflect strong empathic feelings toward others in distress and personal standards for persistence and follow-through in what they undertake.

Loading	Item
0.56	(F14.36) Seeing people cry upsets me.
0.52	(F14.7) I can't feel good if others around me feel sad.
0.51	(F14.12) It upsets me to see helpless people.
0.51	(F14.35) If it is worth starting, it is worth finishing.
0.49	(F14.10) I get very upset when I see an animal in pain.
0.48	(F14.8) The feelings of people in books affect me.
0.48	(F14.21) I get angry when I see someone hurt.
0.47	(F14.28) I feel very bad when I fail to finish something promised.
0.43	(F14.29) I get very involved in my friends' problems.
0.43	(F14.26) The words of a song can move me deeply.
0.37	(F14.2) Every person should give time for the good of the country.
0.35	(F14.18) I get nervous if others seem nervous.

Table 8. Continued

Constructed Variable	Items

	Loading	Item
	0.34	(F14.37) Bringing bad news to others upsets me.
	0.33	(F14.1) It's sad to see a lonely person in a crowd.

Constructed Variable	Items
I. Social Responsibility	A scale consisting of eight items (in F14) from the Social Responsibility Scale developed by Harris (1957) and modified by Berkowitz and Lutterman (1968). Respondents rated their agreement with each item on a 1–4 scale. Responses were coded and summated so that higher scores reflect a higher sense of social responsibility.

V. Mastery

The Mastery measures formed two separate factors reflecting external and internal mastery orientation. The *External Mastery factor* reflected mastery through dependence on external authorities for control of resources. On the discriminant analysis, it ranked fifth and inversely with rescue (-0.35). The *Internal Mastery factor* reflected mastery through reliance on internal resources and ranked sixth as a predictor of rescue (0.30).

Constructed Variable	Items
A. External Mastery	One of two factors emerging from factor analysis to summarize mastery measures. This factor reflects the sense of mastery obtained through compliance with external criteria. Measures loading highly on this factor included Obedience (0.84), Propriety (0.69) and Economic Competence (0.57).
1. Economic Competence	One of four factors that emerged from eleven categories reflecting values learned from father, mother, and significant other adult (in response to questions B12, B22, B32).

	Loading	Item
	0.58	Parental valuing of economic competence
	0.28	Parental valuing of dependability

Constructed Variable	Items
2. Obedience	One of four factors reflecting learned parental values (in response to B12, B22, B32).

	Loading	Item
	0.35	Parental valuing of obedience

Constructed Variable	Items
3. Propriety	A single variable reflecting whether the respondent mentioned propriety as a learned parental value (in response to B12, B22, B32).
B. Internal Mastery	One of two factors emerging from factor analysis to summarize mastery measures. This factor reflects the sense of mastery obtained through dependence on one's internal resources. Measures loading on this factor included Self-Esteem (0.72), Sense of Personal Potency as a Child (0.70), Internal Locus of Control (0.63) and Standing Up for Beliefs before the War (0.35).
1. Internal Locus of Control	A scale consisting of five items (in section F14) from the Internal/External Locus of Control Scale, developed by Rotter (1966) and modified by Gurin, Gurin, and Morrison (1978). Respondents rated their agreement with each item on a 1–4 scale. Responses were coded and summated so that higher scores reflect greater perceived internal locus of control. It measures the extent to which individuals view themselves as able to affect external events through their own efforts.
2. Personal Potency	One of two factors that emerged from ratings of ten self-attributed personal qualities when respondents grew up (C18a–j).

Loading	*Item*
0.68	(C18f) Able to make decisions
0.61	(C18c) Independent
0.58	(C18g) Adventurous
0.53	(C18e) Willing to take chances
0.43	(C18b) Self-confident
0.39	(C18d) Able to take responsibility

Constructed Variable	Items
3. Self-Esteem	A scale consisting of ten items (in F14) from the Self-Esteem Scale, developed by Rosenberg (1965). Respondents rated their agreement with each item on a 1–4 scale. Responses were coded and summated so that higher scores reflect higher self-esteem.

Table 8. Continued

Constructed Variable	Items
4. Stand Up for Beliefs	A single item (D17) in which respondents indicated whether they had ever done anything unusual to stand up for their beliefs before the war.

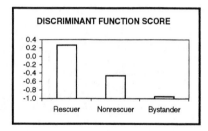

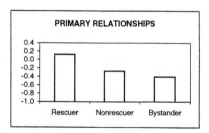

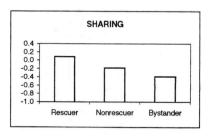

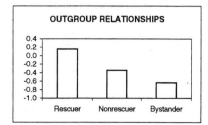

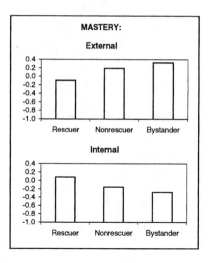

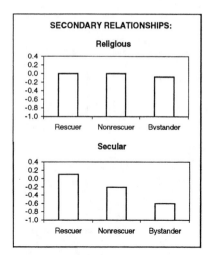

Figure 1: Mean standardized scores on discriminant function and summary factors for rescuers, nonrescuers, and bystanders: Bar graphs.

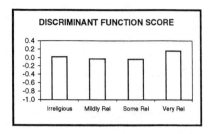

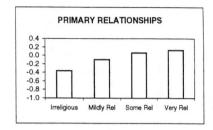

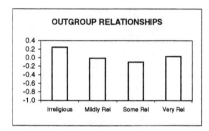

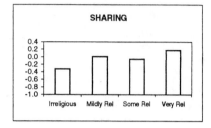

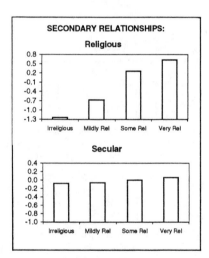

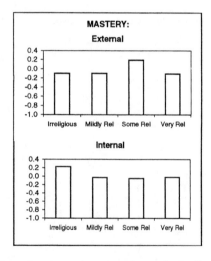

Figure 2: Mean standardized scores on discriminant function and summary factors for irreligious, mildly religious, somewhat religious, and very religious respondents: Bar graphs.

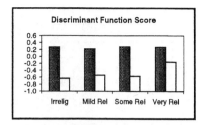

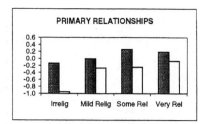

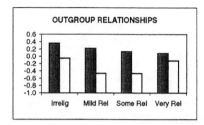

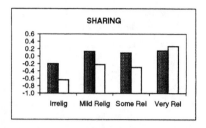

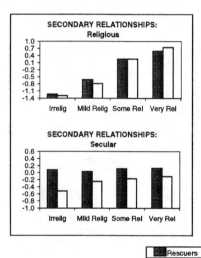

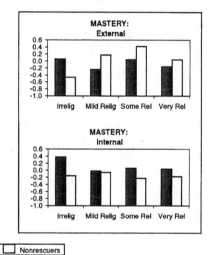

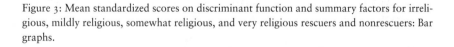

Figure 3: Mean standardized scores on discriminant function and summary factors for irreligious, mildly religious, somewhat religious, and very religious rescuers and nonrescuers: Bar graphs.

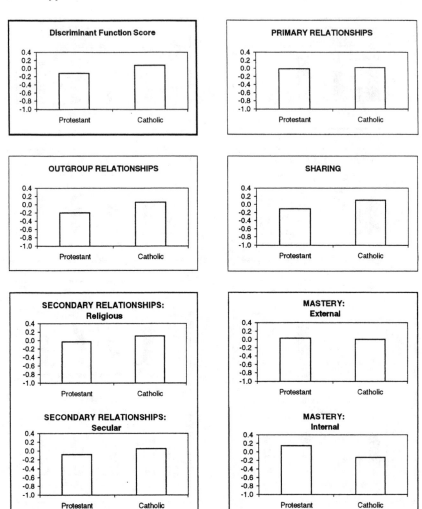

Figure 4: Mean standardized scores on discriminant function and summary factors for Protestants and Catholics: Bar graphs.

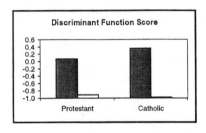

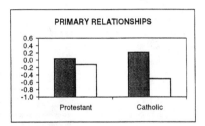

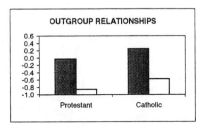

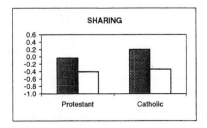

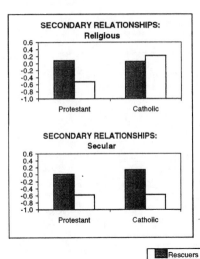

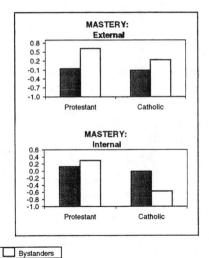

Figure 5: Mean standardized scores on discriminant function and summary factors for Protestant and Catholic rescuers and bystanders: Bar graphs.

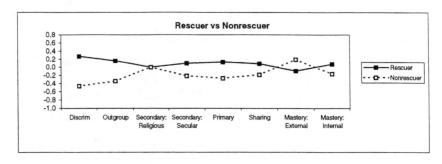

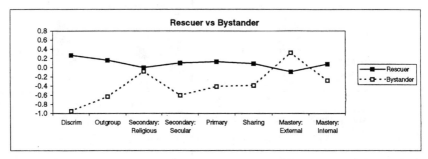

Figure 6: Mean standardized scores on discriminant function and summary factors for rescuers, nonrescuers, and bystanders: Profiles.

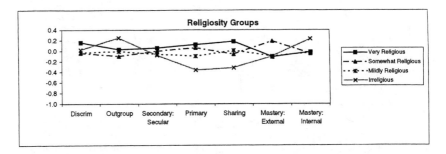

Figure 7: Mean standardized scores on discriminant function and summary factors for irreligious, mildly religious, somewhat religious, and very religious respondents: Profiles.

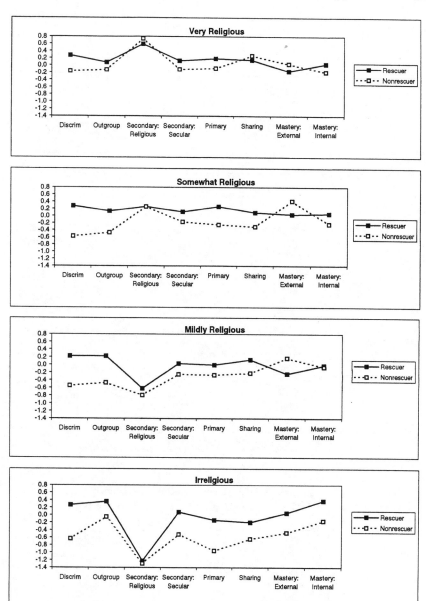

Figure 8: Mean standardized scores on discriminant function and summary factors for irreligious, mildly religious, somewhat religious, and very religious rescuers and nonrescuers: Profiles.

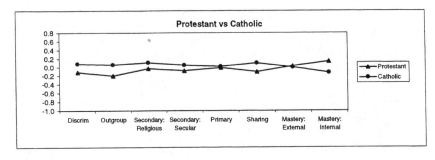

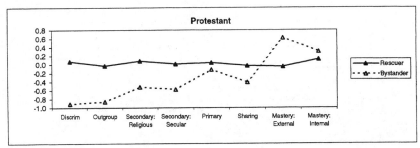

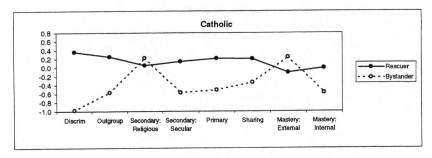

Figure 9: Mean standardized scores on discriminant function and summary factors for Protestants and Catholics, and for Protestant and Catholic rescuers and bystanders: Profiles.

Notes

Chapter 1. Religion and Culture

1. For some examples of descriptions regarding rescuer activities, see Paldiel (1993, 2000); Rittner and Myers (1986); Hallie (1979); Oliner and Oliner (1988); Tec (1986); Baron (1988, 1992, 1995); Gilbert (2002), Monroe (1996, 2004).

2. For discussions of this issue see Barnett (1992); Blumenthal (1999); Carroll (2001); Chary (1970); Conway (1968); Cornwell (1999); Ericksen and Heschel (1999); Gushee (1994); Hilberg (1985); de Jong (1965); Locke, Littell, and Sachs (1996); Littell and Locke (1974); Lubac (1990); Marrus and Paxton (1981); Mastny (1971); McInerny (2001); Modras (1994); Morely (1980); Phayer (2000); Rittner, Smith, and Steinfeldt (2000); Sanchez (2001); Zuccoti (1993).

3. For research on empathy, see Batson (1981); Batson and Oleson (1991); Davis (1994); Eisenberg and Fabes (1990); Eisenberg and Miller (1987); Heshka (1983); Hoffman (1990); Otten and Altabe (1991). For situational variables, see Drake, Finkelstein, and Spolsky (1982); Darley and Latané (1968); Hensley (1981); Latané and Darley (1970); Rappaport (1988); Shotland and Stebbins (1983). For social and personal responsibility studies, see Berkowitz and Daniels (1964); Midlarsky (1984); Penner and Fritzsche (1993). For a comprehensive review of relevant variables and studies see Schroeder et al. (1995). For personality and situational variables related to rescue, see Baron (1995, 1998); Blumental (1999); Gushee (1994); London (1970); Oliner and Oliner (1988); Tec (1986).

4. The Altruistic Personality and Prosocial Behavior Institute, founded by Samuel P. Oliner, is located at Humboldt State University. Sam Oliner serves as its executive director and Pearl Oliner as its research director.

5. Gilbert (2002).

6. Oliner and Oliner (1988), Appendix C: questionnaire, pp. 331–356.

7. Social psychologist Daniel Batson, a major contributor to experimental studies of altruism, regards motivation as all important. Only empathic concern, he concludes — including feelings such as tenderness, sympathy and compassion — produces a real altruistic motivation (Batson 1987).

8. Oliner and Oliner (1988, p. 5).

9. Oliner and Oliner (1988, p. 6).

10. Sober and Wilson (1998).

11. Blum (1980, 1992).

12. For more on this point see Triandis (1995).

13. Hofstede (1994).

14. Tylor (1871).

15. Benedict (1946); Boas (1932); C. Kluckhohn (1949); Mead (1939); Sapir (1957).

16. Almond and Verba (1963); Lasch (1978); Renshon and Duckitt (1997); Wilson (1997).

17. Hofstede (1991, p. 5); Pye (June 1997); Geertz (1973, 1983).

18. Hofstede (1991, p. 8); Swidler (1986); Fiske and Tetlock (1997, p. 261).

19. Triandis (1995, p. 6); Hofstede (1991, p. 18, note 1).

20. Hofstede (1991).

21. Hood, Spilka, Hunsburger, and Gorsuch (1996, p. 4).

22. Wulff (1997); Smith (1963).

23. Geertz (1973).

24. Durkheim (1969); Kurtz (1995, p. 9); Roberts (1995, p. 20); Batson, Schoenrade, and Ventis (1993, p. 8). The "religion as quest" process typically includes questions related to the meaning and purpose of life, relationships to others, death, and self-improvement.

25. See Hill and Hood (1999) for more on measures of religiosity; The concepts "intrinsic" and "extrinsic" were developed by Gordon Allport (1960) and subsequently formed into the Intrinsic/Extrinsic Scale by Feagin (1964). For a summary of efforts to measure religiosity, see Wulff (1997).

Chapter 2. The Very Religious

1. Under the terms of the Armistice that the French signed after their defeat in June 1940, the Germans were to occupy northern France while southern France was to be governed by a French administration. Named after the town of Vichy in which it had its seat, the southern sector Vichy government under head of state Marshal Henri Philippe Pétain was ostensibly neutral. In fact, it actually cooperated with Germany, enacting anti-Jewish legislation on its own as well as rounding up and deporting Jews.

2. Marrus and Paxton (1981, pp. 166–167, 271). For more details on the nightmarish conditions, see Zucotti (1993).

3. Marrus and Paxton (1981) write that Church officials generally did not renew their protests when massive roundups resumed in February 1943 (p. 278).

4. Marrus and Paxton (1981) call it "the clearest voice yet heard in France on the persecution of Jews" (p. 271).

5. The Ausweiss were identification papers that all inhabitants were required to have and present on demand. Intended to discriminate among individuals and groups and to weed out all types of "undesirables," they included complex and detailed personal information, including their religion, ethnicity, and nationality. Jacob's family apparently felt that the Ausweiss they had managed to get assured them permanent safety; Alexander's wife correctly understood that it did not.

6. Baron (1988).

7. Baron (1995b).

8. After completing a cross-cultural political analysis more than forty years ago, sociologist Seymour Lipset (1960) concluded that the personality characteristics of the two extremes, dogmatic fundamentalists and political radicals, were similar in many respects.

9. A study by James A. Christenson (1976) suggests a similar conclusion about the very religious. Restricted to North Carolina and dominantly Protestant subjects, Christenson's study concluded that "stronger adherence to religious values has a consistently positive relation with social compassion issues" (p. 37). Based on their synthesis of several studies, social psychologists Schroeder, Penner, Dovidio, and Piliavin (1995) conclude not only that most religious denominations teach prosocial values and norms, but also that religion is very influential in encouraging prosocial action.

10. Batson (1991, 1993); Davis (1994); Eisenberg and Fabes (1990); Hoffman (1990); Oliner and Oliner (1988). For a summary of the relationship between sharing measures and altruistic behavior, see Schroeder, Penner, Dovidio, and Piliavin (1995).

11. As Barnea and Schwartz (1998) define it more formally, "The egalitarian position bases a rejection of the hierarchical organization of society and the differential distribution of resources on the principles of equality and need. It emphasizes equality among individuals, the well-being of all, and cooperation and mutual responsibility" (p. 22).

12. None identified themselves as Communists, but four were Polish Socialists.

13. Parties were ranked on four variables: economic orientation, political structure, policies concerning minorities generally, and policies concerning Jews specifically.

14. Representative examples of this tendency include the Anti-Revolutionary Party and Christian Historical Union in the Netherlands, Zentrum (Center) Party in Germany, Catholic Action in France, Italian Popular Party in Italy, Christian Democratic Party in Poland, and Slovak Democratic Party in Czechoslovakia. Reluctance to depend on government for income redistribution does not necessarily exclude private giving, however. In the United States, for example, religious commitment tends to be accompanied by a philosophy of minimal government intervention in resource distribution: the Christian religious right traditionally supports lower taxes and less social welfare. But recent U.S. data collected by *Boston Globe* columnist Jeff Jacoby and analyzed by Michael Levine (Levine, 1998) support the notion that among religious Christians personal giving is inversely related to support of government expansiveness — that is, the less supportive they are of government welfare programs, the more generous they are personally. A good deal of such personal generosity in the United States is directed to religious organizations. Statistics from the 1992 United States Bureau of the Census (Independent Sector) led Schroeder, Penner, Dovidio, and Piliavin (1995) to conclude that "In the United States, the most likely recipient of charitable contributions is a religious organization" (p. 236). It seems plausible that like their current American counterparts, very religious respon-

dents were quite ready to share their resources, but like them, too, they preferred to depend on their religious denominations to distribute them appropriately.

15. Several studies suggest that family life is particularly important to the religious (Maton and Wells (1995); McAdoo and Crawford (1991); Stinnett (1979)).

16. Similarly, a number of other studies suggest that the most powerful predictor of children's religiosity is their parents' religious involvement (D. Erickson (1964), Lenski (1953), Newcomb and Svehla (1937), Putney and Middleton (1961), Stark (1963), Weigert and Thomas (1972). Although parents strongly influence children's religious choice and religiosity, they do not necessarily determine it.

17. Greenberg and Pyszczynski (1990) believe that religiosity and patriotism stem from a similar psychological need to allay the anxiety that attends the human condition—what they call the "management of terror." For more on this point see Mizruchi (1998).

18. Reykowski (1997).

19. Reykowski (1997, p. 125).

20. Staub (1997). Staub's conception is very similar to that advanced by Adorno, Frenkel-Brunswik, Levinson, and Sanford (1950) who identified two types of patriotism: "genuine" and "pseudo."

21. Gushee (1994, p. 186) proposes that "one place many people learned to hate Jews was in church." But, he observes, "philo-Semitism" was also evident among several religious communities, including the Reformed Church of Holland (Alexander's community), French Protestants, Ukrainian and Lithuanian Baptists, Hungarian Methodists, and German Plymouth Brethren.

22. One Reformed Church member in our sample explained it this way: "You get Bible history. That starts with the Jews. They were for us God's chosen people. That is the way I was brought up. My father talked about that. At the same time, I knew that part of our mission was to convert Jews."

23. Gushee (1994) notes that Christian rescuers frequently called upon such sources. Featured prominently among them are the Parable of the Good Samaritan (Luke 10:25–37), the Sermon on the Mount, the duty to love of God and neighbor (Matt. 22:34–40), "The Great Judgment" (Matt. 25:31–46), the Golden Rule (Matt: 7:12), and the Cain and Abel story in Genesis (4:8–10), "My brother's Keeper" (Gen 4:8–10). The Isaiah passage that Alexander's family read the night they made their decision was another in the same motif.

24. Glock and Stark (1966).

25. Adorno, Frenkel-Brunswik, Levinson, and Sanford (1950); Allport and Kramer (1946); Pettigrew (1959).

26. See review by Gorsuch and Aleshire (1974).

27. Jewish scholars have written extensively on this topic over many centuries. Among the outstanding Christian leaders of current efforts to purge antisemitism from Christian theology and to forge new and deep bonds of brotherhood with Jews are Franklin Littell (emeritus professor of religion at Temple University and co-founder of the Annual Scholars' Conference on the Holocaust and the Churches), Hubert G. Locke (co-founder of the Annual Scholars' Conference on the Holocaust and the Churches), John K. Roth (Edward J. Sexton Professor of Philosophy at Claremont McKenna College), Carol Rittner (Distinguished Professor of Holocaust Studies at Richard Stockton University), Elizabeth

Maxwell, and Harry James Cargas (the first Catholic appointed to the international advisory board of Yad Vashem, formerly professor of literature and language at Webster University and editor of more than thirty books, most of them on the Holocaust, now deceased). All have published extensively on the Holocaust (see the Bibliography for some of their publications) and together with others too numerous to mention, have exerted extraordinary energy toward making the study of antisemitism a high priority among Christians.

28. Hay (1951), Flannery (1965), Foerster (1962).

29. Eisinga, Felling, and Peters (1990); Friedrichs (1959); Hoge and Carroll (1973); Other studies using different measures of religiosity have also tended to support this relationship, among them Struening (1963) and Wilson (1973). Twenty of the twenty-five studies Gorsuch and Aleshire reviewed in 1974 supported a curvilinear relationship. For a more recent review, see Wulff (1997).

30. Marrus and Paxton (1981, p. 199).

31. Eliach (1998, p. 594).

32. As Nechama Tec (1986) summarizes it, when its posture was less than uniform, a frequent condition, "conventional religion was flexible," and could lead to either destruction or help.

33. It also appears to be consistent with Rokeach's study (1969) done more than forty years ago. Religious subjects, he suggested, often tended to be preoccupied with their own personal salvation and relatively indifferent to issues of social inequality and justice (p. 11).

34. Conway (1968, pp. 81–82).

35. The Pastors' Emergency League was formed in 1933, when Niemöller, then pastor of Berlin's Dahlem Church, alarmed by the State's escalating distortion of Scripture, invited pastors to join him to protest new legislation.

36. Baranowski (1986); Conway (1968).

37. Baranowski (1986); Conway (1968); Weiss (1996).

38. Weiss (1996, p. 226). Baranowski (1986) writes that the Confessing Church was dominated by a conservative elitist group, whose sentiments were similar to that of the "great mass of Germans who agreed with quotas and other measures of exclusion even as they objected to anti-Semitic violence. Legal restrictions were seen, accordingly, not as persecution producing victims as were the action of party militants, but as remedies of injustice" (p. 85). Jürgen's father apparently reflected similar views: "Father was not exactly antisemitic," he said, but he saw himself as a "civil servant in contrast to merchants. Jews are humans too but they play too prominent a part in the country's economy. My father was National Liberal, but in education he personified the Prussian civil servant."

39. Kurek-Lesik (1997). For more on the role of Polish Catholic orders, see Bogner (1999) and Zielinski (1987).

40. After analyzing our sample, Baron (1995) reports that over 60 percent of rescuers in this group reported being originally approached for help by pastors and other church officials, or by close friends and relatives. Almost 80 percent said their family members were also involved in sheltering Jews.

41. Hallie (1979).

42. For a succinct historical summary of rescue in thirteen European countries, see Paldiel (1993).

Chapter 3. The Irreligious

1. Egalitarian principles apparently wound up causing his arrest. A friend asked Andrzej to help his in-laws escape from the ghetto and offered him money. Highly offended, he refused. The reason? "His in-laws were rich and still had money during that time. They could have bought their way out. I told my friend that I was helping only poor people and that he should seek help from those who get paid for helping." His friend became very angry and in retaliation reported him to the Gestapo, and thus his imprisonment in Pawiak.

2. Offered the opportunity from some of his admirers to escape, Korczak chose to perish with his Jewish orphans rather than abandon them; all were gassed in Treblinka in 1942.

3. Korczak's influence is indicated by an account Andrzej gave of a meeting with a young stranger, a Jewish woman, in 1951, six years after the war had ended. By then a journalist in Warsaw, she told him that Dr. Korczak had sent her to him during the war years to ask for help. She never went, she said, because of her general distrust of Poles: too many "were vultures, greedy people who betrayed Jews, and who waited for their prey around the Ghetto." "This," said Andrzej, "the voice of Korczak reaching me after so many years and after his death, was much more memorable for me than all those more or less successful actions."

4. While there was never any effectively single unified underground opposition to the Nazis in the Netherlands, many participants in underground activities did consider themselves members of "The Resistance." Nellie here appears to be distinguishing between those groups who had military goals—the "real Resistance," as she calls them—and those concerned with hiding people. The L.O., the National Organization for Assistance to Divers (Landelijke Organisatie voor Hulp aan Onderduikers), one of the largest Resistance organizations, was intended to coordinate individuals and groups trying to assist those who needed to go into hiding. Founded in late 1942 by a housewife, Mrs. H. Th. Kuipers-Rietberg, and the Rev. F. Slomp, an anti-Nazi Calvinist minister, it focused initially on those trying to escape the labor draft in Germany. Eventually it expanded to include underground workers and Jews. Before the end of the war the L.O. included approximately 15,000 collaborators (Warmbrunn 1972, p. 188).

5. Koestner, Franz, and Weinberger (1990).

6. In the Netherlands, for example, the largest Dutch trade union, the Netherlands Association of Trade Unions (Nederlands Verbond van Vakverenigingen) was allied with the Social Democratic Party. Strongly democratic and socialist, according to Werner Warmbrunn (1963) it had 319,000 members before the invasion. Friendships and contacts among individuals in the union facilitated an underground organization that distributed ration cards, found hiding places for *underdeikers,* and published an underground paper that included information about persecution of Jews.

7. Our findings are consistent with studies in the United States where researchers repeatedly report lowest levels of prejudice among the irreligious (see for example

Adorno, Frenkel-Brunswik, Levinson, and Sanford (1950); Altemeyer and Hunsberger (1992); Hunsberger (1995)).

8. Although not officially established as a new political party until 1947, the PPR (Polska Partia Robotnicza, or Polish Workers Party) was the Polish unified Communist underground organization that emerged in 1942; their underground fighters were known as the People's Army.

9. Staub (1997).

10. Zuccotti (1993) writes that among the left Resistance in France, "The major clandestine Communist paper, *l'Humanité,* referred to Jewish matters only eight times between June 1940 and May 1941 and said nothing at all about German antisemitic ordinances in the occupied zone or about Vichy's racial laws. On October 3, 1940, it welcomed the confiscation of the property of Maurice de Rothschild, predictably calling for a similar policy against all capitalists and declaring, 'Those who oppose these measures, whether done under the guise of anti-Semitism or under other pretexts, are no more than the watchdog of capital." *L'Humanité* finally attacked anti-Semitism as such in May 1941, when it described the arrests of Jewish workers in Paris. But still, it referred to Jewish matters only nine times between May 1941 and September 1942, and not at all between September 1942 and the end of the war. Most French Communists, particularly non-Jews, adhered to the party line: anti-Semitism was an unfortunate by-product of capitalism and a distraction from the class struggle. It and all forms of racism, they believed, would inevitably disappear with the triumph of the workers' revolution" (p. 139). Zuccotti does note that "more specialized Communist newspapers, such as *l'Université libre,* a publication of Parisian intellectuals, and *Notre Voix* (*Unzer Wort* in Yiddish) and *Solidarité,* representing foreign Jews, mentioned the racial persecutions much more frequently" (p. 140).

11. See, for example, Lazare (1996).

12. The British dropped approximately fifty agents in the Netherlands through Englandspiel, their intended mission to commit military and economic sabotage. Unfortunately two of the Dutch agents were arrested and gave the Germans the code, which effectively ended the Englandspiel by the end of 1943. For more, see Warmbrunn (1963).

13. General Winkelman was the Commander in Chief of the Dutch Armed Forces. Advised by him the day after Dutch capitulation that he could no longer assure her safety, Queen Wilhemina and the Dutch governmental ministers left for England. Winkelman thus became the highest governmental authority in the Netherlands.

14. Founded by Anton A. Mussert in 1931, the NSB, the National Socialist Movement of the Netherlands (Nationaal-Socialistische Beweging der Nederlanden), was a Dutch fascist movement that collaborated with the Germans. Increasingly antisemitic, it adopted Nazi race theories after the occupation and assisted in the persecution of Jews.

Chapter 4. The Moderately Religious

1. The cell means for "standing up for beliefs" show a curvilinear pattern for both rescuers and nonrescuers, with lower proportions of the somewhat religious respondents reporting standing up for their beliefs as compared with the not at all religious and very religious respondents.

2. Allport (1959). Extrinsics, said Allport, view religion as a means rather than an end — they use religion as a means to focus on themselves and their own needs for sociability, security, or status. Their orientation contrasts sharply with those who are "intrinsically" religious; for them religion is an end rather than a means. Intrinsics take religion seriously, internalizing its principles and vision and living it. The twenty-item Religious Orientation Scale developed by Allport and Ross (1967) is widely used to assess these orientations. A more recent measure of religiosity has been developed by Batson, Schoenrade, and Ventis (1993). It is called the Religious Life Inventory, and one of the three scales it includes is intended to measure the religious "quest-sensitive individual"; that is, the degree to which the individual recognizes and struggles with religious conflicts rather than accepting ready answers. Batson has provided evidence to suggest that the quest-sensitive individual is more helpful to others and less prejudiced than either the intrinsically or extrinsically oriented individual.

3. The cell means for nonrescuers showed a curvilinear pattern, with somewhat religious nonrescuers scoring highest on parental physical punishment. Rescuers, however, did not show a curvilinear pattern but scored the same regardless of their religiosity level.

4. Horizontal social distance, explains Ruth Cavan (1971), "refers to value differences that members of one religious group feel to exist between them and members of another religious group"; vertical social distance "refers to the degree of acceptability within a hierarchy of social status groups" (p. 94).

5. Among rescuers, religiosity correlates significantly with political party position, and a linear pattern prevails. The less religious rescuers' parties tended to a more leftist economic position and to be more supportive of minorities and Jews, and their relatives' parties reflected a similar pattern. For nonrescuers, religiosity does not correlate significantly to political party direction, and the pattern is curvilinear, with the somewhat religious least inclined to leftist economics and most exclusionary.

6. Ehrlich (December/January 2000, p. 1). For more on the phenomenon of "denial," particularly as it relates to genocides, see Charny (2000).

7. Augoustinos and Walker (1995, p. 222). For a review of current theories regarding the influence of cognition and culture on stereotypes, see Hinton (2000).

8. While earlier investigations concluded that intensity of religious involvement correlated positively with prejudice (e.g., Allport and Kramer 1946; Rosenbluth 1949), later studies reported a curvilinear relationship, that is a relationship consistent with our findings. Based on a comprehensive review of published empirical studies up to the early seventies, Gorsuch and Aleshire (1974) concluded that moderately active church members were likely to be more prejudiced than either nonmembers or highly active church members. They hypothesized that the more "casually" religious — that is, moderately actively church members as compared with the very religious and the irreligious — have weak value positions and tend to select their values from the society at large. Conversely, the very religious and irreligious tend to have strong value positions and can stand outside the value traditions of the larger society. In other words, the moderately religious tend toward conformity, accepting the views of others; the strongly religious and irreligious, by contrast, are prepared to be deviants if necessary, preferring to live according to their own values. But this curvilinear relationship has also been disputed. Altemeyer and

Hunsberger (1992, 1993), for example, claim that the empirical evidence for curvilinearity is weak, and that the relationship is indeed a relatively strong linear one.

Chapter 5. Protestants

1. By autumn of 1941, paths for escape were sealed and deportations were begun. There were several protected categories when deportations began in Germany in 1941: foreign citizens, family members of Jews employed in the defense industries, spouses in mixed marriages, those over fifty and in poor health, and the elderly over sixty. With time, individuals falling within these protected categories also were deported (Lozowick (1999).

2. For more on the behavior of the Norwegian churches, see Abrahamsen (1988).

3. Weber (1958; originally published in 1904–1905); Bruce (1996); Dumont (1986); Kurtz (1995); Lenski (1961); Novak (1993); Robertson (1933); Samuelson (1957); Sombart (1967); Tawney (1926); Triandis (1995).

4. For a fuller elaboration of these points, see *The Columbia Encyclopedia of Religion,* 1993 edition.

5. Kurtz (1995, p. 111).

6. Kurtz (1995, pp. 112–113, 133.)

7. Although the personal potency factor does include "independent" as one of six self-attributed descriptions, a comparison of Protestants and Catholics on "independence" when measured by itself shows no significant difference between them.

8. For a comprehensive review and analysis of classical and contemporary psychological views of religion, see Wulff (1997).

9. Coe (1900), Sheldon (1936).

10. Fromm (1941, 1950).

11. Erikson (1958, p. 263).

12. Jung (1969; first German edition 1952.)

13. Ulanov (1971).

14. Weber in Andreski, ed. (1983). One Calvinist Protestant rescuer put it more simply: "Every Protestant is really a pastor with a Bible in hand."

15. While this might be regarded as a historical issue, no longer relevant in the contemporary scene, it is interesting to note that in comparisons with Catholics, Jews, and nonreligious persons, Rokeach (1969) found some thirty years ago that Protestants ranked salvation as their highest value.

16. Miller (1984).

17. Greven (1977).

18. Weber in Andreski, ed. (1983, p. 115).

19. Weber in Andreski, ed. (1983, pp. 122, 123).

20. Weber in Andreski, ed. (1983, pp. 158–59). In the contemporary Western world, Roberts (1984) writes, "the rational pursuit of wealth (spirit of capitalism) is so thoroughly secularized . . . that it has become independent of any one religious tradition" (p. 278).

21. Murray (1938).

22. Kelvin and Jarrett (1985).

23. For a review of philosophical and empirical work related to the PWE, see Furnham (1990).

24. Furnham (1982, 1983, 1985); MacDonald (1972); Wagstaff (1983); Williamson (1974).

25. Lerner (1980). "Just world" beliefs have been found to correlate positively with many attributes associated with the PWE, as well as authoritarianism, conservative political attitudes, and a strong internal locus of control (the idea that people can control external events through their own internal resources).

26. Furnham (1987).

Chapter 6. Catholics

1. Luke Rothfels (1961, p. 15) reports that in 1939, a Gestapo agent stated in court that in all of Germany, "at least 2,000 boys and girls" were part of such groups.

2. The Croix de Feu was a right-wing-party, reconstituted after 1936 as the Parti Social Français (PSF) with a membership estimated at from 700,000 to 3 million. While Colonel de la Rocque, its leader, repeatedly declared himself not an antisemite, many Jews viewed him and his party with suspicion (Hyman 1979, pp. 226–227). Although definitely a movement of the Right, Marrus and Paxton (1981) point out the new Parti Social fell short "of truly fascist violence and authoritarianism," and refused pointedly to join the anti-Jewish bandwagon, despite the objections of Algerian and Alsatian members as well as more extremist groups (p. 47.) Many right-wing Catholic leaders condemned antisemitism before the war.

3. Dolan (1985); Tracy (1982); Greeley (1990).

4. Greeley (1990); Kurtz (1995, p. 64); Vergote and Tamayo, eds. (1981).

5. Tropman (1995).

6. Tropman (1995, pp. 8, 26).

7. Marty (1996, p. 348).

8. Other terms associated with "collectivist" include "interdependent," "connected," "holistic," "relationship," and "*Gemeinschaft*"; other terms associated with "individualistic" include "independent," "separate," "autonomous," "self-contained," and "*Gesellschaft*" (Toennies 1957).

9. Triandis (1995, pp. 43–44).

10. Tropman (1995).

11. Tropman (1995, p. 76).

12. Weber (1950; first published in 1924).

13. Novak goes on to say that rejection of economics as a primary value is not unique to Catholicism but is rather shared by many groups. "Catholicism is not alone in regarding economic life as a means, as secondary, to a fully human life," he writes, but "so also Protestantism, Judaism, and humanism — and so also Adam Smith, Abraham Lincoln, John Stuart Mill, and many others" (Novak 1993, p. 32).

14. Greeley (1996).

Chapter 7. Patterns and Predictors

1. Strauss and Quinn (2000, p. 91).

2. A discriminant analysis was performed using the five summary factors as predictors of rescuer versus bystander status. The predictors were the factors reflecting Mastery Orientation (Internal/External), Sharing, Primary Relationships, Secondary Relationships (Religious/Secular), and Outgroup Relationships. All of the 346 rescuers and 97 bystanders were included in the analysis, for a total of 443 individuals. One-way univariate analysis of variance verified that the two groups differed significantly on each of the factors, with the rescuers scoring significantly lower than the bystanders on the External Mastery Orientation and significantly higher on each of the other factors. In combination the five summary factors predicted group membership significantly higher than chance, $F_{(6,436)} = 18.57$, $p < 0.001$, eta$^2 = 0.203$. Discriminant function scores were calculated for each respondent based on their scores on the predictor variables, weighted by the discriminant function coefficients. The canonical correlation between the discriminant function scores and group membership was significant, $R_{(436)} = 0.451$, $p < 0.001$. The mean standardized discriminant score was $+0.267$ for the rescuers and -0.952 for the bystanders, indicating that the two groups differed by more than one standard deviation on the discriminant function. When the discriminant scores were used to classify the respondents into predicted rescuer and bystander groupings, with proportions matching the proportions of actual rescuers and bystanders in the sample, 82.4 percent of the individuals were correctly classified. Using the cross-validation procedures, where each individual was classified by the function derived from all other individuals, 80.8 percent of the individuals were correctly classified. These percentages were significantly higher than the 65.9 percent correct classification that would be expected if predictions were made solely by chance, $p < 0.001$.

Chapter 8. Culture and Outgroup Altruism

1. Fiske (1991a, b); Tetlock (1997); Hofstede (1991).

2. Triandis (1995).

3. Hofstede (1994, p. 138).

4. Hofstede (1991).

5. Schwartz (1994a, b).

6. Baron (1995b). Baron writes that "although members of the Reformed Churches constituted only 9 percent of the Dutch population, they accounted for an estimated 25 percent of the rescues of Jews in the Netherlands during the Holocaust." He further concludes that "congregants of these Churches" helped Jews "in disproportionately greater numbers than any other political or religious community in wartime Holland" (p. 1).

7. Kurek-Lesik (1992, 1997) estimates that Polish convents saved as many as 1,200 children. For more on the role of Catholic religious orders in Poland, see Zielinski (1987) and Bogner (1999).

8. Hallie (1979).

9. Ramati (1978).

10. Douglas Huneke (1981–1982) calls these "communal rescues" rather than collectives, and characterizes them as voluntary associations among groups of people who lived in close proximity to one another, shared common, long-established values, and functioned as a cohesive group prior to the war. For more on religious collectivities who supported rescue see Baron (1988), Gushee (1994), and Gross (December 1994).

11. Francis Fukuyama (2000), professor of public policy at the Institute of Public Policy at George Mason University, defines social capital as "an instantiated set of informal values or norms shared among members of a group that permits them to cooperate with one another. If members of the group come to expect that others will behave reliably and honestly, then they will come to *trust* one another. Trust acts like a lubricant that makes any group or organization run more efficiently" (p. 98).

12. See Baron (1995a, b) on this point.

13. Gross (December 1994).

14. Tackling this very point, Lawrence Blum (1980) argues that helping a friend rather than a stranger does not weaken the moral status of the act provided that one does not deny the other's equal entitlements.

15. Oliner and Oliner (1988).

16. While this is a controversial point, Wiggins (1991) and Triandis (1994, 1995) argue that the constructs used to describe personality can also be used to describe cultures.

17. Grondona (2000) argues that this is one of 20 cultural factors essential for economic development.

18. Strauss and Quinn (1997, p. 4).

19. Durkheim (1964; first published 1895).

20. Sober and Wilson (1998, p. 165).

21. Glover (2000), cited in Pinker (Oct. 29, 2000).

22. Hallie (1979).

23. Geertz (1973, 1983).

24. Geertz (2000a, p. 76).

25. Bellah et al. (1985).

26. Browder (1996) used three overlapping samples from all ranks of the SD (the SS security office), from its origins in 1932 to the end of 1934: (1) a sample of all members holding SS officers rank by the end of 1934, (2) a random sample who were either promoted to SS officers rank or entered with SS officers rank in 1936, and (3) a main sample consisting of 526 members in the SD before the end of 1934—approximately 62 percent of the estimated membership by the end of 1934. The primary source of data was the SS and other biographical files in the former U.S. Document Center in Berlin. Browder acknowledges that the data have many problems, among them incomplete information, errors, reliability questions, and a nonrandom sample selection.

27. Browder (1996, p. 11).

28. Kelman (1973); Kelman and Hamilton (1989).

29. Religious cultural leaders are destined to play a critical role in future violent conflicts if political scientist Samuel Huntington (1996), author of *Clash of Civilizations*, is correct.

30. Oliner and Oliner (1992, 1995). For a synthesis of research and application, as well as a teaching curriculum, see Blumenthal (2000).

31. For a view of bystanders, see Barnett (1999).

32. Bauman (1989, pp. 206–207).

33. Levinas, in Levinas and Kearney (1986, p. 31).

34. *New York Times,* "America Enduring," Sept. 11, 2002.

Appendix A. Methodology

1. Gilbert (2002).

2. Oliner and Oliner (1988).

3. The multiple correlation relating the two later measures to the first measure is significant: R $(2,327)$ = 0.761, p $<$ 0.001.

4. Tropman (1995, p. 8).

5. Schwartz (1994a, b). Schwartz derived his conception of mastery through a Guttman-Lingoes smallest space analysis (SSA) and a "configurational verification" approach to survey data he collected from 86 samples drawn from 41 cultural groups in 38 nations during the years 1988–1992. Many of the variables included in the Internal Mastery Orientation appeared similar to those Schwartz identified.

6. Bakan (1966).

7. Wiggins (1991).

8. Schwartz (1994a, p. 103).

9. Wiggins (1991, p. 89).

10. The latter conception appears to be somewhat similar to the opposite pole of Wiggins's (1991) agency metadimension, which he called "passivity."

11. As Strauss and Quinn (1996) put it, they "can tell us what they think others believe, what they take for granted, and the *degree* of sedimentation of cultural understandings, that is, the degree to which they take for granted versus seen as contestable. Public discourses do shape people's understandings" (pp. 264–267).

12. Hofstede (1994, p. x); Triandis (1994, 1995); Wiggins (1991).

Selected Bibliography

Abrahamsen, Samuel (1988). The role of the Norwegian Lutheran Church during World War II. In *Remembering for the Future: Jews and Christians During and After the Holocaust,* Vol. 1. Oxford: Pergamon, 1988, 3–17.

Adamopoulos, J., and Bontempo, R. N. (1984). A note on the relationship between socialization practice and artistic preference. *Cross-Cultural Psychology Bulletin* 18 (2–3): 4–7.

Adorno, T. W., Frenkel-Brunswik, E., Levinson, D. J., and Sanford, R. N. (1950). *The Authoritarian Personality.* New York: Harper.

Allport, Gordon W. (1954). *The Nature of Prejudice.* Cambridge, Mass.: Addison-Wesley.

Allport, Gordon W. (1959). Religion and prejudice. *Crane Review* 2: 1–10. (Reprinted in G. W. Allport (1960) *Personality and Social Encounter: Selected Essays.* Boston: Beacon: 257–267.)

Allport, Gordon W. (1960). *Personality and Social Encounter: Selected Essays.* Boston: Beacon.

Allport, Gordon W. (1966). The religious context of prejudice. *Journal for the Scientific Study of Religion* (Fall): 447–457.

Allport, Gordon W., and Kramer, B. M. (1946). Some roots of prejudice. *Journal of Psychology* 22: 9–39.

Allport, Gordon W., and Ross, J. M. (1967). Personal religious orientation and prejudice. *Journal of Personality and Social Psychology* 5: 432–443.

Almond, Gabriel, and Verba, Sidney (1963). *The Civic Culture.* Princeton, N.J.: Princeton University Press.

Altemeyer, B. (1988). *Enemies of Freedom: Understanding Right-Wing Authoritarianism*. San Francisco: Jossey-Bass.

Altemeyer, B., and Hunsberger, B. (1992). Authoritarianism, religious fundamentalism, quest, and prejudice. *The International Journal for the Psychology of Religion* 2: 113–133.

Altemeyer, B., and Hunsberger, B. (1993). Reply to Gorsuch. *The International Journal for the Psychology of Religion* 3: 33–37.

America enduring. Editorial. *New York Times*, Sept. 11, 2002, p. A34.

Andreski, Stanislav, ed. (1983). *Max Weber on Capitalism, Bureaucracy and Religion: A Selection of Texts*. London: George Allen and Unwin.

Ano, James A. (1990). *The Politics of Righteousness: Idaho Christian Patriotism*. Seattle: University of Washington Press.

Augoustinos, M., and Walker, I. (1995). *Social Cognition: An Integrated Introduction*. London: Sage.

Bakan, David (1966). *The Duality of Human Existence: Isolation and Communion in Western Man*. Boston: Beacon.

Baranowski, Shelley (1986). *The Confessing Church, Conservative Elites, and the Nazi State*. Lewiston: Edwin Mellen Press.

Barnea, Marina F., and Schwartz, Shalom (1998). Values and voting. *Political Psychology* 19 (1): 17–37.

Barnett, Victoria J. (1992). *For the Soul of the People: Protestant Protest Against Hitler*. New York: Oxford University Press.

Barnett, Victoria J. (1999). *Bystanders: Conscience and Complicity During the Holocaust*. Westport, Conn.: Greenwood.

Baron, Lawrence (1988). The historical context of rescue. In Oliner, Samuel P., and Oliner, Pearl, *The Altruistic Personality: Rescuers of Jews in Nazi Europe*. New York: Free Press, 13–40.

Baron, Lawrence (1992). The Dutchness of Dutch rescuers: The national dimension of altruism. In Oliner, Pearl M., Oliner, Samuel P., Baron, Lawrence, Blum, Lawrence A., Krebs, Dennis L., Smolenska, M. Zuzanna, eds., *Embracing the Other: Philosophical, Psychological, and Historical Perspectives on Altruism*. New York: New York University Press, 306–327.

Baron, Lawrence (1995a). The mobilization of moral outrage: Calvinist and Socialist rescue networks for Jews in Nazi-occupied Holland. Paper presented at the Pacific Sociological Association, San Francisco, California, April 9, 1995.

Baron, Lawrence (1995b). Parochialism, patriotism, and philo-Semitism: Why members of the Reformed Churches rescued Jews in the Netherlands during the Holocaust. Paper presented at the Seventh Annual Conference of the Midwest Jewish Studies Association, October 22 and 23, 1995, Macalester College, St. Paul, Minn.

Batson, C. Daniel (1976). Religion as prosocial: Agent or double agent. *Journal for the Scientific Study of Religion* 15: 29–45.

Batson, C. Daniel (1983). Sociobiology and the role of religion in promoting prosocial behavior: An alternative view. *Journal of Personality and Social Psychology* 45: 1380–1385.

Batson, C. Daniel (1987). Prosocial motivation: Is it ever truly altruistic? In Berkowitz, L., ed., *Advances in Experimental Social Psychology*, Vol. 20, San Diego: Academic Press, 65–122.

Batson, C. Daniel (1991). *The Altruism Question: Toward a Social-Psychological Answer*. Hillsdale, N.J.: Erlbaum.

Batson, C. Daniel, Flink, C. H., Schoenrade, P. A., Fultz, J., and Pych, V. (1986). Religious orientation and overt versus covert racial prejudice. *Journal of Personality and Social Psychology* 50: 175–181.

Batson, C. Daniel, Naifeh, S. J., and Pate, S. (1978). Social desirability, religious orientation, and racial prejudice. *Journal for the Scientific Study of Religion* 17: 31–41.

Batson, C. Daniel, and Oleson, K. C. (1991). Current status of the empathy-altruism hypothesis. In M. S. Clark, ed., *Review of Personality and Social Psychology: Prosocial Behavior,* Vol. 12. Newbury Park, Calif.: Sage, 62–85.

Batson, C. Daniel, Schoenrade, Patricia, and Ventis, W. Larry (1993). *Religion and the Individual: A Social-Psychological Perspective*. New York: Oxford University Press.

Batson, C. Daniel, and Ventis, W. Larry (1982). *The Religious Experience: A Social-Psychological Perspective*. New York: Oxford University Press

Bauman, Zygmunt (1989). *Modernity and the Holocaust*. Ithaca, N.Y.: Cornell University Press

Bauman, Zygmunt (1990). *Thinking Sociologically*. Cambridge, Mass.: Basil Blackwell.

Bellah, Robert N., ed. (1973). *Emile Durkheim: On Morality and Society*. Chicago: University of Chicago Press.

Bellah, Robert N., Hodgkinson, Virginia A., and Associates (1990). *Faith and Philanthropy in America*. San Francisco: Jossey-Bass.

Bellah, Robert N., Madsen, Richard, Sullivan, William M., Swidler, Ann, and Tipton, Steven M. (1985). *Habits of the Heart: Individualism and Commitment in American Life*. Berkeley: University of California Press.

Benedict, Ruth (1946). *The Chrysanthemum and the Sword*. Boston: Houghton Mifflin.

Berger, Peter L. (1961). *The Precarious Vision: A Sociologist Looks at Social Fictions and Christian Faith*. New York: Doubleday.

Berger, Peter L., and Ernst Luckmann (1967). *The Social Construction of Reality*. New York: Doubleday.

Berkowitz, L., and Daniels, L. R. (1964). Affecting the salience of the social responsibility norms: Effect of past help on the responses to dependency relationships. *Journal of Abnormal and Social Psychology* 68: 275–281.

Bloom, Irene, Martin, J. Paul, and Proudfoot, Wayne L., eds. (1996). *Religious Diversity and Human Rights*. New York: Columbia University Press.

Blum, Lawrence A. (1980). *Friendship, Altruism and Morality*. London: Routledge and Kegan Paul.

Blum, Lawrence (1992). Friendship, altruism and morality. In Oliner, Pearl M., Oliner, Samuel P., Baron, Lawrence, Blum, Lawrence A., Krebs, Dennis L., and Smolenska, M. Zuzanna, eds., *Embracing the Other: Philosophical, Psychological, and Historical Perspectives on Altruism*. New York: New York University Press.

Blumenthal David R. (1999). *The Banality of Good and Evil: Moral Lessons from the Shoah and Jewish Tradition*. Washington, D.C.: Georgetown University Press.

Boas, Franz (1932). *Anthropology and Modern Life*. New York: Norton.

Boas, Franz, and Benedict, Ruth (1938). *General Anthropology*. Boston: Heath. (Reprinted New York, Johnson Reprint Corporation, 1965.)

Bogner, Nahum (1999). The convent children: The rescue of Jewish children in Polish convents during the Holocaust. In Silberklang, David, ed., *Yad Vashem Studies,* Vol. XXVII. Jerusalem: Yad Vashem, 235–285.

Browder, George C. (1996). *Hitler's Enforcers: The Gestapo and the SS Security Service in the Nazi Revolution.* New York: Oxford University Press.

Bruce, Steve (1996). *Religion in the Modern World: From Cathedrals to Cults.* New York: Oxford University Press.

Burleigh, Michael, and Wipperman, Wolfgang (1991). *The Racial State: Germany 1933– 1945.* Cambridge: Cambridge University Press.

Campbell, Ernest, and Pettigrew, Thomas (1959). *Christians in Racial Crisis.* Washington, D.C.: Public Affairs Press

Carroll, James (2001). *Constantine's Sword: The Church and the Jews.* Boston: Houghton Mifflin.

Cavan, Ruth Shonle (1971). A dating-marriage scale of religious social distance. *Journal for the Scientific Study of Religion* 10 (2): 93–100.

Charny, Israel W. (2000). Innocent denials of known genocides: A further contribution to a psychology of denial of genocide. *Human Rights Review* 1 (3): 15–39.

Chary, Frederick B. (1970). *The Bulgarian Jews and the Final Solution.* Pittsburgh: University of Pittsburgh Press.

Christenson, James A. (1976). Religious involvement, values and social compassion. *Sociological Analysis* 37.

Coe, George A. (1900). *The Spiritual Life: Studies in the Science of Religion.* New York: Eaton and Mains.

Cohen, Abner (1981). *The Politics of Elite Culture.* Berkeley: University of California Press.

The Columbia Encyclopedia of Religion (1993). Fifth edition. New York: Columbia University Press. Distributed by Houghton Mifflin.

Conway, John (1968). *The Nazi Persecution of the Churches.* New York: Basic Books.

Cornwell, John (1999). *Hitler's Pope: The Secret History of Pius XII.* New York.: Viking.

Darley, John M., and Latané, Bibb (1968). Bystander intervention in emergencies: Diffusion of responsibility. *Journal of Personality and Social Psychology* 8: 377–383.

Davis, M. H. (1994). *Empathy: A Social Psychological Approach.* Madison, Wisc.: Brown and Benchmark.

Deutsch, K., et al. (1957). *Political Community and the North Atlantic Area.* Princeton, N.J.: Princeton University Press.

Deutsch, M. (1975). Equity, equality, and need: What determines which values will be used as the basis of distributive justice? *Journal of Social Issues* 31, 137–149.

Deutsch, M. (1985). *Distributive Justice: A Social Psychological Perspective.* New Haven, Conn: Yale University Press.

Diener, E., Diener, M., and Diener, C. (1995). Factors predicting the subjective well-being of nations. *Journal of Personality and Social Psychology* 69: 851–864.

Dittes, J. E. (1969). Psychology of religion. In Lindzey, G. and Aronson, E., eds., *The Handbook of Social Psychology,* Vol. 5, second edition. Reading, Mass.: Addison-Wesley, 602–659.

Dolan, Jay (1985). *The American Catholic Experience.* New York: Doubleday.

Donahue, Michael J. (1995). Catholicism and religious experience. In Hood, Ralph W.

Jr., ed., *Handbook of Religious Experiences*. Birmingham, Ala.: Religious Education Press, 30–48.

Dovidio, J. F., Piliavin, J. A., Gaertner, S. L., Schroeder, D. A., and Clark, R. D., III. (1991). The arousal: Cost-reward model and the process of intervention: A review of the evidence. In Clark, M. S., ed., *Review of Personality and Social Psychology: Prosocial Behavior*, Vol. 12. Newbury Park, Calif.: Sage, 86–118.

Drake, A. W., Finkelstein, S. N., and Spolsky, H. M. (1982). *The American Blood Supply*. Cambridge, Mass.: MIT Press.

Dumont, L. (1986). *Essays on Individualism*. Chicago: University of Chicago Press.

Durkheim, Emile (1964). *The Rules of the Sociological Method*. New York: Free Press. Originally published in 1895.

Durkheim, Emile (1969). *The Elementary Forms of the Religious Life*. Swain, Joseph Ward translator. New York: Free Press. Originally published in 1915.

Ehrlich, Howard J. (December/January 2000). *Perspectives: The Newsletter on Prejudice, Ethnoviolence, and Social Policy* 16: 1.

Eisenberg, Nancy, ed. (1982). *The Development of Prosocial Behavior*. New York: Academic Press.

Eisenberg, Nancy (1986). *Altruistic Emotion, Cognition, and Behavior*. Hillsdale, N.J.: Erlbaum.

Eisenberg, Nancy, and Fabes, R. A. (1990). Empathy: Conceptualization, measurement and relation to prosocial behavior. *Motivation and Emotion* 14: 131–149.

Eisenberg, Nancy, and Miller, P. (1987). The relation of empathy to prosocial and related behaviors. *Psychological Bulletin* 91–119.

Eisinga, Rob, Felling, Albert, and Peters, Jan (1990). Religious belief, church involvement, and ethnocentrism in the Netherlands. *Journal for the Scientific Study of Religion* 29 (91): 54–75.

Eliach, Yaffa (1998). *There Once Was a World: A Nine-Hundred-Year Chronicle of the Shtetl of Eishyshok*. New York: Little, Brown.

Ericksen, Robert, and Heschel, Susannah, eds. (1999). *Betrayal: German Churches and the Holocaust*. Minneapolis, Minn.: Fortress.

Erickson, D. (1964). Religious consequences of public and sectarian schooling. *The School Review* 72: 22–33.

Erikson, Erik H. (1958). *Young Man Luther: A Study in Psychoanalysis and History*. New York: Norton.

Faulkner, Joseph E., and DeJong, Gordon F. (1966). Religiosity in 5-D: An empirical analysis. *Social Forces* 45: 246–254.

Feagin, J. R. (1964). Prejudice and religious types: A focused study of southern Fundamentalists. *Journal for the Scientific Study of Religion* 4: 3–13.

Field, Alexander J. (2001). *Altruistically Inclined?: The Behavioral Sciences, Evolutionary Theory, and the Origins of Reciprocity*. Ann Arbor: University of Michigan.

Fiske, Alan Page (1991a). The cultural relativity of selfish individualism: Anthropological evidence that humans are inherently sociable. In Clark, Margaret S., ed., *Prosocial Behavior: Review of Personality and Social Psychology*, Vol. 12. Newbury Park, Calif.: Sage.

Fiske, Alan Page (1991b). *Structures of Social Life: The Four Elementary Forms of Human Relations*. New York: Free Press.

Fiske, Alan Page, and Tetlock, Philip E. (June 1997). Taboo trade-offs: Reactions to transactions that transgress the spheres of justice. *Political Psychology* 18 (2): 255–297.

Flannery, Edward H. (1965). *The Anguish of the Jews.* New York: Macmillan.

Foerster, Friedrich Wilhelm (1962). *The Jews.* New York: Farrar, Straus and Cudahy.

Freud, Sigmund (1939). Moses and Monotheism: Three Essays. In *The Standard Edition of the Complete Psychological Works of Sigmund Freud,* Vol. 23, 1964, pp. 7–137 (Original German edition 1939).

Friedrichs, R. W. (1959). Christians and residential exclusion: An empirical study of a northern dilemma. *Journal of Social Issues* 15: 14–23.

Fromm, Erich (1941). *Escape from Freedom.* New York: Rinehart.

Fromm, Erich (1950). *Psychoanalysis and Religion.* New Haven, Conn.: Yale University Press.

Fukuyama, Francis (2000). Social capital. In Harrison, Lawrence E., and Huntington, Samuel P., eds., *Culture Matters: How Values Shape Human Progress.* New York: Basic, 98–111.

Furnham Adrian (1982). The Protestant work ethic and attitudes towards unemployment. *Journal of Occupational Psychology* 55: 277–285.

Furnham, Adrian (1983). Attitudes toward the unemployed receiving social security benefits. *Human Relations* 36: 135–150.

Furnham, Adrian (1985). The determinants of attitudes towards social security benefits. *British Journal of Social Psychology* 24: 19–27.

Furnham, Adrian (1987). Work related beliefs and human values. *Personality and Individual Differences* 8: 627–637.

Furnham, Adrian (1990). *The Protestant Work Ethic: The Psychology of Work-Related Beliefs and Behaviors.* London: Routledge.

Galanter, M. (1989). *Cults, Faith, Healing, and Coercion.* New York: Oxford University Press.

Gartner, J. (1983). Self-esteem tests: Assumptions and values. In Ellison C., ed., *Your Better Self: Psychology, Christianity and Self-esteem.* New York: Harper and Row, 98–110.

Geertz, Clifford (1973). *The Interpretation of Cultures: Selected Essays by Clifford Geertz.* New York: Basic.

Geertz, Clifford (1983). *Local Knowledge: Further Essays in Interpretive Anthropology.* New York: Basic.

Geertz, Clifford (2000a). *Available Light: Anthropological Reflections on Philosophical Topics.* Princeton, N.J.: Princeton University Press.

Geertz, Clifford (2000b). *Local Knowledge: Further Essays in Interpretive Anthropology.* New York: Basic.

Gergen, K. J., Gergen, M. M., and Meter, K. (1972). Individual orientations to prosocial behavior. *Journal of Social Issues* 8: 105–130.

Gilbert, Martin (2002). *The Righteous: The Unsung Heroes of the Holocaust.* New York: Doubleday.

Gilligan, Carol (1982). *In a Different Voice: Psychological Theory and Women's Development.* Cambridge: Harvard University Press.

Glock, Charles (1962). On the study of religious commitment. *Religious Education, Research Supplement* 57 (4): S98-S110.

Glock, Charles Y., and Stark, Rodney (1966). *Christian Beliefs and Anti-Semitism.* New York: Harper and Row.

Glover, Jonathan (2000). *Humanity: A Moral History of the Twentieth Century.* New Haven, Conn.: Yale University Press.

Gorsuch, Richard L., and Aleshire, Daniel (1974). Christian faith and ethnic prejudice: A review and interpretation of research. *Journal for the Scientific Study of Religion* 13 (3): 281–307.

Greeley, Andrew M. (1972). *The Denominational Society.* Glenview, Ill.: Scott, Foresman.

Greeley, Andrew M. (1989). Protestant and Catholic: Is the analogical imagination extinct? *American Sociological Review* 54: 485–502.

Greeley, Andrew M. (1990). *The Catholic Myth: The Behavior and Beliefs of American Catholics.* New York: Scribner's.

Greeley, Andrew M. (1996). *Religion as Poetry.* New Jersey: Transaction.

Green, Ronald M. (1988). *Religion and Moral Reason: A New Method for Comparative Study.* New York: Oxford University Press.

Greenberg, J., Pyszczynski, T., Solomon, S., et al. (1990). Evidence for terror management theory II: The effects of mortality salience on reaction to those who threaten or bolster the cultural worldview. *Journal of Personality and Social Psychology* 58: 308–18.

Greven, Philip (1977). *The Protestant Temperament: Patterns of Child-Rearing, Religious Experience, and the Self in Early America.* New York: Knopf.

Grondona, Mariano (2000). A cultural typology of economic development. In Harrison, Lawrence E., and Huntington, Samuel P., eds., *Culture Matters: How Values Shape Human Progress.* New York: Basic, 44–55.

Gross, Michael L. (December 1994). Jewish rescue in Holland and France during the Second World War: Moral cognition and collective action. *Social Forces* 73 (2): 463–496.

Gushee, David (1994). *The Righteous Gentiles of the Holocaust: A Christian Perspective.* Minn.: Fortress.

Hallie, Philip P. (1979). *Lest Innocent Blood Be Shed: The Story of Le Chambon and How Goodness Happened There.* New York: Harper and Row.

Hay, Malcolm (1951). *The Foot of Pride: The Pressure of Christendom on the People of Israel for 1900 Years.* Boston: Beacon.

Hensley, W. E. (1981). The effects of attire, location, and sex on aiding behavior: A similarity explanation. *Journal of Nonverbal Behavior* 6: 3–11.

Herberg, Will (1955). *Protestant-Catholic-Jew.* Garden City, N.Y.: Doubleday.

Heshka, S. (1983). Situational variables affecting participation in voluntary associations. In Smith, D. H., ed., *International Persectives on Voluntary Action Research.* Washington, D.C.: University Press of America, 138–147.

Hilberg, Raul (1985). *The Destruction of the European Jews.* New York: Holmes and Meier, 1985.

Hill, Peter C., and Hood, Ralph W., eds. *Measures of Religiosity.* Birmingham, Ala.: Religious Education Press.

Hinton, Perry (2000). *Stereotypes, Cognition and Culture*. Philadelphia: Taylor and Francis.

Hoffman, M. L. (1990). Empathy and justice motivation. *Motivation and Emotion* 14: 151–172.

Hofstede, Geert (1980). *Culture's Consequences: International Differences in Work-Related Values*. Beverly Hills, Calif.: Sage.

Hofstede, Geert (1991). *Cultures and Organizations: Software of the Mind*. London: McGraw-Hill.

Hofstede, Geert (1994). Foreword. In Kim, Uichol, Triandis, Harry C., Kagitcibasi, Cigdem, Choi, Sang-Chin, and Yoon, Gene, eds. *Individualism and Collectivism: Theory, Method, and Applications*. Newbury Park, Calif.: Sage, ix–xiv.

Hoge, D. R., and Carroll, J. W. (1973). Religiosity and prejudice in northern and southern churches. *Journal for the Scientific Study of Religion* 12: 181–187.

Hood, Ralph, W. Jr., Spilka, Bernard, Hunsburger, Bruce, and Gorsuch, Richard (1996). *The Psychology of Religion*. New York: Guilford.

Horowitz, D. L. (1985). *Ethnic Groups in Conflict*. Berkeley: University of California Press.

Huneke, Douglas (1981–82). A study of Christians who rescued Jews during the Nazi era. *Humboldt Journal of Social Relations* 9 (1): 144–149.

Hunsberger, Bruce (1995). Religion and prejudice: The role of religious fundamentalism, quest, and right-wing authoritarianism. *Journal of Social Issues* 51 (2): 113–130.

Huntington, Samuel P. (1996). *The Clash of Civilizations: Remaking the World Order*. New York: Simon and Schuster.

Hyman, Paula (1979). *From Dreyfus to Vichy: The Remaking of French Jewry, 1906–1939*. New York: Columbia University Press.

Inglehart, R. (1990). *Cultural Shift in Advanced Industrial Society*. Princeton, N.J.: Princeton University Press.

Inkeles, Alex (1990–1991). National character revisited. *The de Tocqueville Review* 12: 83–117.

Inkeles, A., and Levinson, D. J. (1978–1979). National character: The study of modal personality and sociocultural systems. In Lindzey G., ed., *The Handbook of Social Psychology*, Vol. 4., second edition. Reading, Mass.: Addison-Wesley, 428–506.

Jahoda, M. (1958). *Current Concepts of Positive Mental Health*. New York: Basic.

Jensen, J. P., and Bergin, A. E. (1988). Mental health values of professional therapists: A national interdisciplinary survey. *Professional Psychology: Research and Practice* 19: 290–297.

Jong, Louis de (1990). *The Netherlands and Nazi Germany*. Cambridge, Mass.: Harvard University Press.

Jung, Carl G. (1969). Answer to Job. In *The Collected Works of C. G. Jung*, Vol. 11, second edition. Princeton, N.J.: Princeton University Press, 355–470. First German edition 1952.

Kagitcibasi, C., and Berry, J. W. (1989). Cross-cultural psychology: Current research and trends. *Annual Review of Psychology* 40, 493–531.

Kanter, Rosabeth (1972). *Commitment and Community*. Cambridge, Mass.: Harvard University Press.

Kegan, Robert (1982). *The Evolving Self: Problems and Process in Human Development*. Cambridge, Mass.: Harvard University Press.

Kelman, Herbert C. (1973). Violence without moral restraint: Reflections on the dehumanization of victims and victimizers. *Journal of Social Issues* 29: 25–62.

Kelman, Herbert C., and V. Lee Hamilton (1989). *Crimes of Obedience: Toward a Social Psychology of Authority and Responsibility*. New Haven, Conn.: Yale University Press.

Kelvin, P., and Jarrett, J. (1985). *Unemployment: Its Social Psychological Effects*. Cambridge: Cambridge University Press.

Kim, Uichol, Triandis, Harry C., Kagitcibasi, Cigdem, Choi, Sang-Chin, and Yoon, Gene, eds. (1994). *Individualism and Collectivism: Theory, Method, and Applications*. Thousand Oaks, Calif.: Sage.

Kluckhohn, Clyde (1949). *Mirror for Man: The Relation of Anthropology to Modern Life*. New York: Whittesey.

Kluckhohn, Richard, ed. (1962). *Culture and Behavior: Collected Essays of Clyde Kluckhohn*. New York: Free Press.

Koestner, Richard, Franz, Carol, and Weinberger, Joel (1990). The family origins of empathic concern: A 26 year longitudinal study. *Journal of Personality and Social Psychology* 58: 709–717.

Kurek-Lesik, Ewa (1992). The role of Polish Nuns in the rescue of Jews, 1939–1945. In Oliner, Pearl M., Oliner, Samuel P., Baron, Lawrence, Blum, Lawrence A., Krebs, Dennis L., and Smolenska, M. Zuzanna, eds. (1992). *Embracing the Other: Philosophical, Psychological, and Historical Perspectives on Altruism*. New York: New York University Press, 328–334.

Kurek-Lesik, Ewa (1997). *Your Life Is Worth Mine: How Polish Nuns Saved Hundreds of Jewish Children in German-Occupied Poland, 1939–1945*. New York: Hippocrene.

Kurtz, Lester (1995). *Gods in the Global Village: The World's Religions in Sociological Perspective*. Thousand Oaks, Calif.: Pine Forge.

Lasch, Christopher (1978). *Culture of Narcissism: American Life in an Age of Diminishing Expectations*. New York: Norton.

Latané, Bibb, and Darley, John M. (1970). *The Unresponsive Bystander: Why Doesn't He Help?* New York: Appleton-Century Crofts.

Lazare, Lucien (1996). *Rescue as Resistance: How Jewish Organizations Fought the Holocaust in France*. Translated by Jeffrey M. Green. New York: Columbia University Press.

Lehr, E., and Spilka, B. (1989). Religion in the introductory psychology textbook: A comparison of three decades. *Journal for the Scientific Study of Religion* 28: 366–371.

Lenski, Gerhard Emmanuel (1953). Social correlates of religious interest. *American Sociological Review* 18: 533–544.

Lenski, Gerhard Emmanuel (1961). *The Religious Factor: A Sociological Study of Religion's Impact on Politics, Economics, and Family Life*. Garden City, N.Y.: Doubleday.

Lepp, Ignace (1963). *Atheism in Our Time*. New York: Macmillan.

Lerner, Michael (1980). *The Belief in a Just World: A Fundamental Delusion*. New York: Plenum.

Leuba, J. H. (1921). *The Belief in God and Immortality: A Pscyhological, Anthropological and Statistical Study*. Chicago: Open Court. Originally published in 1916.

Levinas, Emmanuel, and Kearney, Richard (1986). Dialogue with Emmanuel Levinas. In Cohen, Richard A., ed., *Face to Face with Levinas.* Albany, N.Y.: State University of New York Press.

Levine, Michael (July 17, 1998). Charity is at home in the Bible Belt. *San Francisco Chronicle,* p. A23.

Linton, Ralph (1936). *The Study of Man.* Englewood Cliffs, N.J.: Prentice Hall.

Lipset, Seymour (1960). *Political Man.* Garden City, N.Y.: Doubleday.

Littell, Franklin H., and Locke, Hubert C., eds. (1974). *The German Church Struggle and the Holocaust.* Detroit, Mich.: Wayne State University Press.

Locke, Hubert G., and Littell, Marcia Sachs, eds. (1996). *Holocaust and Church Struggle: Religion, Power and the Politics of Resistance,* Vol. XVI: *Studies in the Shoah.* Washington, D.C.: University Press of America.

Lomax, A., and Berkowitz, N. (1972). The evolutionary taxonomy of cultures. *Science* 177: 228–239.

London, Perry (1970). The rescuers: Motivational hypotheses about Christian who saved Jews from the Nazis. In Macaulay, J., and Berkowitz, L., eds., *Altruism and Helping Behavior.* New York: Academic Press, 241–250.

Lozowick, Yaacov (1999). Malice in action. In Silberklang, David, ed., *Yad Vashem Studies,* Vol. XXVII. Jerusalem: Yad Vashem, 287–330.

Lubac, Henri de (1990). *Christian Resistance to Anti-Semitism: Memories from 1940–1944.* Translated by Sister Elizabeth Englund, O.C.D. S.F.: Ignatius. Originally published as *Resistance Chretienne a l'antisemitisime,* Librairie Artheme Fayard, 1988.

MacDonald, A. (1972). More on the Protestant ethic. *Journal of Consulting and Clinical Psychology* 39: 116–22.

Malony, H. Newton (1992). Religious diagnosis in evaluations of mental health. In Schumaker John F., ed., *Religion and Mental Health.* New York: Oxford University Press, 245–258.

Marcuse, Herbert (1974). *Two-dimensional Man: An Essay on the Anthropology of Power and Symbolism in Complex Society.* Berkeley: University of California Press.

Marrus, Michael R., and Robert O. Paxton (1981). *Vichy France and the Jews.* New York: Basic.

Marty, Martin (March 20/27, 1996). Review of the Catholic ethic in American society: An exploration of values. *Christian Century* 346–349.

Masters, Kevin S., and Bergin, Allen E. (1992). Religious orientation and mental health. In Schumaker, John F., ed. *Religion and Mental Health.* New York: Oxford University Press, 221–232.

Maton, Kenneth I., and Wells, Elizabeth A. (1995). Religion as a community resource for well-being: Prevention, healing, and empowerment pathways. *Journal of Social Issues* 51 (2): 113–130.

McAdoo, H., and Crawford, V. (1991). The black church and family support programs. *Prevention in Human Services* 9: 193–203.

McBrien, Richard P. (1980). *Catholicism.* 2 vols. Minneapolis, Minn.: Winston.

McCrae, Robert R., and Costa, Paul T. Jr. (May 1997). Personality trait structure as a human universal. *American Psychologist* 52 (5): 509–516.

McCrae, Robert R., and John, Oliver P. (1992). An introduction to the five-factor model and its applications. *Journal of Personality* 60 (2): 175–215.

McInerny, Ralph (2001). *The Defamation of Pius XII.* South Bend, Ind.: St. Augustine's Press.

Mead, Margaret (1939). *From the South Seas.* New York: Morrow.

Meloen, J. (1994). State authoritarianism world wide. Paper presented at the Conference of the Dutch Society of Political Psychology, October 21, 1994, Amsterdam, The Netherlands.

Midlarsky, Elizabeth (1984). Competence and helping. In Staub, E., Bar-Tal, D., Kary-lowski, J. and Reykowski, J. (eds.). *Development and Maintenance of Prosocial Behavior.* New York: Plenum.

Midlarsky, Elizabeth (1991). Helping as coping. In Clark, M. S., ed., *Review of Personality and Social Psychology,* Vol. 12: *Prosocial Behavior.* Newbury Park, Calif.: Sage: 238–264.

Mikula, G., ed. (1980). *Justice and Social Interaction.* New York: Springer-Verlag.

Miller, Alice (1984). *For Your Own Good: Hidden Cruelty in Child-Rearing and the Roots of Violence.* New York: Farrar, Straus and Giroux.

Mizruchi, Susan (1998). *The Science of Sacrifice: American Literature and Modern Social Theory.* Princeton, N.J.: Princeton University Press

Modras, Ronald (1994). *The Catholic Church and Antisemitism: Poland, 1933–1939.* Langhorne, Penn.: Harwood Academic Publishers.

Monroe, Kristen Renwick (1996). *The Heart of Altruism: Perceptions of a Common Humanity.* Princeton: Princeton University Press.

Monroe, Kristen Renwick (2004). *The Hand of Compassion: Portraits of Moral Choice during the Holocaust.* Princeton: Princeton University Press.

Morley, John (1980). *Vatican Diplomacy and the Jews during the Holocaust, 1939–1945.* New York: Ktav.

Mosher, D. L. (1965). Interaction of fear and guilt in inhibiting unacceptable behavior. *Journal of Consulting Psychology* 29: 161–167.

Murray, H. (1938). *Explorations in Personality.* New York: Oxford University Press.

Newcomb, R. M., and Svehla, G. (1937). Intra-family relationships in attitude. *Sociometry* 7 (1): 180–205.

Nisbett, R. E. (1980). The trait construct in lay and professional psychology. In Festinger, L., ed., *Retrospections in Social Psychology.* New York: Oxford University Press: 109–130.

Norman, W. T. (1963). Toward an adequate taxonomy of personality attributes: Replicated factor structure in peer nomination personality ratings. *Journal of Abnormal and Social Psychology* 66: 574–583.

Novak, Michael (1993). *The Catholic Ethic and the Spirit of Capitalism.* New York: Free Press.

Nucci, Larry P., Saxe, Geoffrey B., and Turiel, Elliot, eds. (2000). *Culture, Thought, and Development.* Mahwah, N.J.: Erlbaum.

Ogburn, William F. (1922). *Social Change with Respect to Culture and Original Nature.* New York: Huebsch. Reprinted 1966, New York, Dell.

Oliner, Samuel P., and Oliner, Pearl (1988). *The Altruistic Personality: Rescuers of Jews in Nazi Europe.* New York: Free Press.

Oliner, Pearl M., and Oliner, Samuel P. (1992). Promoting extensive altruistic bonds: A conceptual elaboration and some pragmatic implications. In Oliner, Pearl M., Oliner,

Samuel P., Baron, Lawrence, Blum, Lawrence A., Krebs, Dennis L., and Smolenska, M. Zuzanna, eds. (1992). *Embracing the Other: Philosophical, Psychological, and Historical Perspectives on Altruism*. New York: New York University Press, 369–389.

Oliner, Pearl M., and Oliner, Samuel P. (1995). *Toward a Caring Society: Ideas into Action*. Westport, Conn.: Praeger.

Oliner, Pearl M., Oliner, Samuel P., Baron, Lawrence, Blum, Lawrence A., Krebs, Dennis L., and Smolenska, M. Zuzanna, eds. (1992). *Embracing the Other:Philosophical, Psychological, and Historical Perspectives on Altruism*. New York: New York University Press.

Otten, C. A., Penner, Louis, A., and Altabe, M. N. (1991). An examination of therapists' and college students' willlingness to help a psychologically distressed person. *Journal of Social and Clinical Psychology* 7: 34–41.

Paldiel, Mordecai (1993). *The Path of the Righteous: Gentile Rescuers of Jews During the Holocaust*. N.J.: Ktav.

Paldiel, Mordecai (2000). *Saving the Jews*. Rockville, Md.: Schreiber.

Paloutzian, Raymond F., and Kirkpatrick, Lee A. (1995), issue eds. *Religious Influences on Personal and Societal Well-Being: Journal of Social Issues* 51 (2).

Peabody, D. (1985). *National Characteristics*. Cambridge: Cambridge University Press.

Pelto, P. J. (April 1968). The difference between "tight" and "loose" societies. *Transaction:* 37–40.

Penner, Louis A., and Fritzsche, Barbara A. (1993). Magic Johnson and reactions to people with AIDS: A natural experiment. *Journal of Applied Social Psychology* 23: 1035–1050.

Penner, Louis A., Fritzsche, Barbara A., Craiger, J. Philip, and Freifeld, Tamara S. (1995). Measuring the prosocial personality. In Butcher, J., and Spielberger, C. D., eds., *Advances in Personality Assessment*, Vol. 10. Hillsdale, N.J.: Lea.

Pettigrew, Thomas F. (1959). Regional differences in anti-Negro prejudice. *Journal of Abnormal and Social Psychology* 59:28–36.

Phayer, Michael (2000). *The Catholic Church and the Holocaust, 1930–1965*. Bloomington: Indiana University Press.

Pinker, Steven (October 29, 2000). Jonathan Glover: Humanity: A moral history of the twentieth century. *New York Times Book Review,* p. 14.

Potvin, Raymond (1985). *Seminarians of the Eighties: A National Survey*. Washington, D.C.: National Catholic Educational Association.

Potvin, Raymond, and Suziedelis, Antanas (1969). *Seminarians of the Sixties: A National Survey*. Washington, D.C.: National Catholic Educational Association.

Putney, S., and Middleton, R. (1961). Rebellion, conformity, and parental religious ideologies. *Sociometry* 24: 125–135.

Pye, Lucian W. (June 1997). Introduction: The elusive concept of culture and the vivid reality of personality. *Political Psychology* 18 (2): 241–254.

Ramati, Alexander (1978). *The Assisi Underground: The Priests Who Rescued Jews*. New York: Stein and Day.

Rappaport, A. (1988). Provision of step-level public goods: Effect of inequality in resources. *Journal of Personality and Social Psychology* 54: 432–440.

Reddy, R. D. (1980). Individual philanthropy and giving behavior. In Smith, D. H., and

Macaulay, J., eds., *Participation in Social and Political Activities*. San Francisco: Jossey-Bass, 370–399.

Redfield, Robert (1957). *The Primitive World and Its Transformations*. Ithaca, N.Y.: Cornell University Press.

Renshon, Stanley, and Duckitt, John (June 1997). Cultural and cross-cultural political psychology: Toward the development of a new subfield. *Political Psychology* 18 (2): 233–240.

Reykowski, Janusz (1994). In Kim, Uichol, Triandis, Harry C., Kagitcibasi, Cigdem, Choi, Sang-Chin, and Yoon, Gene, eds., *Individualism and Collectivism: Theory, Method, and Applications*. Newbury Park, Calif.: Sage 276–292.

Reykowski, Janusz (1997). Patriotism and the collective system of meanings. In Bar-Tal, Daniel, and Staub, Ervin, eds. *Patriotism in the Lives of Individuals and Nations*. Chicago: Nelson-Hall, 108–128.

Rittner, Carol, and Myers, Sandra (1986). *The Courage to Care: Rescuers of Jews during the Holocaust*. New York: New York University Press.

Rittner, Carol, Smith, Stephen D., and Steinfeldt, Irena, eds. (2000). *The Holocaust and the Christian World: Reflections on the Past, Challenges for the Future*. London: Kuperard.

Roberts, Keith (1984). *Religion in Sociological Perspective*. Homewood, Ill.: Dorsey Press.

Roberts, Keith (1995). *Religion in Sociological Perspective*. Third edition. Belmont, Calif.: Wadsworth Publishing.

Robertson, Hector Menteith (1933). *Aspects of the Rise of Economic Individualism: A Criticism of Max Weber and His School*. Cambridge, England: The University Press. First published 1933.

Rochat, Francois, and Modigliani, Andre (Fall 1995). The ordinary quality of resistance: From Milgram's laboratory to the village of Le Chambon. *Journal of Social Issues* 51 (3): 195–211.

Rokeach, Milton (1960). *The Open and Closed Mind*. New York: Basic.

Rokeach, Milton (1969). Religious values and social compassion. *Review of Religious Research* 11: 24–39.

Romer, D., Gruder, C. L., and Lizzardo, T. (1986). A person-situation approach situation to altruistic behavior. *Journal of Personality and Social Psychology* 51: 1001–1012.

Ross, Marc Howard (June 1997). The relevance of culture for the study of political psychology and ethnic conflict. *Political Psychology* 18 (2): 299–326.

Ross, Murray (1950). *Religious Beliefs of Youth*. New York: Association Press.

Roth, John K., and Berenbaum, M., eds. (1989). *Holocaust: Religious and Philosophical Implications*. St. Paul, Minn.: Paragon House.

Rothfels, Luke (1961). *The German Opposition to Hitler: An Assessment*. Translated from the German by Lawrence Wilson. London: Oswald Wolff.

Rousso, Henry (1991). *The Vichy Syndrome: History and Memory in France Since 1944*. Cambridge, Mass.: Harvard University Press.

Sampson, E. E. (1975). On justice as equality. *Journal of Social Issues* 31: 45–64.

Samuelson, Kurt (1957). *Religion and Economic Action*. New York: Basic.

Sánchez, José M. (2001). *Pius XII and the Holocaust: Understanding the Controversy*. Washington, D.C.: Catholic University of America.

Sapir, Edward (1957). *Culture, Language and Personality: Selected Essays*. Mandelbaum, David G., ed. Berkeley, Calif.: University of California Press. Originally published in 1949.

Schroeder, David A., Penner, Louis A., Dovidio, John F., and Piliavin, Jane A. (1995). *The Psychology of Helping and Altruism: Problems and Puzzles*. New York: McGraw-Hill.

Schwartz, Shalom H. (1994a). Are there universal aspects in the structure and contents of human values? *Journal of Social Issues* 50: 19–46.

Schwartz, Shalom H. (1994b). Beyond individualism-collectivism: New cultural dimensions of values. In Kim, Uichol, Triandis, Harry C., Kagitcibasi, Cigdem, Choi, Sang-Chin, and Yoon, Gene, eds., *Individualism and Collectivism: Theory, Method, and Applications*. Newbury Park, Calif.: Sage, 85–119.

Schwartz, Shalom H., and Bardi, Anat (June 1997). Influences of adaptation to communist rule on value priorities in Eastern Europe. *Political Psychology* 18 (2): 385–410.

Schwartz, S. H., and Howard, J. A. (1981). A normative decision-making model of helping behavior. In Rushton, J. P. and Sorrentino, R. M., eds. *Altruism and Helping Behavior*. Hillsdale, N.J.: Erlbaum, 189–211.

Schwartz, S. H. and Howard, J. A. (1982). Helping and cooperation: A self-based motivational model. In Derlega, V. J., and Grzelak, J., eds., *Cooperation and Helping Behavior: Theories and Research*. New York: Academic Press, 327–353.

Schwinger, W. (1980). Just allocation of goods: Decision among three principles. In Mikula, G., ed., *Justice and Social Interaction*. New York: Springer-Verlag.

Sheldon, William H. (1936). *Psychology and the Promethean Will*. New York: Harper.

Shotland, R. Lance, and Huston, T. L. (1979). Emergencies: What are they and how do they influence bystanders to intervene. *Journal of Personality and Social Psychology* 37: 1822–1834.

Shotland, R. Lance, and Stebbins, Charles A. (1983). Emergency and cost as determinants of helping behavior and the slow accumulation of social psychological knowledge. *Social Psychology Quarterly* 46: 36–46.

Smith, Peter Bovington, and Bond, Michael Harris (1994). *Social Psychology Across Cultures: Analysis and Perspectives*. Boston: Allyn and Bacon.

Smith, Wilfred Cantwell (1963). *The Meaning and End of Religion: A New Approach to the Religious Traditions of Mankind*. New York: Macmillan.

Snyder, M. (1992). Of persons and situations, of personality and social psychology, *Psychological Inquiry* 3, 94–98.

Sober, Elliott, and Wilson, David Sloan (1998). *Unto Others: The Evolution and Psychology of Unselfish Behavior*. Cambridge, Mass.: Harvard University Press

Sombart, Werner (1967). *Luxury and Capitalism*. Ann Arbor: University of Michigan Press.

Spiro, Melford E. (1987). Collective representations and mental representations in religious symbol systems. In Kilborne, B., and Langness, L., eds., *Culture and Human Nature: Theoretical Papers of Melford E. Spiro*. Chicago: University of Chicago Press, 161–184. Originally published in 1982.

Starbuck, E. D. (1899). *The Psychology of Religion; An Empirical Study of the Growth of Religious Consciousness*. New York: Scribner's.

Stark, R. (1963). On the incompatibility of religion and science: A survey of American graduate students. *Journal for Scientific Study of Religion* 3: 3–21.

Staub, Ervin (1971). Helping a person in distress: The influence of implicit and explicit "rules" of conduct on children and adults. *Journal of Personality and Social Psychology* 17, 137–144.

Staub, Ervin (1997). Blind versus constructive patriotism: Moving from embeddedness in the group to critical loyalty and action. In Bar-Tal, Daniel, and Staub, Ervin, eds., *Patriotism in the Lives of Individuals and Nations*. Chicago: Nelson-Hall.

Staub, Ervin (2002). The psychology of bystanders, perperators, and heroic helpers. In Newman, Leonard S. and Erber, Ralph, eds., *Understanding Genocide: The Social Psychology of the Holocaust*. New York: Oxford University Press.

Stinnett, N. (1979). Strengthening families. *Family Perspective* 13: 3–9.

Strauss, Claudia (2000), The culture concept and the individualism-collectivism debate: Dominant and alternative attributions for class in the United States. In Nucci, Larry P., Saxe, Geoffrey B., and Turiel, Elliot, eds., *Culture, Thought, and Development*. Hillsdale, N.J.: Erlbaum, 85–114.

Strauss, Claudia, and Quinn, Naomi (1997). *A Cognitive Theory of Cultural Meaning*. New York: Cambridge University Press.

Struening, Elmer (1963). Anti-democratic attitudes in Midwest University. In Remmers, H. H., ed., *Anti-Democratic Attitudes in American Schools*. Evanston, Ill.: Northwestern University Press, 210–258.

Swidler, Ann (1986). Culture in action: Symbols and strategies. *American Sociological Review* 5: 273–286.

Tawney, Richard H. (1926). *Religion and the Rise of Capitalism*. New York: Harcourt, Brace & Co.

Tec, Nechama (1986). *When Light Pierced the Darkness: Christian Rescue of Jews in Nazi-Occupied Poland*. New York: Oxford University Press.

Tetlock, Philip E., and Fiske, Alan (1997). Taboo trade-offs: Reactions to transactions that transgress the spheres of justice. *Political Psychology* 18 (2): 255–297.

Thurstone, L. L., and Chave, Ernest J. (1929). *The Measurement of Attitude: A Psychophysical Method and Some Experiments with a Scale for Measuring Attitude Toward the Church*. Chicago, Ill.: University of Chicago Press.

Tracy, David (1982). *The Analogical Imagination*. New York: Crossroad.

Triandis, Harry C. (1994). Theoretical and methodological approaches to the study of collectivism and individualism. In Kim, Uichol, Triandis, Harry C., Kagitcibasi, Cigdem, Choi, Sang-Chin, and Yoon, Gene, eds. *Individualism and Collectivism: Theory, Method, and Applications*. Newbury Park, Calif.: Sage, 41–51

Triandis, Harry C. (1995). *Individualism and Collectivism*. Boulder, Colo.: Westview.

Triandis, Harry C., Bontempo, R., and Villareal, M. (1988). Individualism and collectivism: Cross cultural perspectives on self-in-group relationships. *Journal of Personality and Social Psychology* 54: 323–338.

Tropman, John E. (1995). *The Catholic Ethic in American Society: An Exploration of Values*. San Francisco: Jossey-Bass.

Tupes, E. C., and Christal, R. E. (1961). *Recurrent personality factors based on trait ratings*. USAF ASD Tech. Rep. No. 61–97. Lackland Air Force Bases, Tex.: U.S. Air Force.

Tylor, Edward B. (1871). *Primitive Culture*. London: Murray.

Ulanov, Ann B. (1971). *The Feminine in Jungian Psychology and in Christian Theology*. Evanston, Ill.: Northwestern University Press.

Ventis, W. Larry (1995). The relationships between religion and mental health. *Journal of Social Issues* 51 (2): 33–48.

Vergote, Antoine, and Tamayo, Alvaro, eds. (1981). *The Parental Figures and the Representation of God: A Psychological and Cross-Cultural Study.* The Hague: Mouton.

Vernon, G. M. (1968). The religious nones: A neglected category. *Journal for the Scientific Study of Religion* 7: 219–229.

Vojtech Mastny (1971). *Czechs Under Nazi Rule: The Failure of National Resistance 1939–1942.* New York: Columbia University Press.

Wagstaff, G. (1983). Attitudes to poverty, the Protestant ethic, and political affiliation: A preliminary investigation. *Social Behavior and Personality* 11: 45–47.

Warmbrunn, Werner (1972). *The Dutch under German Occupation: 1940–1945.* Stanford, Calif.: Stanford University Press.

Weber, Max (1950). *General Economic History.* Translated by Frank H. Knight. London: Allen and Unwin. Originally published in 1924.

Weber, Max (1958). *The Protestant Ethic and the Spirit of Capitalism.* Translated by Talcott Parsons. New York: Scribner's. Originally published in 1904–1905.

Weber, Max (1976). *The Agrarian Sociology of Ancient Civilizations.* Translated by R. I. Frank. London: New Left Books. Originally published in 1909.

Weber, Max (1983a). The end of capitalism. Excerpted in Andreski, Stanislav, ed. *Max Weber on Capitalism, Bureaucracy and Religion: A Selection of Texts.* London: George Allen and Unwin, 158–59. Originally published in 1904–1905.

Weber, Max (1983b). Protestantism and the spirit of capitalism. Excerpted in Andreski, Stanislav, ed. *Max Weber on Capitalism, Bureaucracy and Religion: A Selection of Texts.* London: George Allen and Unwin. Originally published 1904–1905.

Weigert, A. J., and Thomas, D. L. (1972). Parental support, control, and adolescent religiosity: An extension of previous research. *Journal for the Scientific Study of Religion* 11: 389–393.

Weiss, John (1996). *Ideology of Death: Why the Holocaust Happened in Germany.* Chicago: Ivan R. Dee.

Whitehead, Alfred North (1926). *Religion in the Making.* New York: Macmillan.

Wiebe, K. F., and Fleck, J. R. (1980). Personality correlates of intrinsic, extrinsic, and nonreligious orientations. *The Journal of Psychology* 105: 181–187.

Wiggins, Jerry S. (1991). Agency and communion as conceptual coordinates for the understanding and measurement of interpersonal behavior. In Dante Ciccheti, ed., *Thinking Clearly About Psychology: Essays in Honor of Paul E. Meehl.* Minneapolis: University of Minnesota Press, 89–113.

Williamson, J. (1974). Beliefs about the motivation of the poor and attitudes towards poverty policy. *Social Problems* 21: 634–649.

Wilson, Glenn (1973). *The Psychology of Conservatism.* London: Academic Press.

Wilson, Richard W. (June 1997). American political culture in comparative perspective. *Political Psychology* 18 (2): 483–502.

Wulff, David M. (1991). *Psychology of Religion: Classic and Contemporary Views.* New York: John Wiley.

Wulff, David M. (1997). *Psychology of Religion: Classic and Contemporary.* Second edition. New York: John Wiley.

Wuthnow, Robert (1991). *Acts of Compassion: Caring for Others and Helping Ourselves.* Princeton, N.J.: Princeton University Press.

Wuthnow, Robert, Hodgkinson, Virginia A., and Associates (1990). *Faith and Philanthropy in America: Exploring the Role of Religion in America's Voluntary Sector.* San Francisco: Jossey-Bass.

Yang, K. (1988). Will social modernization eventually eliminate cross-cultural psychological differences? In Bond, M., ed., *The Cross-Cutural Challenge to Social Psychology.* Newbury Park, Calif.: Sage.

Yinger, Milton (1969). A Structural Examination of Religion. *Journal for the Scientific Study of Religion* 8: 88–99.

Zielinski, Zygmunt (1987). Activities of Catholic orders on behalf of Jews in Nazi-Occupied Poland. In Kulka, Otto Dov, and Mendes-Flohr, Paul R., eds., *Judaism and Christianity Under the Impact of National Socialism.* Jerusalem: The Historical Society of Israel and the Zalman Shazar Center for Jewish History, 381–394.

Zuccotti, Susan (1993). *The Holocaust: The French and the Jews.* New York: Basic.

Index

accommodation, and bystanders, 36, 127

Alexander, as very religious rescuer, 1, 2, 21–24, 109

Alice, Sister, as very religious rescuer, 18–21, 37

Allport, Gordon, 14–15, 75

Almond, Gabriel, 10

altruism: attitudes and values associated with, 118, 144; and care, 160; consequential, 161–162; cultural context of, 2, 154–155; definition and description of, 7–8; and internal orientation, 15. *See also* ingroup altruism; outgroup altruism

Altruistic Personality and Prosocial Behavior Institute, 6–7, 164

Andrzej, as irreligious rescuer, 46–49, 64

Annette, as irreligious nonrescuer, 62–65

antifascism, and the irreligious, 48, 49, 51

antisemitism, 81–82; of nonrescuers, 81–82, 85–86; in Poland, 51–52; of Protestant bystanders, 113; and religiosity, 31–33. *See also* Jews

Armand, as moderately religious rescuer, 87–89

authorization, and cultural change, 158–159

autonomous cultures, 150

Baron, Lawrence, 23

Batson, C. Daniel, 14

Bauman, Zygmunt, 161

beliefs, assertion of, 25–26

Benedict, Ruth, 10

Bible, Christian, and religious kinship with Jews, 23–24, 31–32, 63, 109

Boas, Franz, 10

bolstering, and cultural change, 158–159

Browder, George, 157–158

Bund (Jewish Youth Organization), 46

Bündische Jugend, 43

bystanders, 6; and accommodation, 36, 127; attitudes of, toward Jews, 108; and family relationships, 141; and obedience, 106–107, 127, 145

bystander syndrome, 161